The Gulf Migrant Archives in Kerala

The Gulf Migrant Archives in Kerala

Reading Borders and Belonging

MOHAMED SHAFEEQ KARINKURAYIL

OXFORD
UNIVERSITY PRESS

OXFORD
UNIVERSITY PRESS

Great Clarendon Street, Oxford, OX2 6DP,
United Kingdom

Oxford University Press is a department of the University of Oxford.
It furthers the University's objective of excellence in research, scholarship,
and education by publishing worldwide. Oxford is a registered trade mark of
Oxford University Press in the UK and in certain other countries

Published in the United States of America by Oxford University Press
198 Madison Avenue, New York, NY 10016, United States of America

British Library Cataloguing in Publication Data
Data available

Library of Congress Control Number is on file at the Library of Congress

ISBN 9780198908258

DOI: 10.1093/9780198910619.001.0001

POD

When in fourth standard, there was this boy who, unable to contain his excitement at the story of Oedipus a teacher narrated, wanted to share with me the narrative and the thrill of narration. We were in different divisions and would meet only during the lunch break. As all the other hostellers found their way to the mess hall, we stayed by the path to the mess, stricken by the life of a boy who would live his destiny. By the time Oedipus blinded himself, the lunch time was over. 'We will have to eat air', he said, and gaped in demonstration. I followed suit. This book is dedicated to that boy, Fazil MHKP (1983–2022), and all the other storytellers in my life.

Contents

Acknowledgements

Of the many possibilities, your reading this book has become a reality. Thank God.

In some ways, this work is a continuation of my PhD dissertation. The monograph starts where my dissertation ended, with an acknowledgement that the large-scale migration of the labour to the Arab Gulf ushered in a new era for Kerala. This new era is the subject of this book. The foundation for much that has gone into this book was forged in the years I spent with the Department of Cultural Studies at the English and Foreign Languages University (EFLU, formerly CIEFL), Hyderabad. I acknowledge with gratitude my PhD supervisor Satish Poduval who continues to be a source of support and counsel; M. Madhava Prasad who praised with grace and encouraged with humour; K. Satyanarayana for all the memorable classes and for pushing me to present a paper at a conference for the first time ever; Uma Maheswari Bhrugubanda for all the encouragement and especially for that one afternoon she sat me down and talked me out of my decision to quit academics; Parthasarathi Muthukaruppan who is more of an elder brother comrade; Sujith Parayil for the affection and encouragement.

I acknowledge the emotional, material, and intellectual support offered over the years by friends from Hyderabad and my school and college batchmates.

I thank friends and colleagues from the two places I taught immediately after my PhD—the Department of English and Comparative Literature at the Central University of Kerala (CUK), and the Centre for Comparative Literature at the University of Hyderabad (UoH) for making my life easier and happier at a testing time.

Had it not been for the work culture of Manipal Centre for Humanities, where I have been working these past few years, I probably would have never sat down to write this monograph. I thank Nikhil Govind for his engagement and appreciation of my works in general; E. Dawson Varughese for pushing me to write this monograph, and for co-editing with me the *Journal of Commonwealth Literature* symposium on the 'Gulf–Kerala Literary Publics' which helped further channel me towards this monograph; Gayathri Prabhu for her steadfast support at all times; Neha Chatterji and Ashokan Nambiar for their care, conversations, and feedback with specific parts of this volume; Ketaki Chowkhani, Vishal Pratap Singh Deo, Jagriti Gangopadhyay, Shining Star Lyngdoh, Raghu Menon, Prabodhan Pol, and Anubhav Sengupta for the great conversations from time to time. The role of my former colleagues at Manipal was crucial in orienting me towards writing and publishing; I thank Mrinal Kaul for continuing to be there for me as a source of counsel, support, and anecdotes; Meera Baindur, Chandan Bose, and Ranjana Saha for the tips on writing, rewriting, and the logistics of publishing.

Many thanks to all my students who were and continue to be a source of joy and inspiration, and especially the doctoral students working with me, Anagha Anil, Abeer Khatoon, and Samseer Mambra.

Parts of this monograph were presented at various conferences, workshops, or as independent talks: at *Nation, Gender and History: Asian Cinemas in Perspective*, Centre of Oriental Studies, University of Vilnius, 7–9 September 2017; at the *25th European Conference on South Asian Studies (ECSAS 2018)*, European Association for South Asian Studies (EASAS), with Centre for South Asian Studies, Paris, 24–27 July 2018; at the *Fourth Annual Research and Orientation Workshop and Conference on Global Protection of Migrants & Refugees*, organized by Mahanirban Calcutta Research Group in collaboration with Rosa Luxemburg Stiftung, Kolkata, 25–29 November 2019; at DOT Talks (online), organized by Tetso College, Dimapur, Nagaland, 12 May 2020; at *Mezzaterra* (online) organized by Christ (deemed to be University), Bengaluru, 20 May 2020; (online) at *Research Methodology and Syllabus Making in Migration and Forced Migration Studies* organized by Mahanirban Calcutta Research Group, Kolkata, in collaboration with IWM, Vienna, 12 December 2020; at *WoCiCo 2021 I World Cinema International Conference* (online), organized by University Complutense of Madrid, 15–16 June 2021; (online) at the University of Potsdam, 7 December 2021; (online) at Center for Humanities at Tufts University, 10 March 2022; at *Writing Worlds, Worlds Writing* organized by the Department of English, St Joseph's College (Autonomous), Bengaluru, 16–18 June 2022; British Academy Writing Workshop, Kohima, 12–14 December 2022; *Manipal Centre for*

Humanities meets the Centre for South Asian Studies, University of Toronto (online), 1–3 February 2023; *Researchers at Work Conference* (RAW. Con) organized by the Centre for Comparative Literature, University of Hyderabad, India, 27–19 March 2023; and at New York University Abu Dhabi on 26 September 2023. I thank the organizers and the respondents in each of these events for their questions, suggestions, and comments, especially Aby Abraham, Afeef Ahmed, Achuth Ajit, Elika Assumi, Samata Biswas, Vindhya Buthpithiya, Ira Bhaskar, Priya Chandran, Sajaudeen Chapparban, Sowmya Dechamma, Christoph Emmrich, Ann George, William Gould, Hephzibah Israel, Shail Jha, Niveditha Kalarikkal, Mona Kareem, Nuaiman Keeprath Andru, Joseph Koyippally, Awanish Kumar, Mithilesh Kumar, M.T. Ansari, Mallika Leuzinger, Mara Matta, Darshana Sridhar Mini, Meharban Mohammed, Sanal Mohan, Aparna Nandakumar, Arya Parakkatte Vijayaraghavan, Sreebitha Payattu Valappil, Christopher Pinney, Anupama Prabhala, Srilata Raman, Florian Schybilski, S.V. Srinivas, Justin Stearns, John Thomas, Deepak Unnikrishnan, Deimantas Valanciunas, Valentina Vitali, and John Zavos.

For their help with resources, I thank Sabika Afsal, Afeefa Amariyil, Muhthasim Billah, Nusarath Jahan, Haneefa Mangadan, Ranees P.P., Basheera Sarqui, and Hafsath Tharammal. Thanks to Laure Assaf, Bindu Menon, Manishankar Prasad, Ratheesh Radhakrishnan, Muhammed Afzal P., Sadique P.K. Mampad, Manohar Reddy and Kena Wani for engaging with my work in various capacities. I acknowledge my debt to friends who amplify my voice on social media.

Permissions:

Fig. 1.1 is reproduced here thanks to K. K. Abdul Razaq.

Fig. 3.1 is reproduced here thanks to Sageer.

Parts of a section of Chapter 2 was published earlier as 'The Islamic Subject of Home Cinema of Kerala', *BioScope: South Asian Screen Studies* 10, no. 1 (2019): 30–51. Reproduced by permission of Sage Publications India Private Limited.

I thank Barun Sarkar, Darshana Sarkar, Natasha Sarkar, and Meghali Banerjee at Oxford University Press and Praveena A for holding my hand through the publication.

I acknowledge my debt to the extended family, relations, and parents' friend circle for helping me with their resources. This book owes much to their goodwill. I thank my colleagues, parents, siblings Shaheer and

Shahida, Riyas, Mediha, my nephew Tasin, my sons Aman Razi and Aysar Razi, and my partner Jumi, for being the world around me and the heart of my well-being.

I am indebted to every person and situation who has made this book possible. Thank you!

Introduction

A Rumour at the Borders

In the beginning there was rumour. 'Rumours of a land which har-
vests gold' was how the introductory voice-over in the Malayalam film
Vilkkanundu Swapnangal (*Dreams for Sale*) (Azad, 1980) called it. The
rumoured land was 'Dubai'. The film showed its audience the less-than-
desirable conditions of labour and life in the Gulf. But it also conjured the
fabled riches of the Gulf too, and the undreamt of rise it can bestow on
those who are willing to take their chances. The film showed the Dubai
dream. That was 1980.

Cut to the present, and that dream supposedly has begun to fade.
Malayalam Gulf cinemas resort to voice-over, again and again, in the beginning or in the end of the film, to establish authoritatively the 'truth'—
the bitter truth—of migration.[1] All of these voice-overs establish the Gulf
as a place of hardship and distress. All of them say it as if it is a revelation.
The reality of the Gulf seems to be a truth that needs to be told over and
over again.

Rumour and revelation will occupy us in this chapter. The bond that is
produced in the hissing of a rumour or the largesse of a revelation, that
performative exclusion and inclusion, is the synecdoche of what this
book attempts to study—the formation of collectivities in the sharing of a
secret. For us, that secret is the Gulf in Kerala.

---

[1] Examples include *Visit Visa* (Shafi Orange, 2014), *Passport* (Manoj Mohan Mynagappally,
2015), or the hugely popular *Shawarma* (Jimmy Joseph, 2018). For a discussion on Gulf Malayali
film productions for their quality of empathy, see Darshana Sreedhar Mini, 'Transnational
Ethical Screens: Empathetic Networks in Malayalam Short Films from the Gulf', *Film History* 32,
no. 3 (2020).

The Gulf Migrant Archives in Kerala. Mohamed Shafeeq Karinkurayil, Oxford University Press. © Mohamed Shafeeq
Karinkurayil 2024. DOI: 10.1093/9780198910619.003.0001

The Lie of the Land

Kerala is situated in the deep southwest corner of India. With the Arabian Sea on one side and the Western Ghats on the other, one could read the region as naturally endowed with a common unique destiny. The state of Kerala is, however, the result of the linguistic reorganization of states undertaken by the Union Government of India in response to the vociferous demands for such reorganization from the various dominant linguistic communities of south India.[2] The state of Kerala came into existence in 1956 through a merger of the Malabar District of the Madras Presidency with the two former princely states of Cochin and Travancore. Provinces were added to or cut off from these provinces through negotiations with the would-be states of Karnataka and Tamil Nadu, both of which were also formed through the same reorganization and through mergers of former princely states with parts of the former presidencies as well as through partitions of previously continuous territorial units.

Malayalam, one of the languages of Kerala, has near complete dominance within its dominion. A little more than 97 per cent of the population of Kerala speak the language.[3] In Malayalam the word 'Malayalam' also means 'the knowable' and 'the known'. To evoke 'Bhoomi Malayalam' is to evoke the whole earth, or at least what is known of it. An alliterative saying goes Manja chera malarnnu kadichal malayalathi marunnilla— 'there is no cure in the known (Malayalam as a language and as the world) for the bite of a supine rat snake. But to evoke the known earth need not always be to place oneself in the centre of the world; it could be to signal the growth of the self into the world.[4] Placed along the trade routes of the Indian Ocean, Kerala has a rich history of maritime relations with the East as well as the West of the Old World, and across ages. The first Jews supposedly came during the reign of King Solomon (r. 970–931 BCE).

---

[2] The demand for the recognition of linguistic communities as territorial blocs dates back to the pre-independence period, at least to the 1920 conference of the Indian National Congress which was held at Nagpur.

[3] https://censusindia.gov.in/nada/index.php/catalog/10209 Last accessed 02 December 2023.

[4] Malayalam, however, did not always exist as the name of a language of a people. The connection between Kerala and its various communities was made bypassing the language question. See G. Arunima, 'Imagining communities – differently: Print, language and the (public sphere) in colonial Kerala', Indian Economic Social History Review 43, no.1 (2006), doi: 10.1177/001946460504300103.

The archaeologists dig up coins of the Roman Empire once in a while. St Thomas the Apostle is supposed by some to have made his escape to the shores of Kerala in 52 CE as he fled the Roman Empire. A few churches claim that they were built by the saint, and therefore the first ones in South Asia. This, some would take the pleasure of reminding you, is a few centuries before Christianity became the official religion of the Roman Empire, and many more before it became the heritage of Europe. The more widely accepted narrative is the arrival of Thomas of Cana, whose arrival is dated to the fourth century CE.

Similarly, the first mosque in India is in Kerala. The Cheraman Perumal Masjid in Kodungallur (formerly Cranganore) is believed to have been built in 629 CE by a group of Muslim traders from Arabia led by Malik Deenar. This was in the final years of the Prophet Muhammad's lifetime. Legend has it that the incumbent Zamorin (Samudiri, as he is called in Malayalam, the title of the Chera king) happened to see the miracle of the splitting of the moon undertaken by the Prophet in response to a challenge by the unbelievers in Makkah. Several years later the Zamorin hears the backstory to the miracle he had witnessed and thus comes to know of the Prophet and his faith. Zamorin then divides his vast kingdom among his chieftains and left for Makkah. The legend has it that he met the Prophet, was given the name of Tajuddin, or 'the Crown of Faith' and passed away on his way back.[5] He is now buried in Salalah in Oman, where the hills, the hanging clouds, and the banana plantations evokehis homeland across the ocean.[6]

Kappad, near the coastal town of Kozhikode (formerly known as Calicut), was the site of the arrival of the first Portuguese fleet that made its way to the East Indies. Led by Vasco da Gama (c.1469–1524), this fleet signalled a shift in the power equations of the Old World. As the Portuguese set out on a path of belligerence provoked also by their experience of dealing with many Muslim kingdoms along the African coast,[7] the Islamic scholars residing in the region, part of Zamorin's dominion,

[5] Sebastian R. Prange, *Monsoon Islam: Trade and Faith on the Medieval Malabar Coast* (New Delhi: Cambridge University Press, 2018), 1–2.

[6] This is not to imply that the location was chosen for this reason. For an account of the final resting place of Tajuddin, see Wilson Chacko Jacob, *For God or Empire: Sayyid Fadl and the Indian Ocean World* (Stanford, CA: Stanford University Press, 2019).

[7] Sanjay Subrahmanyam, *The Career and Legend of Vasco Da Gama* (Cambridge: Cambridge University Press, 1998).

called on the Muslims of the land and the Muslim kings in other parts of peninsular India to fight the Portuguese, for this was an attack on the abode of Islam ruled by a benevolent Hindu king.[8] At the end of a phase of rapacious assault in the sea and on land, the trade in the Indian Ocean was lost from the hands of the Arabian traders who would soon be labelled pirates. The hero of the age, Kunjali Marakkar IV (d. 1600), naval commander of the Zamorins who engaged the Portuguese on the sea, would soon fall as the colonizers reached a deal with the Zamorin, and was hanged to martyrdom in Goa. The Portuguese period was followed by the Dutch, and a century later peninsular India would be the stage of the British–French rivalry as well as the native kingdoms, in intricate and intriguing alliances. Meanwhile the defeat of Tipu at the hands of the British in 1792 meant that British dominion was established over parts of Kerala known as the Malabar district, initially a part of the Bombay Presidency, and transferred to the Madras Presidency in 1800. This part would merge with the two princely states of Cochin and Travancore to form Kerala in 1956.

Colonial Kerala had one of the worst practices of caste discrimination in India. Not only was untouchability prevalent, but there was also unseeability. This refers to the practice in which members of certain castes should not come within the sight of any member of the upper caste. 'The highest-status groups forced their underlings to display servility in a host of ways, while lower groups in turn exacted similar marks of respect from others held to be still lower than themselves.'[9] The caste system dictated the choice of one's job and sustenance, the houses one could build, and

---

[8] Sheikh Zainuddin Makhdoom II (c.1531–1583), a Ponnani-based Islamic scholar with Hadramawti origins, wrote his *Tuhfat-al-Mujahideen* (c.1583) as a call to each Muslim to defend the abode of Islam and as a plea to Muslim rulers in India to join Zamorin's fight against the Portuguese. Another Islamic scholar from the region, Qadi Muhammad bin Abdul Aziz, composed his *Fathul Mubyn* a few years later, denouncing the Muslim kings for refusing to fight the Portuguese, and dedicating his work to Zamorin whom he calls a most just ruler. Interestingly, the former book was dedicated to Ali Adil Shah, who later broke off the alliance with Zamorin, prompting the denunciation in the latter.

For some recent studies on these texts, see Engseng Ho, 'Custom and Conversion in Malabar: Zayn Al-Din Al-Malibari's Gift of the Mujahidin', in *Islam in South Asia in Practice*, ed. Barbara Daly Metcalf (Princeton, NJ: Princeton University Press, 2009); Mahmood Kooria, 'An Abode of Islam under a Hindu King: Circuitous Imagination of Kingdoms among Muslims of Sixteenth-Century Malabar', *Journal of Indian Ocean World Studies* 1 (2017); P. K. Yasser Arafath, 'Muslim Ulema in the Shafiite Cosmopolis: Fitna, Piety and Resistance in the Age of Fasad', *The Medieval History Journal* 21, no. 1 (2018).

[9] Robin Jeffrey, *Politics, Women and Well-Being* (New York: Palgrave Macmillan, 1992), 2. Much of what follows in this section is informed by Jeffrey, occasionally with details from other sources indicated in such instances.

even the clothes one could wear.[10] The nineteenth century saw a series of revolts against the caste system over a range of issues such as the sartorial codes (for example the Channar Revolt) and access to public roads which were denied to the outcastes (agricultural strike by Ayyankali). The series of Mappila militant outbreaks throughout the nineteenth century against the colonial state came to a close with the popular uprising of 1921, which was also a rebellion against the arbitrary evictions of the peasants.[11]

The late nineteenth century and the early twentieth century were periods of intense social transformation. Some of the leaders who provided political and spiritual leadership of this period were Narayana Guru, Ayyankali, K. P. Karuppan et al. The period is marked by the intense churning within communities, anti-caste consciousness,[12] family reform, and the end of the matrilineal system signalling the arrival of modern familial structure represented by the figure of the father.[13] It also witnessed the disintegration of earlier grove-based rural traditions and the emergence of rigid communal identities,[14] the emergence of Malayalam as a common language among the different communities of Kerala, and thereby the creation of a Malayali identity and public sphere, the literary and imaginative cosmopolitanism which were influenced by ideas from across the world fostered through the experiences of migration and exile, institutions such as the Church and Communist Party, [15] expansion of public education, and the intimations of a welfare state.[16]

---

[10] Thus while the lower castes and Mappila Muslim men could not cover their upper body, certain outcastes/Dalits were required to wear necklaces with stone beads. See Bernard S. Cohn, *Colonialism and Its Forms of Knowledge: British in India* (Princeton, NJ: Princeton University Press, 1996), 138–143.

[11] K. N. Panikkar, *Against Lord and State: Religion and Peasant Uprisings in Malabar, 1836–1921* (New Delhi: Oxford University Press, 1989).

[12] Jeffrey, *Politics, Women and Well-Being*.

[13] G. Arunima, *There Comes Papa: Colonialism and the Transformation of Matriliny in Kerala, Malabar, c. 1850–1940* (Hyderabad: Orient Blackswan, 2008).

[14] Jeffrey, *Politics, Women and Well-Being*; Dilip M. Menon, 'Becoming "Hindu" and "Muslim": Identity and Conflict in Malabar', Working Papers id:2921, *eSocialSciences*, 2010.

[15] For discussions, see Seema Alavi, *Muslim Cosmopolitanism in the Age of Empire* (Cambridge, MA and London: Harvard University Press, 2015); Arunima, 'Imagining Communities – Differently'; Dilip M. Menon, 'A Local Cosmopolitan: Kesari Balakrishna Pillai and the Invention of Europe for a Modern Kerala', *Tapasam* 2, nos 3–4 (2007); J. Devika, 'Migration, transnationalism, and modernity: Thinking of Kerala's many cosmopolitanisms', *Cultural Dynamics* 24, nos 2–3 (2012); J. Devika, 'Cochin Creoles and the Perils of Casteist Cosmpolitanism: Reading *Requiem for the Living*', *The Journal of Commonwealth Literature*, 51, no. 1 (2016); Jacob, *For God or Empire*; Udaya Kumar, *Writing the First Person: Literature, History, and Autobiography in Modern Kerala* (Ranikhet: Permanent Black in association with Ashoka University, 2016).

[16] Manali Desai, 'Indirect British Rule, State Formation, and Welfarism in Kerala, India, 1860–1957', *Social Science History* 29, no. 3 (2005); Vipin K. Kadavath, *Historicising Kshemam: A*

After its formation in 1956, Kerala became only the second place in the world to vote the Communists to power. It earned the epithet of being the Yenan of India. In the ensuing decades the social relations were thoroughly transformed. As Robin Jeffrey notes with reference to a gesture of obsequiousness of the lower castes, 'the servile hand before the mouth gave way to the challenge of the shaken fist'.[17] While led by an upper caste leadership, the Communist movement in Kerala was 'certainly the most, and possibly the only, successful instance of lower-class organization in postcolonial India'.[18] The Communist rule in Kerala has been credited with the implementation of the Land Reforms (introduced in 1969 and implemented in the 1970s) which significantly altered the landholdings in Kerala and paved the way for acquisition of land by newly mobile communities. In the mid-1970s Kerala was upheld as a model for achieving high levels of social development—'both the birth rate and the infant mortality rate were falling, where average life expectancy was approaching 70 years, where the large majority of women and men could read and write, and where women indeed outnumbered men'[19]—despite the low level of economic development.[20] This came to be known as the 'Kerala Model'. The Communist Party also brought in the decentralization of power in Kerala and set up the foundation for a welfare state. Today Kerala is known as the bastion of progressive politics and is the only state in India where the Communist parties hold any significant electoral influence.

Study of Vernacular Political Discourse, Unpublished PhD Diss., English and Foreign Languages University, 2015.

[17] Jeffrey, *Politics, Women and Well-Being*, 2.

[18] Patrick Heller, *The Labor of Development: Workers and the Transformation of Capitalism in Kerala, India* (Ithaca, NY and London: Cornell University Press, 2000), 13–14.

Taking stock of this period in Kerala's history and the role of the Communist movement in Kerala in popular struggles of the period, Nissim Mannathukkaren argues that the thesis which posit governmentality and passive revolution as the modes through which India's subalterns encounter modern political ideas does not hold in the case of Kerala. See Nissim Mannathukkaren, *Communism, Subaltern Studies and Postcolonial Theory: The Left in South India* (London and New York: Routledge, 2022).

[19] Jeffrey, *Politics, Women and Well-Being*, 4.

[20] Centre for Development Studies, *Poverty, Unemployment and Development Policy: A Case Study of Selected Issues with Reference to Kerala* (Bombay: Orient Longman, 1977).

Despite the progressive public sphere which upholds the values of egalitarianism and secularism, scholars have noted that caste has persisted in modern-day Kerala albeit in disguise. Aspects such as 'the caste division of labour and endogamous marriages, were left unchallenged and unchanged'.[21]

> Production continues to retain characteristics linking it to status: Izhava caste status is still linked to definitions of the community as 'toddy-tappers'; the most popular form of employment among Brahmans is school-teaching; most agricultural labourers are Pulayas. All this makes employment a less promising and significant arena for escape from caste hierarchy and for construction of a new identity than consumption.[22]

The persistence of caste along the lines of occupation also meant the persistence of the semiotic association between certain occupations and the position the occupation seemed to suggest in the social hierarchy.[23] The insistence on class in Kerala's intellectual discourse has blinded itself towards engaging with caste as a lived reality. The reality of caste with its denial in the public sphere leads to a state of double life where, there is an avowed ideology of equality but it is at the cost of erasing particularities. Anyone was capable of emerging as a liberated subject as long as they kept their occupation—as if the Malayali renaissance was echoing the Kantian injunction[24]—in the realm of the private.

There was, however, a way in which the professions could enter the realm of the public, and that was through unionization. The unions could organize rallies, demonstrations, and put pressure on the state, thus turning the private into a zone of the public, even while concerning

---

[21] Anna Lindberg, *Experience and Identity: A Historical Account of Class, Caste and Gender among Cashew Workers of Kerala, 1930–2000* (Lund: Department of History, University of Lund, 2001), 161, quoted in J. Devika, 'Egalitarian Developmentalism, Communist Mobilization, and the Question of Caste in Kerala State, India', *The Journal of Asian Studies* 69, no. 3 (2010): 807.

[22] Filippo Osella and Caroline Osella, *Social Mobility in Kerala: Modernity and Identity in Conflict* (London: Pluto Press, 2001), 118.

[23] An important aspect of the intra-community reformations of the late nineteenth and early twentieth centuries in Kerala has been to exhort the followers to leave those jobs which were considered inferior or immoral, such as Sree Narayana Guru's call to his followers to give up toddy tapping.

[24] Immanuel Kant, 'An Answer to the Question: "What is Enlightenment?"', in *Kant: Political Writings*, ed. H. S. Reiss, trans. H. B. Nisbet (Cambridge: Cambridge University Press, 1991).

themselves with the workplace conditions. It is still a private concern making demand on a public institution, rather than an active translation into a public genre.[25]

The public sphere, understood as such, was the space of universality, whose idioms had to be conjured in the absence of any historical precedence. Commenting on the articulation of Kerala identity by Elamkulam Manakkal Sankaran Namboodiripad (popularly known as EMS), the tallest Communist leader Kerala has produced, Devika notes that 'even as traditional caste servitude was challenged, upper-caste culture and social norms were not only largely spared, but actually reclaimed as the unifying "core" of Kerala's national culture'.[26] The efficacy of markers of dignity, symbolized for example by the white *mundu* (wraparound for the lower half of the body) adopted by communities towards the beginning of twentieth century as a symbol of respectability, lies in its uniformity, which was, however, of an upper caste provenance.[27]

---

[25] Thus, while issues like inflation or the price of specific commodities, say coconut or areca nut, takes the form of public discourse, the question of wages is understood to be a private affair. It is pertinent to note here that the word 'public' is translated as 'pothu' ('common') in Malayalam which thereby already assumes the space of the public to be one concerned with common rather than particular concern. Essentially what we are looking at here is how the question of livelihood stepped back from being a common concern. For a discussion on the word 'public' in early twentieth-century Kerala, see Udaya Kumar, 'Ambivalences of Publicity: Transparency and Exposure in K. Ramakrishna Pillai's Thought', in *The Public Sphere From Outside the West*, eds Divya Dwivedi and Sanil V. (New Delhi: Bloomsbury, 2015).

But seen differently, this withdrawal of labour from the sphere of public to unions that constituted the sphere of the workplace was in itself the signalling of the crisis of radical politics which had to overcome caste in the interest of a universal citizen while also articulate a working-class politics. Considering the organic link between caste and occupation, the symbolic measures to overcome it ironically made working class a public rhetoric anyone could identify with while work itself became a private affair.

[26] Devika, 'Egalitarian Developmentalism', 809. For a scathing criticism of the caste affiliations of EMS's imagination of Kerala, see also Dilip M. Menon, 'Being a Brahmin the Marxist Way: EMS Nambudiripad and the Pasts of Kerala', in *The Blindness of Insight* (Chennai: Navayana, 2006).

[27] For more on the sociopolitical dimensions of *mundu*, see Mohamed Shafeeq Karinkurayil, 'A Strangeness One Can Occupy: Clothes and Their Codes in the Photographs of Gulf Migrants from Kerala', in *Migration in the Making of the Gulf Space: Social, Political, and Cultural Dimensions*, eds Antia Mato Bouzas and Lorenzo Casini (New York and Oxford: Berghahn Books, 2022).

Similar was the case with the saree for women. The point, however, is that whether *mundu* or saree, its universality also lies in its availability to express the particular. Thus, if one were to read Basheer's *Ntuppuppakkonandarnnu* along sartorial lines, it was about the transition of saree from being a non-Muslim sartorial option to it being an option that can be universal while also convey a Muslim particularity, in the way in which Kunjupathumma, the female protagonist of the novel, pulls the end of the saree and places it on her head (thus signifying the Muslim headcovering). See Vaikom Muhammad Basheer, *Ntuppuppakkoranandarnnu* (Kottayam: DC Books, 2008). The *mundu* can similarly convey a Muslim particularity when its outer fold opens towards the left rather than the right.

Despite the seismic shifts that had transformed Kerala from the late nineteenth century, despite the arrival of a clamorous and assertive public, Kerala did not have much to offer its struggling classes. For most, the landholdings were far too few for gainful agriculture, and employment were hard to come by.[28] The economic crisis caused by the less developed capitalist sector meant that the working classes had to renegotiate the revolutionary impulse with class compromise.[29] The radical tendencies in the early communism was soon supplanted by a developmentalist ideology framed by the nation state which left behind any revolutionary change.[30] The question of redistribution of wealth was replaced with developmentalism. The new ideology called for the extension of the infrastructure of the state, and not the radical democracy it was supposed to be. The developmental logic operated on governmental categories. Thus, while the ideas of uniformity and non-particularity were essential to the public sphere, the developmental logic worked by demarcating this public into separate gender, region, tribes, castes, and communities and through operations which targeted or prioritized some gender, region, tribe, caste, or community over the other. At the same time, communities became an important pivot in politics by the 1970s when the hegemony of an earlier technocratic model of nation-building was unravelling.[31] The need to exert pressure to gain resources from a state which regulated its economy often resulted in these associations existing along prior faultlines, such as that of caste and community. This made caste and community as an

---

[28] The modi operandi of Land Reforms have been credited with the continuing landlessness and marginalization of Dalits. The bestowal of ownership was marginal. The governments found itself left with less and less lands identified as excess lands to be redistributed to the landless. See Jeffrey, *Politics, Women and Well-Being*.

[29] Heller, *The Labor of Development*.

[30] Dilip M. Menon, 'Lost Visions? Imagining a National Culture in the 1950s', in *Land, Labour & Rights: Daniel Thorner Memorial Lectures*, ed. Alice Thorner (New Delhi: Tulika Books, 2001).

[31] Sudipta Kaviraj, *The Imaginary Institution of India: Politics and Ideas* (New York: Columbia University Press, 2010).

Heller claims that Kerala does not fit into this model because of its unique agrarian history of class formation. Heller, *The Labor of Development*, 48–49. Such a thesis rests on the idea that class identification has trumped communitarian identification. However, communities have always existed as a pressure bloc in Kerala's electoral system, and the limited traction that the Communist movement has among Christians and Muslims in Kerala suggests that class identification has not been as triumphant as it is imagined to be.

identity a visible public force both as an object of governmentality and the subject of democratic politics.[32]

A corollary of the developmental politics is the citizen–subject divide. The Indian nationalist struggle in its moment of popularization was predicated on a pedagogical function which created the ideal Indian.[33] The nascent Indian state took on this pedagogical function. While citizenship was universal in India, when it came to voting rights, cultural citizenship was one in which the populations had to be trained. Cultural citizenship posited certain competencies which were understood to be a result of one's ability to transcend one's private sphere of belonging. A secular modern education was both a sign of this and the means to achieve such a universality. The idea of the *modern* Malayali was predicated on a continuity between her mind and of her surroundings. Udaya Kumar[34] illustrates this point with reference to the early Malayalam novel *Indulekha* (1889). The eponymous Nair heroine's refined sensibility is in evidence around her, in the painting that hangs on the wall, and the books on the shelf. To surround oneself with objects that one has understood to be of high cultural value is not therefore just an index of economic mobility, but also to suggest one's acknowledgement of modern sensibility, and hence a bid to make invisible one's caste particularity. Thus, cultural citizenship became something that could be and is to be demonstrated through the objects one had around oneself. [35] Added to this is the thrust on consumerism in the 1980s that was adopted as a national ideology which replaced pedagogy with consumerism as the basis for the formation of a national cultural citizenship.[36] The consumer became the locus of the proof of development and the spectral presence of the simultaneity

---

[32] It is not implied here that these formations have to take an explicit electoral party character. They are more often than not communities represented by their proxies in the electoral field, or as pressure blocs within existing parties.

[33] Partha Chatterjee, *Nationalist Thought and the Colonial World: A Derivative Discourse* (London: Zed Books, 1986).

[34] Kumar, *Writing the First Person*.

[35] While Nairs are caste Hindus and would be considered upper caste in popular parlance today, Udaya Kumar notes, with reference to early literary histories of Malayalam in circulation around the time of Indulekha, that in the Brahmin/non-Brahmin dichotomy of the period, the non-Brahmin position was elided to be Nair by default. See Udaya Kumar, 'Shaping a Literary Space: Early Literary Histories in Malayalam and Normative Uses of the Past', in *Literature and Nationalist Ideology*, ed. Hans Harder (New Delhi: Social Science Press, 2010).

[36] William Mazzarella, *Shoveling Smoke: Advertising and Globalization in Contemporary India* (Delhi: Oxford University Press, 2003).

of the nation, replacing the thrust on state developmental effort meant to produce the enlightened citizen in the earlier era.

The Promise of Migration

Migration from the region that constitute present-day Kerala in search of job and sustenance has been an ongoing process. In the beginning of the twentieth century, Ceylon was the target. There were efforts to settle in Brazil, though in much smaller numbers. In the mid-twentieth century, Malaya and Singapore were the prime targets of migration. Devika comments that migration in the early twentieth century, and the critical cosmopolitanism that came to accrue through the experience of migration has been the understudied aspect of the modernity in Kerala.[37] In the dominant accounts, Kerala modernity beginning at the end of the 19th century, which is usually called the Malayali renaissance, is attributed to the unification of language, print modernity and national consciousness (the way in which we recounted it in the earlier section), completely overlooking the role of migrations.

The migration to the Gulf, which began through British intermediaries in the 1940s and in smaller numbers,[38] began to achieve mass proportions in the late 1970s, enabled by the oil boom in the Gulf and complemented with a labour crunch. This was the time, as shown earlier, when radical politics in Kerala had settled for class compromise and developmental state.[39] The securitization and depoliticization of oil rigs by the British companies in the 1950s and the need to avoid workplace unrest such as the strikes by the local (*khaleeji*) labour force in the 1960s played a major role in aiding this large-scale flow of migrants to the Arabian Gulf.[40] The typical migrant to the Gulf was drawn from among populations which were understood by the state as not yet possessing the

---

[37] Devika, 'Migration, transnationalism, and modernity'.

[38] Ian J. Seccombe, 'Labour migration to the Arabian Gulf: evolution and characteristics 1920–1950', *British Society for Middle Eastern Studies. Bulletin* 10, no. 1 (1983).

[39] The 1970s was also the time of the militant Communist movement, popularly known as Naxalism in some parts of Kerala, infusing some radicalism back to Communism. Aiming for the 'thunder of spring', the mobilization, as a popular movement, was a short-lived one.

[40] Wright, *Between Dreams and Ghosts*, 147.

cultural competency to represent India abroad.[41] Many of the early migrants reached the shores of the Gulf through extra legal means. They were later regularized through the efforts of the Indian authorities in the Gulf. While there were around ten thousand Keralan migrants in the Gulf region by the late 1950s, the figure rose to around two hundred thousand by the late 1970s. [42] By 1998, the Gulf region accounted for almost 94 per cent of the total international migrants from Kerala. The number of Keralan migrants in the Gulf for 2014 is around two million.[43]

Gulf migration has been credited with being the single most important factor which contributed to the reduction of unemployment, the alleviation of poverty, and redistribution of wealth in Kerala since the 1970s.[44] The early migrants to the Gulf were mostly drawn from the economically and socially deprived,[45] and migration was understood to be one of the avenues of improving one's social location. As Robin Jeffrey noted in 1992, 'the "Gulf boom" has in a sense provided the hope that politics held out in the 1940s and 1950s'.[46] The wage differential involved in Gulf migration, that one can earn a lot more money in the Gulf doing an inferior job than many respectable jobs in Kerala, severed the link between occupation and remuneration. Migration bracketed one's work while allowing its results to circulate in the public sphere. The migrant could now accumulate luxurious good around him. The Gulf is credited with being the source for the introduction or popularization of gadgets such as cassette recorders, still and movie cameras, washing machines, etc. 'The proportion of "luxurious" and "very good" houses is much higher among households with an emigrant or a return emigrant.'[47] Similarly, houses with emigrants are more likely to possess consumer durables such as television, refrigerator, phones, and motorcycles.[48] Conspicuous consumption

---

[41] For a discussion on cultural citizenship and the pedagogical and protective role of the state in relation to Gulf migrants from India, see Andrea Wright, *Between Dreams and Ghosts: Indian Migration and Middle Eastern Oil* (Stanford, CA: Stanford University Press, 2021), 21–48.

[42] K. C. Zachariah and Irudaya Rajan, *Kerala's Gulf Connection, 1998–2011: Economic and Social Impact of Migration* (Hyderabad: Orient Blackswan, 2012), 2–3.

[43] K. C. Zachariah and S. Irudaya Rajan, *Emigration from Kerala: End of an Era* (Kochi: RedInk, 2018), 57.

[44] B. A. Prakash, 'Gulf Migration and Its Economic Impact: The Kerala Experience', *Economic and Political Weekly* 30, no. 50 (1998).

[45] P. R. Gopinathan Nair, 'Asian Emigration to the Middle East: Emigration from India', Working Paper no.180, Centre for Development Studies, Trivandrum, 1983.

[46] Jeffrey, *Politics, Women and Well-Being*, 12.

[47] Zachariah and Rajan, *Kerala's Gulf Connection*, 84.

[48] Zachariah and Rajan, *Kerala's Gulf Connection*, 88.

and excessive spending in life-cycle rituals were strategies through which migrants from lower social orders try to better their social status in the face of the public back home.

The increasing importance of consumption is also linked both to migration and to economic liberalization, which have brought new and more expensive goods into the villages. For migrant workers in particular, who form the vanguard of consumption activity, sites of production are hidden, far removed from the village; this works to their advantage as public attention turns on spending behaviour where they take a prominent role in consumption, rather than on their labour, likely to be low or unskilled work.[49]

While migration played an important role in the redistribution of wealth, it also drew its grammar and efficacy from the value system of a hierarchical society. The turn to religion as well as masculinity[50] can be seen as the assumption of respectability. However, these strategies work only to a certain extent, as caste in a bounded society is not easy to shrug off from public memory.[51] The Gulf had to contend with the local realities in Kerala which would not allow it to be a living reality, let alone a model for life.

The invisibility of production could also be read as the unavailability of a public discourse to speak about labour. The fact that the only way in which one's profession could break into the public sphere, through unionization, was not a possibility in the case of the Gulf migrants because migration essentially did not fit into the existing logic of unionization, which is premised on the (now unravelling) fit between the worker and the citizen. Migration brought about a break in this fit in that it divorced citizenship from labour. One belonged somewhere and laboured elsewhere. The invisibilization of the Gulf can therefore be read as the deprivation of a public language of rights to speak about the Gulf.

To return to the film with which we began this chapter, *Vilkkanundu Swapgnangal*, which referred to Dubai as a rumour—the film begins with

---

[49] Osella and Osella, *Social Mobility in Kerala*, 118.

[50] Filippo Osella and Caroline Osella, 'Migration, Money and Masculinity in Kerala', *The Journal of Royal Anthropological Institute* 6, no. 1 (2000).

[51] Osella and Osella, *Social Mobility in Kerala*.

a group of men finding their way to Khor Fakkan on a small dhow. These means of arriving at the Gulf was undocumented. Typically, the migrant of the late 1960s reached the Gulf outside the state's ambit. They travelled without documents and reached a land which had not yet attained its present political contours. The state as the trainer and the protector of the Gulf migrants was not so in the case of these early migrants. This break between the state and labour made the Gulf a public secret in that it did not fall under the domain of a public discussion. As far as the state and the civil society discourse which was tied to the state were concerned, the Gulf migration did not exist.

This privatization of the Gulf in the public sphere of Kerala meant that while the Gulf is much spoken about, it is spoken about as if it is a private affair. This was a genre of speaking as if in private, and not really a discourse which was confined spatially to the public sphere (say, in the private confines of one's home). An important aspect of this privatization is how the effects of Gulf, when inhabiting the genres of the private, can take on idioms and tropes that would be considered irrational as public talk, but has force in the public as occulted knowledge precisely because it belongs to the private.[52] These idioms and tropes tried to explain the almost miraculous mobility that was made possible by the Gulf. The migrant who found a treasure, the rich Arab man who gave his everything to a migrant because of immense trust, as well as the fabulous characters of the wise Arab, the terribly cruel Arab, or the incredibly stupid Arab are all part of this private talk, and so are the fabulous cunning migrant, the

---

[52] With reference to the formation of the public sphere in Kerala in the early twentieth century, Udaya Kumar has shown how it was created with reference to the state (in this case, the Thiruvithamkoor state). Matters understood to be private, such as one's sex life, of the public functionaries, was leveraged in newspapers towards public end, thereby complicating any neat separation between the private and the public in postcolonial contexts. Kumar refers to such items as scandals. The newspaper presents these item as if these are public secrets even though these may be uttered for the first time by the newspaper itself. Considering that the newspapers in the early twentieth century were bringing a public into existence, the 'private' can be considered a constitutive element of the public itself in that the public sphere was also to be the sphere of visibility and exposure. See Kumar, 'Ambivalences of Publicity'.

It is important to take into account the added force a news item acquires by sustaining the clandestine nature of its information even as the very utterance makes it public. As Michael Taussig illustrates with reference to Franco's Spain, genres such as rumour, gossip, and silence play an important part in sustaining the state because they appear private and intimate. Michael Taussig, *Defacement: Public Secrecy and the Labor of the Negative* (Stanford, CA: Stanford University Press, 1999). However, what we see in the early phase of Gulf migration is the labelling of a knowledge systems as rumour, gossip, and tall tales because the experience of migration could not be expressed adequately in the rational public speech.

sincere-to-death migrant, the thieving migrant, the all-sacrificing migrant as well as the migrant who would sell his very own people to Arab lust. The Gulf was, basically, a genre considered private, with all its force, emotions, and affect, but devoid of a public language other than that of remittance. It was part of this very privatization of the Gulf that the Gulf became a space of exaggeration in Kerala—that everything in the Gulf is better and bigger ('our *puttu*[53] is this much, but in the Gulf their *puttu* is *this* much', the street narrator would say and gesture the wide expanse with his hands to show the bigness of puttu in the Gulf; that people travel there in planes like we do in buses, etc.).

These conditions gave rise to paradoxical forms of visibility for the Gulf. On the one hand, the Gulf as a source of remittance allowed one to try their hand at cultural citizenship. The developmental thrust along governmental lines together with communitarian mobilization in politics meant that the Gulf money came to be invested in Kerala as community capital for projects such as schools, colleges, and hospitals, and such funding were made possible in the Gulf through organizations along communitarian lines, such as in the case of the Kerala Muslim Cultural Centre, which is affiliated to the political party Muslim League which is influential among the Muslims of Kerala. At the same time, as a place of labour with its own experiences, the Gulf had to occupy a private genre of discourse in Kerala, as all professions devoid of unions were. The occupational struggles of the Gulf migrant worker did not find a channel in Kerala. The migrant's tears, sweat, dreams, miseries, were all private affairs. As far as the public sphere was concerned, the Gulf was a source of remittance alone.

This 'secretive' nature of the Gulf made the Gulf migrant an object of fantasy and contradiction. He was the suffering rich! The Gulf migrant was a sought-after groom, a fact played to hilarious effects in the comedy films of the late 1980s. In the social realist mode, the Gulf migrant became the symbol of illicit wealth and a threat to the goodness of the older ways of life.[54]

---

[53] Steamed cylindrical rice flour cakes usually consumed as breakfast food.

[54] Dilip M. Menon, 'Things Fall Apart: The Cinematic Rendition of Agrarian Landscape in South India', *The Journal of Peasant Studies* 32, no. 2 (2005).

Towards the closing years of the twentieth century, migrant narratives began appearing in the mainstream discourse. Malayalam newspapers ran accounts of Gulf migrant lives. Babu Bharadwaj published his Saudi memoirs with the well-established Mathrubhumi Press in 2000. In the early years of the twenty-first century, the newly founded Kairali television channel aired *Pravasalokam* (*The World of Expatriates*). This programme spoke about the difficult conditions faced by many migrants in the Gulf and offered its viewers the opportunity to phone in and share their woes about missing migrants, cases of unpaid labour, harassment, etc. in the Gulf.[55] In the process it relied on a network of migrants. In 2008, Benyamin's debut novel of *Aatujeevitham*[56] was published to unprecedented success. The novel narrated the harrowing story of Najeeb who worked as a goatherd in Saudi Arabia, and was ostensibly based on the real-life experiences of a migrant by the same name.

All this points to a change in the earlier configuration of the public domain with respect to the Gulf. It is not coincidental that we now finally have the breaking out of the Gulf into the public discourse of Kerala. There have been vast changes between the conditions that existed in the late 1960s and the 1970s and those that exist now. The profile of the migrant has changed thanks to a new generation who have been trained with an eye on the opportunities in the Gulf. The state measures such as making matriculation a necessary qualification for migration to the Gulf also changed the educational profile of the migrants. The Gulf migrants have also started unionizing and putting pressure on the Indian state. The state has stretched its reach among the migrants through agencies such as the Non Resident Keralites Affairs (NoRKA) initiative of Kerala state. Moreover, the Gulf itself has changed considerably in its profiles, changing its image to tourism destinations and bureaucratic corporation states, thus making the Gulf of the migrant memoirs a thing of the past.

Surely, the Gulf could now be spoken about in the public as an experience and not just as a place of abstract labour. However, what was interesting about this new visibility—with the exception of the television programme *Pravasalokam*—was that it took the form of revelation. It

---

[55] For more on this television programme, see Darshana Sreedhar Mini, 'Public Interest Television and Social Responsibility: The Search for the Missing Person in Indian Television', *International Journal of Digital Television* 7, no. 2 (2016).

[56] Benyamin, *Aatujeevitham* (Thrissur: Green Books, 2008).

was always a matter of opening the eyes of Malayali towards the reality of the Gulf. Thus, Salam Kodiyathur, who would put forth the Gulf experience as the major plank of his independent film movement,[57] would begin his first ever Gulf film, *Parethan Thirichu Varunnu* (*The Revenant*), with visuals of rubbish pickers in the Gulf. Benyamin would speak of *Aatujeevitham* in biblical terms, as the Christ who has arrived to redeem generations of Gulf migrants from their muteness regarding the reality of their migrant lives.

The idiom of revelation suggests that though the Gulf as an experience of life could now find representation in mainstream Malayalam public discourse, it still had to resort to a poetics of secrecy. It was still about the disclosure of a secret. Such a performative revelation, rather than being a movement from a private genre of speech to a public one, is in fact a continuity of the private genre, albeit in modes that are different hitherto. The personal address and *bildungsroman* nature of the novel, the primacy of the individual and his loneliness in the memoir, and the individual rather than collective address that marks the new cinema, all indicate that the Gulf continues to be spoken about in the mode of a rumour. Perhaps then, rather than treating the private nature of the Gulf as an aberration of the public sphere, one should see it as constitutive of the condition of migration itself.

Andrea Wright, in her study of the migrant Indian oil labourers in the Gulf, emphasizes the role of networks in the lives of the migrants, and argues that the conceptual weight put on migrants as those in need of protection or as brand bearers accord primacy to statist epistemic infrastructure at the cost of recognizing transnational communities that the conceptual infrastructure of network brings to light.[58] The insistence on the individual is not specific to academic study alone. Rather, the migrant experience in itself, as narrated in photographs, memoirs, novels, and films, etc. is thoroughly individuated in its epistemic coordinates. Even as migration is facilitated and sustained through a network, the individual is supposed to be the fulcrum of migrant world-making. This is not to deny that a host of migrants appear as one's support system in the narrative. However, migrants also appear in other forms, as touts, tricksters,

---

[57] See Chapter 2 in this volume.
[58] Wright, *Between Dreams and Ghosts*, 65–66.

exploiters, spies of one's employer, etc. Ultimately, it is the individual story, heroic or tragic, of facing the world with all its different characters.

The Temporariness of the Gulf Migration

An appreciation of this cognitive limit of narrating migration has to be sought not in Kerala alone, but also in the structural conditions in the Gulf. The early 1970s saw the stabilization of the Gulf region, now known as the countries of the Gulf Cooperation Council (GCC), into its present territorial contours. While the Kingdom of Saudi Arabia was established as early as 1932, and Kuwait in 1946, the other constituents namely Bahrain, Qatar, and the United Arab Emirates (UAE), came into existence in 1971, and the period of political turbulence in Oman ended in 1975. The GCC was formed in 1981.

What makes the migration to the Gulf countries different from the other targets of Keralan economic migration—Malaya (now Malaysia) and Singapore up to the 1960s, or North America, Europe, and Australia today—is the impossibility of any hope of being citizens one day in the countries of the Arabian Gulf. The Gulf countries have a migrant population many more times the size of its population. Philippe Fargues tells us that the Gulf countries adopted three policies to safeguard itself in the wake of the large-scale migration to their countries from the various parts of the world. The first of these was to deny the migrants citizenship. The second was to promote the birth rate among natives. And the third was to build a local workforce by investing in education. The second and the third did not work owing to the inherent contradictions. A state that was welfare-centric and educationist kept away the women from their assumed role as reproducers, and the citizens from work. Ultimately it was the first policy alone, that of protecting a zone of citizenship that came with its privileges which upheld the national coherence.[59] This refusal of citizenship to migrants is the central plank of nation-building in the Gulf. This peculiar nature of migration to the Gulf therefore makes it circular

---

[59] Philippe Fargues, 'Immigration without Inclusion: Non-Nationals in Nation-Building in the Gulf States', *Asia and Pacific Migration Journal* 20, nos 3–4 (2011). Also see James Sater, 'Citizenship and migration in Arab Gulf monarchies', *Citizenship Studies* 18, nos 3–4 (2013).

by compulsion.[60] The migrant to the Gulf cannot think of settling permanently in the Gulf, s/he is not allowed think so. The temporariness of the migrants is ensured through a labour contract system known as *kafala*. The term:

> originally refers to a contract where a guarantor conjoins a guaranteed person (*makfūl*) and assumes liability for that person in various specified terms. *Kafala* is meant to provide an assurance of the fulfilment of an obligation of the guaranteed person. This can be to guarantee the payment of the guaranteed person's financial liability (*kafala bi-al-māl*) (as in a surety guaranteeing the repayment of a debt). It could also be to guarantee the presence of a certain person at a specified time and place (*kafala bi-al-nafs*) or the appearance of a certain person, as in the case of a lawsuit (*kafala bi-al-wajh*) (as in guaranteeing bail money). It could be a guarantee for the delivery of goods (*kafala bi-al-taslīm*) or a guarantee for the purchase of goods sold (*kafala bi-al-darak*). In short, the guarantor assumes responsibility for a certain liability due by the guaranteed that will include the *kafīl* as a representative of the guaranteed (*makfūl*) in front of the state and other government institutions and take responsibly for any breach of the law perpetrated by the guaranteed. [61]

With its etymology in Islamic and tribal customs where the guest has to be accounted for by someone who belongs to the host tribe, this currently translates to a system in which the migrant labourer has to have a native sponsor, known as a *kafeel*. The migrant is bound to his *kafeel*, or the sponsor. In practice this means that s/he cannot change jobs or return from the Gulf, without the approval of the *kafeel*. Often, though it is against the law, the migrant might even have to surrender his passport to the *kafeel*. At the hands of a merciless *kafeel*, the migrant labourer might end up in a precarious state, working with no salary, and often at gunpoint, metaphorically, or perhaps even literally.[62] The system of *kafala* is

---

[60] This is in theory. Practically, many families manage to live their entire lives in the Gulf through a combination of employment and visit visas, in a state of perpetual temporariness.

[61] Ray Jureidani and Said Fares Hassan, *Migration and Islamic Ethics: Issues of Residence, Naturalisation and Citizenship* (Leiden and Boston, MA: Brill, 2019), 94.

[62] Rejimon Kuttappan, '"He Held a Gun to My Neck": Modern Slavery and Forced Labour in the GCC', in *Uncertain Journeys: Labour Migration South Asia*, ed. A. S. Pannerselvan (New Delhi: Speaking Tiger, 2018), 23–38.

part of GCC policymaking in place 'to ensure that the large foreign work-force currently dominating the national labor market remains strictly temporary'.[63] The desperation and precarity created by the system, and the extraction of wealth in terms of costs of a visa attached to a *kafeel*, the bargaining power of visa mafias vis-à-vis the visa seeker, the low wages, and the precarious state these conditions subject the migrant worker to, have made one observer call the Gulf states 'slave states'.[64]

In the absence of the liberal democratic framework which gives the citizen an active stake in the running of the country, the fact that a large population is denied citizenship in itself makes citizenship worthy. [65] The fact that the migrants will not be granted citizenship makes it a ra-cial privilege. Race as an axis of differentiation and discrimination af-fects not just the legal status in the Gulf but also every sphere of life. Race plays a part in the kind of job one gets, the wages one can expect, the part of the city one lives in, or even the ways in which one negotiates the roads[66] in visa regimes, and avenues of entertainment and leisure one has at one's disposal.[67] The natives and Westerners enjoy vast privileges in the system, often at the cost of those at the lower end. The bulk of the

---

[63] Zahra Babar, 'Migration Policy and Governance in the GCC: A Regional Perspective', in *Labor Mobility: An Enabler for Sustainable Development*, eds Ali Rashid Al-Noaimi and Irena Omelaniuk (Abu Dhabi and Cambridge: The Emirates Centre for Strategic Studies and Research and Cambridge University Press, 2013), 121–142.

[64] Yasin Kakande, *Slave States: The Practice of Kafala in the Gulf Arab Region* (Winchester: Zero Books, 2015). See also, Bina Fernandez, 'Racialised institutional humiliation through the Kafala', *Journal of Ethnic and Migration Studies*, 2021, doi.: 10.1080/1369183X.2021.1876555.

Many of these laws are now changing, unevenly, across the Gulf states. Business establishments in Saudi Arabia need not have a native sponsor if one could pay a (hefty) fee to change ownership, a recent law forbids the employer from keeping custody of employee's passport in the UAE, the employees can now change jobs without the consent of the employer in Qatar, etc.

[65] John Willoughby, 'Ambivalent Anxieties of the South Asian – Gulf Arab Labor Exchange', *Revista de Economia Mundial* 14 (2006).

[66] David Kendall, 'Always let the road decide: South Asian labourers along the highways of Dubai, UAE: a photographic essay', *South Asian Diaspora* 4, no. 1 (2012), doi: 10.1080/19438192.2012.634561.

[67] Neha Vora, *Impossible Citizens: Dubai's Indian Diaspora* (Hyderabad: Orient Blackswan, 2013); Laavanya Kathiravelu, *Migrant Dubai: Low Wage Workers and the Construction of a Global City* (New York: Palgrave Macmillan, 2016).

André Naffis-Sahely, a writer born to an Iranian father and an Italian mother, and raised in Abu Dhabi, makes a scathing satire on the perversity of the racial entitlements, when he writes that the comfort of life that the 'Jumeirah Janes', the wives of the white men in the Gulf, makes it impossible for them to even have a sustained cribbing party. However, the arbitrariness of the system is felt by even the white folks, as seen in Naffis-Sahely's satire ('The Return') of the Municipality's ever-changing rules for partitions in one's house. See, André Naffis-Sahely, *The Promised Land: Poems from Itinerant Life* (London: Penguin Books, 2017).

migrant labourers are men who cannot afford to take their families to the Gulf with them, and are known as 'bachelors'. They are segregated into labour camps or bachelor residences, and live in arduous, exploitative, and excluded conditions. While race is a defining factor, the low-wage nature of these workers intersects with the racial difference such that these workers do not even have the means to approximate the affluent ways of life. 'Some places such as malls, the zoo, the souk, or the Corniche promenade, are forbidden to bachelor workers on Friday, the only day off in the week ... South Asian workers, who all are bachelors, are particularly targeted as other bachelors, whether Arab or Westerners, encounter no problems on entering malls.'[68] They are viewed as a threat to the integrity of those living with their families, and to the racial stability that governs the Gulf establishment.[69]

The system is designed to keep the lowest of the migrants marginalized, but also prevents, through a system of national/linguistic segregation, any transnational solidarity. The segregationist model is at the heart of migrant management. '[M]ost companies are careful to draw labor from a variety of different regions, for these linguistic, national, cultural, and ethnic differences help build a fragmented and more docile workforce—a workforce with less ability to organize and strike.'[70] 'At dormitory level and often at canteen level, the division among migrants is based on nationality.'[71]

'I am here only for working', runs the title of an investigative piece by William T. Vollmann on the labour conditions in the oil fields of the Gulf.[72] To state one's purpose as 'only for working' is to also enact a detachment over what is happening around them. The temporary nature of migration, and the segregationist model that is followed by the Gulf countries, together with the networked nature of migration and its collateral effects have contributed to a ghettoization that one commentator on

---

[68] Tristan Bruslé, 'What Kind of place is this? Daily Life, Privacy and Inmate Metaphor in a Nepalese Workers Labour Camp (Qatar)', *South Asia Multidisciplinary Academic Journal* 6 (2012), doi: 10.4000/samaj.3446.

[69] Kathiravelu, *Migrant Dubai*.

[70] Andrew M. Gardner, *City of Strangers: Gulf Migration and the Indian Community in Bahrain* (Ithaca, NY and London: Cornell University Press, 2010), 63.

[71] Bruslé, 'What kind of place is this?', 7.

[72] William T. Vollmann, 'I am here only for working: Conversations with the petroleum brotherhood in the UAE', *Harper's*, December 2017. https://harpers.org/archive/2017/12/i-am-here-only-for-working/ Last accessed on 11 May 2021.

the Gulf has noted: 'it is not unusual for adults in their social lives to only associate with those of the same nationality, religion or ethnicity.'[73]

Given these conditions, there have been a few vigorous deliberations on what public life could mean for the migrants in the Gulf. Neha Vora's conception of consumer citizenship, which factors in migrants as accounted in the public sphere in their capacity as consumers is one such attempt to think beyond citizenship in the narrowly statist terms.[74] Gardner's study of the migrant media posits a migrant public sphere in the context of Bahrain.[75] Extending the discussion on citizenship in the Gulf, M. H. Ilias, [76] with reference to the labour unrest in Dubai in 2007 in which Indian labourers were prominent, observes how the non-citizenry aspect of Gulf migration has still managed to give rise to a right-based politics among the migrants in the Gulf. More studies which take as its pivot the denial of citizenship to migrants by the Gulf countries, note that the immigrants nevertheless manage to create places of belonging using the possibilities of these cityscapes, such as empty parking lots or under the shade of the flyovers,[77] and map their own zones of belonging in literature[78] and radio.[79]

Kerala as a Borderland

The perversity of the system of *kafala* ensures that the migrant is not a bounded entity separable from the oppressive system. In fact, the migrant is hardly innocent of the system. A lot of people, labour brokers, middlemen, the sponsor, and even the state stands to gain by the perpetual precarity.[80] The existence of the middlemen undermines any easy

---

[73] Willoughby, 'Ambivalent Anxieties', 37.
[74] Vora, *Impossible Citizens*.
[75] Gardner, *City of Strangers*.
[76] Ilias, M. H. 'South Asian Labour Unrests and Non-Citizenry Aspects of Popular Politics in the Gulf', in *Asianization of Migrant Workers in the Gulf Countries*, eds S. Irudaya Rajan and Ginu Zacharia Oommen (Singapore: Springer, 2020).
[77] Laure Assaf, ' "Abu Dhabi is my sweet home": Arab youth, interstitial spaces, and the building of a cosmopolitan locality', *City* 24, nos 5–6 (2020), doi: 10.1080/13604813.2020.1837562; Kendall, 'Always let the road decide'.
[78] Christiane Schlote, 'Writing Dubai: Indian labour migrants and taxi topographies', *South Asian Diaspora* 6, no. 1 (2014), doi: 10.1080/19438192.2013.828500.
[79] Irene Ann Promodh, 'FM radio and the Malayali diaspora in Qatar: at home overseas', *Journal of Ethnic and Migration Studies* 47, no. 9 (2021), doi: 10.1080/1369183X.2020.1838268.
[80] Gardner, *City of Strangers*.

binarization of the native and the migrant and brings forth the porousness of community boundaries. As Neha Vora puts it: 'In fact, without the large number of expatriate employers and managers in the Gulf, the *kafala* system of migration sponsorship that underpins Gulf economic and political systems would not be able to function as it does.'[81]

Migration generates and is generated out of faultlines. Wright illustrates how Gulf migration is often fuelled by the feeling that one is discriminated at home and can only achieve a level of equality by moving elsewhere.[82] But the elsewheres are hardly clean slates. Not only do divisions of language, class, and hierarchies thereby established within the migrants, the fault lines from their homelands get carried to the Gulf. The circular migration also demands that we think of migration in newer ways than the 'absolute discontinuity'[83] that it was supposed to be. The constant movement of people, images, and ideas make localities uncontainable within the frame of the nation states.[84] The continuities between home and Gulf established because of circular and 'temporary' migration, such that one feels Dubai is not separate from India or vice versa[85], also means that the migrant mind is not a *tabula rasa* from which new solidarities can emerge. The networked structure of migration to the Gulf means that even though the migrant may come home only once in two or three years, his transactions with home are kept alive through letters and gifts passed on through the network.[86] The networked nature of migration also means that affinities at home gets carried over into the migrant life.[87] Vora gives us an example of the prejudices that exist within the migrant community in the Gulf:

---

[81] Vora, *Impossible Citizens*, 110–111.

[82] Wright, *Between Dreams and Ghosts*.

[83] Ranajit Guha, *The Small Voice of History: Collected Essays* (Delhi: Permanent Black, 2002), 648.

[84] Arjun Appadurai, 'Disjuncture and Difference in the Global Cultural Economy', in *Modernity at Large: Cultural Dimensions of Globalization* (Minneapolis, MN: University of Minnesota Press, 1996), 27–47.

[85] Vora, *Impossible Citizens*.

[86] Prema Ann Kurien, 'Non-Economic Bases of Economic Behaviour: The Consumption, Investment and Exchange Patterns of Three Emigrant Communities in Kerala, India', *Development and Change* 25 (1994), doi: 10.1111/j.1467-7660.1994.tb00535.x. See also Mufsin Puthan Purayil and Manish Thakur, 'The strength of strong ties: wasta and migration strategies among the Mappila Muslims of northern Kerala, India', *Journal of Ethnic and Migration Studies* (2022), doi: 10.1080/1369183X.2022.2069090.

[87] Thomas Chambers, 'Continuity in Mind: Imagination and Migration in India and the Gulf', *Modern Asian Studies* 52, no. 4 (2018), doi: 10.1017/S0026749X1700049X.

Hindu and Muslim Indians also felt solidarity as well as difference with one another. While Muslim Indians expressed a sense of belonging to a transnational Muslim community (ummah), they also lamented the fact that they did not have the strong ethno-national social associations that their Hindu and Christians compatriots did. On the other hand, Hindus and Christians were often under the impression that Muslims from South Asia had advantages they did not and were able to assimilate with Emiratis, although no Muslim Dubai Indians confirmed this assumption.[88]

Over the decades the networked nature of migration has also resulted in a division of labour among the migrant communities. Within Kerala for example, one is more likely to find a migrant from Kasaragod engaged in business in the Gulf and a migrant from Malappuram in a low-salaried job than otherwise. M. H. Ilias notes that the mobilization of migrants in the Gulf along the political fault lines in Kerala, that between a Communist Party oriented front and the Indian National Congress-centric one, as impactful both at home and in the Gulf.[89]

While the fault lines at home gets carried to the places where one migrates to, migration can also create its own lines of separation, the one between the migrant and the non-migrant being one of them. The image of the migrant as someone who has left his home with much pain not just to him but also to those around him is so strong that we tend to ignore the fact that migration creates a dividing line between those who migrate and those who remain at home. The *kafala* system, with its retinue of middlemen, is operationalized on this division. The yet-to-be migrant is yet one more chip to be cast into the business. The earlier migrant preys on the new migrant. More often than not, it is with the earlier migrant that the new migrant has to negotiate his life ahead. The system gives rise to a discourse of insecurity and victimization. The insecurity of migration involves the imagined or real betrayal by someone close to oneself, such as a friend, or one's wife. The migrant community's insecurities are not always from an already defined outside—the natives, other

---

[88] Vora, *Impossible Citizens*, 83.

[89] M. H. Ilias, 'Malayalee Migrants and Translocal Kerala Politics in the Gulf: Reconceptualising the "Political"', in *Diasporas of the Modern Middle East: Contextualising Community*, eds Anthony Gorman and Sossie Kasbarian (Edinburgh: Edinburgh University Press, 2015).

migrant communities, the state apparatus, etc. The outside and the inside, the hostilities and solidarities do not have predefined contours, concerns, or targets.

Like ghettoization among the migrants and between the migrants and the natives in the Gulf, this fault line between a migrant and non-migrant in Kerala, too, is a border. An example of the migrant's perspective on those at home can be seen in the films of Kodiyathur, where the (non-migrant) men in Kerala are usually just loitering around all the time, investing all their energies in spreading rumours about the family of the migrants (see Chapter 2 in this volume). The migrants on the other hand are shown to be brothers for each other, sticking together, and forging a life in the face of multiple impediments. Both the migrant and the one at home accuse each other of pleasures. The temporariness of migration goes round in a comic and cruel circle. Kerala and the Gulf become the fantasy land for each other for their own lacks. The one back in Kerala associates the migrant with the wonders of the world, no doubt aided by the goodies which the migrant brings as well as the visible material improvement in the migrant's family in terms of clothes they wear or the gadgets they use, etc. The migrant's vocabulary, for those at home, is filled with sounds he doesn't know, making it both a declaration of distinction, and the markers of many pleasures that await the migrant in the Gulf.

The migrant on the other hand associates the one staying at home as someone who is privileged to be staying back home, someone who can continue to enjoy the natural beauty bestowed on one's homeland, doesn't have to work every single day without taking a day off just so that one can afford to spend a couple of months at home, and one who can partake of the general benefit including those very gadgets brought in by the migrant who has to, to use a local expression, turn his sweat into blood by working.

For the low wage workers in the Gulf, taking their family to stay with them was an impossibility, practically and legally. These 'bachelors' are targeted in the rumours about the 'loose morals' of the 'Gulf wives', a term that refers to the left-behind wives of these 'bachelors'. In the 1977 song known as 'Dubai *Kathupattu*', a sensational song in the format of letters between the migrant husband in the Arabian Gulf and the left-behind wife at home, a stanza, ostensibly from the wife to the husband has the wife warning the husband in fruit-laden imagery that she is after all a human and has bodily needs and her husband being away might give way to other temptations. The song, which set off the trend of letter songs and later phone songs, sings of the tragedy of migration, that in the pursuit of money, one's youth is lost. S. A. Jameel, the author of this song, an amateur psychologist, claims that a large number of migrant husbands returned after hearing this song.[90]

One cannot ignore the suffusion of pleasure that marks either the coveting or the assumed loss on either side. Pleasure, the succulence of tropical fruits, the fullness of blushes is the means through which the (possible) breach of an imaginable community is made intelligible. Gossip and rumours thus produce contradicting knowledge about the Gulf in Kerala. Some of these contradictions can be seen as driving the fascination for migration in the Gulf.

Beyond the language of contract or right, it is enjoyment, the lack of it while there is an abundance of it on the other side, that spurs action in this world. The thought of the Other's secret enjoyments fuels our collectivities.[91]

---

[90] P. K. Yasser Arafath, 'Cassetted emotions: intimate songs and marital conflicts in the age of *pravasi* (1970–1990)', in *Cultural Histories of India: Subaltern Spaces, Peripheral Genres, and Alternate Historiography*, ed. Rita Banerjee (New York: Routledge, 2020), 138.
The enforced bachelorhood is one of the points of vulnerability in migrant narratives. The absence of women is acutely felt in many of the narratives. Babu Bharadwaj's *Pravasiyude Kurippukal* is dedicated to women. An early chapter of the memoir recalls the author's discomfort at seeing the apparent ease with which the women who belonged to the Arab landlord was teasing him (20–24). In another episode, Bhardwaj recalls the time of bliss he and his workers, all of them men, experienced at the sight of a woman's face at one of their construction sites (41–44). See Babu Bharadwaj, *Pravasiyude Kurippukal*, 3rd edn (Kozhikode: Mathrubhumi Books, 2013). In some narratives, the men, yearning for female company, often end up being cheated by the women. A thriving sex market is another feature of the enforced bachelorhood in migrant narratives. The lead character of Sadiq Kavil's *Outpass* spends a considerable time as an undocumented migrant manning the sex workers most of whom were trafficked with false promises. The female sex worker is a looming figure in Sabin Iqbal's *Shamal Days*. See Sabin Iqbal, *Shamal Days* (Noida: Harper Collins, 2021); Sadiq Kavil, *Outpass* (Kottayam: DC Books, 2014). The left-behind wife leaving her migrant husband for someone else (including another migrant) is another anxiety in the Gulf migrant narratives. Examples include Shamlal Puri's *Dubai on Wheels*, Nisamudheen Ravuthar's *Arabyayile Atima* (*A Slave in Arabia*), Deepak Unnikrishnan's *Temporary People*. See Shamlal Puri, *Dubai on Wheels: Speeding Headlong on a Dangerous, Slippery Road* (New Delhi: Diamond Books, 2010); Nisamudheen Ravuthar, *Arabyayile Atima* (Thrissur: Green Books, 2013); Deepak Unnikrishnan, *Temporary People* (Brooklyn, NY: Restless Books, 2017). For ethnographies of left-behind wives of Gulf migrants, see Leela Gulati, *In the Absence of their Men: The Impact of Male Migration on Women* (New Delhi: Sage Publications, 1993); Nusarath Jahan, 'Transnational relationships and virtual technology: an ethnographic study of the left-behind wives in Kerala', *Gender, Technology and Development* 25, no. 2 (2021), doi: 10.1080/09718524.2021.1928875.
[91] Slavoj Žižek, 'Enjoy Your Nation as Yourself!', in *Tarrying with the Negative: Kant, Hegel, and the Critique of Ideology* (Durham: Duke University Press, 1993), 200–238.

Translating the Borders

The book argues that the nature of conditions on both sides of the link-
ages in the labour migration process gives rise to peculiar forms of cultural products and subjectivities—'the *trans*versal, the *trans*actional,
the *trans*lational and the *trans*gressive', to recollect the various crossings
listed by Aihwa Ong.[92] The rumour/gossip that characterize the Gulf
migrant experience can be directly related to the structural conditions
of Kerala–Gulf migration. These interrelated conditions are: (i) the private and personal nature through which the Gulf migration took place
in Kerala; (ii) the kinship networks that migration to the Gulf continues
to depend upon; (iii) the denial of the possibility of citizenship for the
migrants in the Gulf countries which more often resulted in circular migration; (iv) *kafala* as an extremely exploitative system of bonded labour
which operates through middlemen who are more often than not migrants themselves; and (v) the system of segregation on ethnic and linguistic bases that is prevalent and ordained by the employers in the Arab
Gulf among the low class migrants. These structural conditions produce
a situation in which: the obligation of the final return from the Gulf often
means that one must go back where one came from; the fact that a migrant community cannot be taken for granted as a resource of solidarity
or resistance against exploitation precisely because the members of the
community themselves are facilitators of the system; the ghettoization of
communities in particular lines of work because of the networked nature
of recruitment; and the inability to form a broad migrant front due to the
ethnic and linguistic differences.

As much as one recognizes the affective intensities of the gossip and
rumours that cannot be reduced to what can and cannot be talked about
in the public domain, this book wagers that the 'silence' that had characterized the Gulf migration, and the revelations associated thereof, is
an instance of cognitive borders put in place by global capitalistic conditions. The private nature of the Gulf in the public discussions in Kerala
has much to do with the depoliticization of the public sphere, characteristic of governmentality, on the question of livelihood. But this privacy is

---

[92] Aihwa Ong, *Flexible Citizenship: The Cultural Logics of Transnationality* (Durham, NC and
London: Duke University Press, 1999), 4. *Emphasis in the original.*

also refracted as affect, matters of pleasure and trust, envy, and insecurity. It has to do too with local forms of knowledge and discussion beyond the state which cannot find space in the rational public domain except as rumours and gossip. Similarly, the *kafala* system itself may be understood as a regional variation of a global condition under contemporary capitalism. Andrew Gardner notes that the *kafala* system is a local variant of the deportation industry.[93] Similarly, Wright illustrates how the conditions of *kafala* are part of the neoliberal labour policies rather than any cultural eccentricity of the Arab states. The conditions of *kafala* as well as of the segregation of labour were drawn up by the transnational oil corporations in the middle of the twentieth century, and (only) subsequently attached to the stability of the Gulf monarchies.[94]

This book finds Kerala and the Gulf to be borderlands where the migrants among themselves and in relation to non-migrants are divided by epistemic fault lines. A border is where different epistemes coexist and struggle against each other. The borderland is characterized by communities of gossip, rumour, and revelation which have a communal existence and provide space for exclusive belonging and pleasure.[95] To study Kerala as a borderland is also to move away from the constriction of the idea of the border to those dividing the nation states. It is to study Kerala as one of the regions in which the intensification, diversification, and heterogenization of labour, caught as it is in global capital, produce political, economic, and cognitive borders. The scope of this book is to study this in relation to the literary and visual narratives in Kerala pertaining to the Gulf migration. The expansion of the frontiers of capital, with regions replacing nations as its significant economic unit, the divorce between jurisdiction and territory effected due to carving out special zones and variation in applicable labour codes, the factoring of ethnicity, gender, political status, etc. in the labour process have all led to heterogenization of labour. [96] In effect, multiple borders, along political, economic, and cognitive axes characterize the abstract labour today, which the living

---

[93] Gardner, *City of Strangers*, 68.

[94] Wright, *Between Dreams and Ghosts*.

[95] For a study of the role of rumours in a situation of acute communal rivalry, see Veena Das, *Life and Words: Violence and the Descent into the Ordinary* (Berkeley and Los Angeles, CA and London: University of California Press, 2006).

[96] Sandro Mezzadra and Brett Nielson, *Border as Method, or, Multiplication of Labor* (Durham, NC and London: Duke University Press, 2013).

labour have to negotiate.[97] 'In the *fabrica mundi* of the contemporary world, borders are instrumental in producing space, labor power, markets, jurisdiction, and a variety of other objects in ways that converge on the production of subjectivity.'[98]

Once we recognize the centrality of borders to late capitalism and the struggles against it, we see that there is a dialectic process at work between the capitalist border reinforcements on the one hand, and border struggles on the other. But precisely because the idea of the border does not correspond to the idea of nation state any more, one should also move away from positing the state as the theatre of the struggles. Rather, in the very disjuncture between territory, nation, and jurisdiction, the border struggles find themselves to be operating locally. The border struggles are about devising new forms of forging newer horizons of intelligibility, the scale of operation of which does not fit with that of the state. Mezzadra and Neilson call this act of negotiating the borders, 'translation'.

Mezzadra and Neilson do not understand translation as the replacement of codes of one established language with another. For them, the paradigm of translation is the cocreation of language that happens between foreigners.[99] To illustrate this, they refer to the creations of Creole on slave ships as narrated by Édouard Glissant. The language that is created out of the condition that mirrors modern labour force—that slaves are chosen deliberately across languages to stop them from acting on their own in coordination—does not originally belong to any of them. It is that activity through which one's untranslatability becomes the source for a continual process of translation. Untranslatability is in the first place a predicate of the need to translate itself. Thus, rather than seeing untranslatability as the *cul-de-sac* of translation, one must see it as the starting point. Moreover, it is the untranslatability that is one's singularity. Rather than think of the singularity as that which is to be overcome in the eventuality of successful translation, it is to be thought of as that point of discontinuity that makes translation an ongoing process. As is clear, the

---

[97] Mezzadra and Nielson, *Border as Method*, 87–93.

[98] Mezzadra and Nielson, *Border as Method*, 280.

[99] Naoki Sakai's distinction between homolingual (assumes homogenous language communities) and heterolingual (assumes heterogeneity in language and otherwise) serves as the theoretical apparatus for this notion of translation. Naoki Sakai, *Translation and Subjectivity: On 'Japan' and Cultural Nationalism* (Minneapolis, MN: University of Minnesota Press, 1997).

idea of translation is not premised on the arrival at a final stage of transparency in which all singularities have vanished. Rather, the idea of translation is premised on bordering itself along the various axes which will continue to produce discontinuities.

The opacity that is cast on the Gulf and the staging of bringing the other side to light, a characteristic of the Gulf migrant archives, is to be read as part of this translational relation which erects borders, some conspicuously staged, and others stealthily operationalized, as well as struggle against them in an act of articulating common destinies. The paradigm of border brings to the fore the need to study the publics, the intimate publics, and the counterpublics, recognizing that the very condition of border gives rise to pleasurable bonds, but also make the inside and outside of these bonds tentative and unstable.[100] Borders give rise to binaries incapable of dialogue, of non-mutuality of speech, but also uncanniness of sounds and gestures. Borders are spaces and processes marked by the breakdown of public speech, the cleavages of rumours, the double-speak under surveillance, and the hesitancy of confidence thanks to the looming figure of the informer. Studying the border demands of us that we be sensitive of the inconsistency of characters, the fluidity of speech, the arresting of signifiers before they could turn to meanings, and the congealing of affect around the quotidian.

While the cultural archives of Gulf migration are located in the conditions of the global capital, this book is about reading them in Kerala. That is, the archives of Gulf migration are read as they are decoded in the sociocultural milieu of Kerala. The opacity that characterizes the Gulf–Kerala is one produced among others by the institutions of literature.[101] This book expands this insight to look into the crucial role such an opacity plays in configuring the quotidian and the mundane as well the spectacular and the evental in Kerala. Thus, while the form of the Gulf migrant

---

[100] Not only are borders not set in stone, they are also not impermeable. Borders are selective enactments of passability and opacity. And since they are passable, the borders are also not at the edge, but inbetween, as something that divides rather than something that marks the absolute end of anything. As a process, the border does not merely include and exclude, but also recirculates, and is therefore inbetween rather than at the edge, is in motion as it can be permeable or can in itself be moved, and that which cannot be reduced to space. See Thomas Nail, *Theory of the Border* (New York: Oxford University Press, 2016).

[101] E. Dawson Varughese and Mohamed Shafeeq Karinkurayil, 'Editorial', *Journal of Commonwealth Literature* 58, no. 1 (2023).

archives in Kerala takes shape in an expanding capitalism crossing and producing borders of language and knowledge, it is determined crucially by the language in which it takes form, Malayalam, and by an assumption in these archives of that language belonging to a specific territory—Kerala. The circular migration, obtained due to the state regulations in the Gulf, thus directs its imagination back home. The translation, transaction, and transgression between the two orders of language: one, in the Gulf, Malayalam as the cryptic tongue of an exclusive group in an arrangement which hinders world-making through linguistic transaction across linguistically divergent groups, and two, in Kerala, Malayalam as the universal language of state and public deliberation, shall occupy us centrally in this book.

The point of the book is to take the form of the epistemic disjuncture created by the structural conditions of global capital—*rumour*—in literature, film, photographs, and other material figurations of the Gulf as its starting point, and see what it allows or not in building collectives and imagining a future. These products and subjectivities are to be placed in the contradictory pulls of the discursive and material power effects and cannot be assumed to be assimilative or resistant by default.

As such the 'reality' of the Gulf, which also at the same time stages an epistemic border between the Gulf migrant and the non-migrant in Kerala, is the very difference which lends singularity to the Gulf migrant as caught between the two realities. It is what constitutes her as a singularity. This singularity is the untranslatability of the Gulf experience while it is, at the same time, that which is in constant need of translation in order to forge a common of the various singularities. But insofar as the borders are multiple and along different axes, such a common cannot be equated with an (impossible) universal, and should be located in the continual action on a tentative ground. The task of this book is to illustrate the operation of the epistemic borders in the form of migrant narratives belonging to various media genres and to illustrate the translation that is made possible within this bordering. How are these epistemes sites of translation? In what frames can such a translation be attempted? Within what horizon of imagination? What are the stakes involved?

Under the weight of the increasing number of border crossings and the migrant 'crisis' that has come to haunt the First World, the recent years have seen a renewed engagement with the idea of cosmopolitanism.

Originally meaning a condition in which the world (*cosmos*) is one's city (*polis*), the condition meant an ability to belong to the world wherever one goes. Because of this easy amenability to new places, cosmopolitanism has been understood as rootlessness. However, if one were to look at how the idea is developed in the philosophy of Immanuel Kant,[102] one sees the weight of cosmopolitanism slide towards the responsibility of the state. The cosmopolitan right is the right of the traveller to travel to a foreign land and establish relations with people there. Though a right of the traveller, the right in itself can only be guaranteed by the state. Because of the centrality of the state as the guarantor of rights, the neo-Kantians like Seyla Benhabib[103] insist on a mode of activism that aims for state-driven expansion of citizenship. Others, however, insist on the need to forge people's solidarities and people-driven reforms.[104] Such a critical cosmopolitanism points out the crossing borders of ideas that allows various peoples to come together for common good.

A notion of cosmopolitanism which has as its premise the sedentariness of the nation state or the audibility and intelligibility of speech in a public sphere ignore the regime of movement, at the level of individual as well as that of society[105] that characterizes the present world. While studying the enactment of borders, this book is also an attempt to study cosmopolitanism which is premised on patiency and on the condition of being minor. The concept of patiency, formulated in another context by William Mazzarella,[106] describes the power to be moved. As such, it is both an assertion of power while also conceptualizing this as a power to respond to an external stimulus. Patiency is therefore the 'other' of agency because it does not propose a *tabula rasa* on which man can exert his power of world-making. At the same time, it does not deny power either,

---

[102] H. S. Reiss (ed.), *Kant: Political Writings* (Cambridge: Cambridge University Press, 1991), 41–53 and 93–130.

[103] Seyla Benhabib, *Another Cosmopolitanism* (Oxford: Oxford University Press, 2006).

[104] For example, see Lilie Chouliaraki, 'Cosmopolitanism as Irony: A Critique of Post-Humanitarianism', in *After Cosmopolitanism*, eds Rosi Braidotti, Patrick Hanafin, and Bolette Blaagaard (New York: Routledge, 2013); Patrick Hanafin, 'A Cosmopolitics of Singularities: Rights and the Thinking of Other Worlds', in *After Cosmopolitanism*, eds Rosi Braidotti, Patrick Hanafin, and Bolette Blaagaard (New York: Routledge, 2013); Bonnie Honig, 'Another Cosmopolitanism? Law and Politics in the New Europe', in *Another Cosmopolitanism*, ed. Seyla Benhabib (Oxford: Oxford University Press, 2006).

[105] Thomas Nail, *The Figure of the Migrant* (Stanford, CA: Stanford University Press, 2015).

[106] William Mazzarella, *The Mana of Mass Society* (Chicago, IL and London: The University of Chicago Press, 2017), 103.

but instead posits the possibility of giving rise to the new in allowing oneself to be swayed by the power that resides without rather than within. This book notes the power of the migrants to respond to a world in which they enjoy only minimal freedom, and the ways in which they stand forth in languages that defy the normative. In keeping with this object of study, the book moves beyond the binary of migrant/citizen, agency or the lack of it, the centrality of the nation state as the locus of belonging, or the figure of the migrant as always already resistant or regressive.

Chapterization

This book follows recent attempts to query the cultural dimension of migration. The call of dreams, the work of imagination, the push of aspiration, the promise of freedom, etc. have been recognized in recent years as factors driving migration.[107] More precisely, this book is an attempt to resituate the Gulf in Kerala, from a source of remittance, to one that is in continuing relations of translation and transaction with the arc of the everyday in Kerala.

This book deals with a host of Gulf migrant archives drawn from literature and visual culture. The effort in this book is to read them as conditioned by the structures of exclusion and inclusion in the Gulf and Kerala. In general, the method has been that of formal and thematic analysis of select portions from the text which can highlight acutely the staging of epistemic boundaries and their translation. This book does not aim to provide a comprehensive account of the Gulf migrant archives in Kerala or of the individual texts it reads. Rather, the attention is paid to select moments in the texts for what they show about the operation of epistemic disjuncture and its un/successful translation into the language of commons.

---

[107] Examples include Jørgen Carling and Francis Collins, 'Aspiration, desire and drivers of migration', *Journal of Ethnic and Migration Studies* 44, no. 6 (2018), doi: 10.1080/1369183X.2017.1384134; Noel Salazar, 'The Power of Imagination in Transnational Mobilities', *Identities: Global Studies in Culture and Power* 18 (2011): 576–598, doi: 10.1080/1070289X.2011.672859; the Realm Project by Caroline Osella, (https://blogs.soas.ac.uk/osella-realm/en/), etc.

The nature of these texts demand that our methodological tools are medium specific. Thus, the literary texts are closely read drawing its apparatus from literary theory, while films and photography base themselves on theories from film and visual culture studies. Even as this is a work of close-reading and occasionally revels in indulgence at the level of a word or a gesture, the thrust of the work is on a worldly reading, mobilizing only as much semantic depth and expanse as can be warranted at a synchronic moment. The book takes recourse to anthropological and historical details in the service of such a worldly reading.

The book has four chapters. In Chapter 1, the focus is on the most prolific of Gulf migrant expressions beginning from the late1970s—the migrant photographs. Perhaps only the personal letters written by migrants are more in number than the migrant photographs. At a time when even television was rare, it was through photographs that the Gulf made itself a presence in Kerala. With the coming of the cheap still cameras in the late 1970s, photographs became a medium within reach of almost everybody. Unlike literature or film, the photograph, shot by the amateur, had the democratic potentials that Walter Benjamin posited,[108] and, contra Benjamin, could also produce an aura around the subjects in the photograph. The Gulf itself was produced as wondrous by these photographs, through a borrowing of the syntax of popular films. The intermedial nature of the photographs is crucial to comprehend the nature of the affects mobilized by these photographs. While analyzing the components of this intermediality, this chapter also looks at the ways in which these photographs refracted the Gulf in the Kerala milieu. The effort of the chapter is to demonstrate the multiple entanglements in which the photograph, supposed to be an indexical medium, got itself coded into.

Chapter 2 looks at the representation of the Gulf and the Gulf migrant in Malayalam cinema. Beginning with *Vilkkanundu Swapnangal* (Azad, 1980), the first section of the chapter proceeds to present in broad brushstrokes the representation of the migrant in mainstream Malayalam cinema. The migrant was a butt of jokes for his gaudy tastes and his show-off nature in these films. His new-found wealth was threatening to the moral universe of the Keralan villages. This one-dimensional image of

---

[108] Walter Benjamin, 'The Work of Art in the Age of Mechanical Reproduction', in *Illuminations*, trans. Harry Zohn (New York: Schocken Books, 1968), 217–258.

the migrant undergoes a change in the late 1990s, with the arrival of the poor migrant on the scene. With the coming of new technologies in the early twenty-first century, there is a shift, and perhaps one could claim a democratization. The Home Cinema, associated with Salam Kodiyathur, is an emblem of this new energy in narrating the migrant story.

Many more mainstream Malayalam films are now shot in the Gulf, and the migrant has acquired narrative agency in the diegetic universe of these films. The last section of Chapter 2 is a reading of the effect of the Gulf on Malayalam cinema even as the Gulf was largely absent as a diegetic space in Malayalam cinema until the 2000s. Looking closely at the genre of laughter films which was the dominant trend from the mid-1980s to the mid-1990s, this section attempts a recuperative reading of the absent migrant in Malayalam cinema.

Chapter 3 and 4 are on Keralan Gulf migrant literature. The texts discussed in Chapter 3 are Sageer's *Gulfumpadi PO*, [109] Khadeeja Mumthas's *Barsa*,[110] Krishnadas's memoir *Dubaipuzha* and his novel, *Katalirampangal*,[111] and Sonia Rafeek's *Herbarium*.[112] The chapter will illustrate the modes of speaking about the Gulf experience in these literary works, their contradictions and deadlocks, and their attempts to forge a communal existence in the face of the structural difficulties they face within the form of these texts and without. Amitav Ghosh,[113] reviewing the novel *Cities of Salt* by Abdul Rahman Munif,[114] made the observation that the world of oil encounter 'poses a radical challenge not merely to the practice of writing as we know it, but to much of modern culture: to such notions as the idea of distinguishable and distant civilizations, or recognizable and separate "societies".'[115] The world of oil encounter is mute because it is bafflingly multilingual. This multilinguality, and the borders created thereby, is also a calculated measure by the powers-that-be in their interest. Chapter 4 analyzes the dead ends of public speech to explore the

[109] Sageer, *Gulfumpadi PO* (Kottayam: Don Books, 2021).

[110] Khadeeja Mumthas, *Barsa*, 3rd edn (Kottayam: DC Books, 2021).

[111] Krishnadas, *Dubaipuzha*, 20th edn (Thrissur: Green Books, 2019); Krishnadas, *Katalirampangal* (Thrissur: Green Books, 2010).

[112] Sonia Rafeek, *Herbarium* 4 edn (Kottayam: DC Books, 2018).

[113] Amitav Ghosh, 'Petrofiction: The Oil Encounter and the Novel', in *The Imam and the Indian: Prose Pieces*. (Delhi: Ravi Dayal Publisher and Permanent Black, 2002).

[114] Abdul Rahman Munif, *Cities of Salt*, trans. Peter Thoreaux (Vintage International, 1989).

[115] Ghosh, 'Petrofiction', 79.

possibility of affective communities. The analysis there extends to works of fiction by Benyamin and Deepak Unnikrishnan. The staging of the impossibility of a stable community, the performance of epistemic borders, and the pleasures of the border are the points of discussion in the chapter. *Temporary People* is not a Malayalam work in original, but has been included because of the vital uses it makes of Malayalam as a language in communicating the migrant experience in Gulf, apart from the fact that Keralans form the bulk of the characters in the book, and Kerala an important setting for the narrative.

This book does not aim to be a comprehensive historical presentation of the Gulf migration from Kerala, nor provide an objective macro-level assessment of its economic and social implications. Rather, this book draws from a variety of sources to recentre migration as a mode of being and a lived experience that is irreducible to the economic role of the migrants or the passivity they have been accorded as victims of cruel fate and unjust labour conditions. This book highlights the migrant creativity, their take on their own condition, and an attempt to factor them into the daily life in Kerala from which they were ostensibly away. It is an attempt to recreate the life-worlds of a lost time of migration; lost not because no one spoke about it, but that even in the abundance of the spoken and shown, the migrant life could not find for itself a place at home in Kerala except as the tunes and murmurs of a private and intimate world. The simultaneity of Kerala and the Gulf in this life-world of migrants and those around them, the public nature of the materials, memories, anxieties, care, and prayers that separate and bring them together, is the concern of this book.

1

The Thrills of Migrant Photography

If, before the turn of the century, the Gulf was thought of in Kerala as
fantastically rich, it is mostly due to the Gulf photographs. This chapter
analyzes the role of photographic representation in privatizing the Gulf
experience in Kerala, marking this as a deviation from the other popular
representation of the Gulf in popular songs. Taking the Mappila Muslim
milieu of south Malabar as its context, this chapter locates the photographs of the Gulf by the Gulf migrants in the wider cultural context of
visuality in which the migrants and their families participate. The characteristics of visual culture detailed here are based on my belonging to the
community and spending a good part of my life so far in the region and
among the community members.

The Cassetted Migrant

In the 1970s and 1980s, when the Gulf literature exploring the pathetic
migrant lives had not blossomed as it has now,[1] there was still an intimation of the Gulf as an inhospitable terrain in the few that existed in
the popular realm. Popular song was one such medium where the Gulf
was animated in harsh metonymies. The popular song culture itself was
undergoing a shift in the 1980s thanks to the coming of tape recorders
which were brought to India by the Gulf migrants. Tape recorders as a
technology soon changed the face of the Indian music industry both at
the infrastructural and the superstructural level. While India became
the second largest manufacturer of cassettes in a matter of years, the new

---

[1] See Chapter 3 for discussion on Malayalam Gulf literature.

The Gulf Migrant Archives in Kerala. Mohamed Shafeeq Karinkurayil, Oxford University Press. © Mohamed Shafeeq
Karinkurayil 2024. DOI: 10.1093/9780198910619.003.0002

technology also gave rise to technological reproduction of local music forms and singers, and gave rise to new voices and genres in the dominant film music industry.[2]

Two new genres of songs connected to Gulf migration from Kerala arose from the late 1970s in the Mappila song tradition.[3] The first of these is the *kathupattu*, or the letter song, which has a longer history in the Mappila tradition. This genre of songs is composed like a personal letter from one person to another, with generic salutations and endings, but understood to be composed for popular singing rather than individual perusal. In 1979, an amateur psychologist S. A. Jameel composed the trend-setting *Dubai Kathupattu* which, while in the tradition of the letter songs, was composed as a letter from the left-behind wife of a Gulf migrant to her husband in Dubai. In the song, which Jameel claims was based on conversations that he has had with left-behind wives of migrants,[4] the woman reminds her husband that in the pursuit of money they were letting go of their youth. She is unable to sleep in the night as

---

[2] Indians became consumers of recorded music at an unprecedented level. While recorded songs sold for 1.2 million US dollars in 1980, by 1986 the figure stood at 12 million dollars. By the late 1980s, there were around 500 music-producing companies in India. The rise in the number of cassette recorders produced and the volume of trade was similarly astronomical—from 1.65 million rupees worth in 1983 to almost 100 million in 1987. See Peter Manuel, *Cassette Culture: Popular Music and Technology in North India* (Chicago, IL and London: University of Chicago Press, 1993), 62.

[3] The Muslims are the most numerous among the migrants to the Gulf from Kerala; the northern districts of Kerala, where the Mappilas are the most dominant among Muslims, contribute the bulk of the migrants to the Gulf. The Mappilas are a Muslim community mostly concentrated in the region extending from Mangalore in south Karnataka to Kochi in Kerala. Mappilas are generally understood to have risen out of the marriage of local women with Arab maritime traders. While the Mappilas are generally taken to be traders, the Mappilas of south Malabar, the region in focus in this chapter, are mostly of peasant origins. Roland Miller's study of the community is considered a classic. See Roland Miller, *Mappila Muslims of Kerala* (Bombay: Orient Longman, 1976).

Mappila song refers to an established song tradition among the community. For discussions see Balakrishnan Vallikkunnu and Dr Umar Tharamel, *Mappilappattu: Paadavum Padanavum (Mappila Songs: the Message and the Enquiry)* (Kottayam: DC Books, 2006); M. H. Ilias and Shamshad Hussain, 'Literate Illiterates', in *Cosmopolitan Cultures and Oceanic Thought*, eds Dilip M. Menon and Nishat Zaidi (Oxford and New York: Routledge, 2023); Dr M. N. Karassery, *Pulikkottil Krithikal (Works by Pulikkottil)* (Thrissur: Kerala Sahitya Akademi, 1979); V. M. Kutty, *Mappilappattinte Charitrasancharangal (The Historical Trajectory of Mappila Songs)* (Kozhikode: Lipi Publications, 2007).

[4] P. K. Yasser Arafath, 'Cassetted emotions: intimate songs and marital conflicts in the age of *pravasi* (1970–1990)', in *Cultural Histories of India: Subaltern Spaces, Peripheral Genres, and Alternate Historiography*, ed. Rita Banerjee (New York: Routledge, 2020).

For an analysis of songs by men in the first person feminine and their difference from women's folksongs, see Asha Singh, 'Of Women, by Men: Understanding the "First Person Feminine" in Bhojpuri Folksongs', *Sociological Bulletin* 64, no.2 (2015).

she has dreams of the time he was home, the marital home has turned into a prison, and she can't bear it when their son asks for his father. The song is a passionate plea to the husband, who is a migrant, to leave Dubai and come back to her.

Due to its formal feature, the letter song genre implied that letters are always paired, one as the reply to another. In the *Marupadipattu*, the reply song to *Dubai Kathupattu*, the migrant reminds the wife of the life of hardship before the Gulf, and how he has been regular with his remittance. 'Haven't you been receiving regular money orders?' The money order thus transforms into a kinship material which substitutes for the migrant's physical presence with his wife.[5]

The song was immensely popular, and it is said that many migrants abandoned their migrant lives influenced by the song, to settle back for a life with their spouse. Part of its popularity was the controversy generated by some of the lines in the song in which the wife, after likening her body to a fruit which, while she will not let anyone else have, reminds the migrant that she is after all not an angel. A recipe for much heartburn, the song is an early instance in which the fidelity of the left-behind wife of the Gulf migrant comes under scrutiny. By foregrounding the figure of the wife, the letter song transformed migration into an intimate affair, one that cuts out the kinship network in favour of the personal and the private. The wife becomes the figure around which the border between the migrant and the non-migrant is drawn in Kerala. It is only the wife who seems to share the sentiments of the migrants. It is interesting that it is not the parents but the wife who understands the migrant. Considering that the wife does not belong to the family, and is essentially an outsider whose loyalty is not a given, the wife figure serves two functions. The first function is to contrast the cruelty of the people one considers one's own. The other function is to imagine relations of affiliation, highlighted by the sympathetic wife, over that of filiation, thereby registering the breakdown of the older order and the arrival of a new subjectivity. The sympathetic

---

[5] Wright discusses gold as a kinship material in the Gulf migrant context. See Andrea Wright, *Between Dreams and Ghosts: Indian Migration and Middle Eastern Oil* (Stanford, CA: Stanford University Press, 2021), 93–112. For the role of gold as condensation and facilitator of social bonds between Dubai and Malabar, see Nisha Mathew, 'Layered Cities, Shared Histories: Gold, Mobility and Urbanity between Dubai and Malabar', in *Routledge Handbook of Indian Transnationalism*, eds. Ajaya Sahoo and Bandana Purkayastha (London: Routledge, 2019).

wife as opposed to the greedy or cruel parents and blood relations is a stock motif of the time, as can be seen in other migrant narratives too, such as the films by Salam Kodiyathur (see Chapter 2). A third function of the sympathetic wife may be to alleviate the anxieties around marital fidelity. The left-behind wife of the Gulf migrant is an object of gossip; her movements and contacts are open to speculation and easy material for tall tales. Discussing the popularity of letter songs, P. K. Yasser Arafath has attributed their social efficacy to a host of reasons, in addition to the migrants' easy access to cassette technology. These include the sexual anxieties fuelled by the rise of prostitution and access to erotic video and television channels for the migrants in the Gulf, the coming of intimate literature in Malayalam periodicals, and the rise of an Islamic discourse in Kerala around the purity of marital relations.[6] The wife figure becomes an index of not just the material prosperity of the Gulf migrant, but also the insecurities around it, especially of not being at home physically to be beside one's wife. As we have already noted in the Introduction, this separation is structural in that the law in the Gulf does not permit the lower-class male migrant to bring his wife to the Gulf. The emasculation that the husband is always at the verge of is deeply entrenched in the condition of the Gulf migration.

Soon, the letter song was supplanted by a new genre of Mappila song, one which did not have any direct precedent—the phone songs. Here, it is the conventions of the phone conversation which frame the song. Unlike the letter songs, the phone songs are duets, turning it into a two-way conversation. A famous song of the period began with 'Hello I am Shafeeq and I am calling from Kuwait'. The content remained the same desperation—the agony of separation on the one hand, the need for money for any life of dignity on the other. Two technologies—the telephone and the cassette—that represented the changed times and moreover the migrant's self-consciousness as riding the crest of modernity, came together in the phone songs.

In the 1980s, when the letter songs and phone songs were popular, both phone and cassette technologies, however, came with limitations

---

[6] Arafath, 'Cassetted Emotions'.

for popular use. While the phone songs put to tune intimate conversations, the phone conversations were rarely intimate in the practical sense considering that phones were not yet personal devices. The telephonic intimacy was an aspiration rather than a reality. The telephone penetration in rural India was thin until the post-1991 liberalization. Those few houses that had phones would become the point of contact in the neighbourhood where the families of migrants would come at pre-decided times to receive phone calls. In its very placement, the phone was not considered personal. The phones would often be placed in the living room, and at times extendable to windows when, in some instances, those waiting for the call were not expected to enter the house to receive the call.

While the new song genres became popular thanks to the new tape-recording technology coming to India making local song genres consumable at an industrial level, another use to which the cassette was put was as recordings of personal letters. The rerecordable nature of the cassette as well as its double sides made it amenable as a medium of personal communication, in which the same cassette could be used multiple times, and each of the interlocutors could keep using one of the sides of the cassette. However, cassette letters were not as popular as regular written letters. One can make informed guesses as to why. Cassettes were inconvenient as a personal medium. Even if the technology existed for private listening, tape recorders were not a private device. Its place was that of a public entertainer. In the crowded rooms where the unskilled and the semi-skilled migrants stayed, it was difficult for this device to switch between private and public uses. The second possible reason is in the very ephemerality of the spoken word itself. Writing over the cassette with new recording makes it inaccessible as a document one could go back to. The letters between migrants and their close ones back home were also manuals that called for archiving and retrievability for a while. These are documents not just of love and longing, but also of the details regarding expenditure of remittance, obligations owed to people, instructions on things to be done on the migrant's behalf, etc. Usually an envelope carried multiple letters, addressed to separate individuals, and listing separate tasks to be done at home.

The Photographic Truth

The coming of cheap photography in the late 1970s in the Gulf shifted the orientation of the representation based on labour and toil. While photography was already a prevalent technology among the well-to-do classes by the 1930s,[7] it became truly popular only with the Gulf migration. Arguably the most numerous of the Gulf migrant cultural artefacts, photographs represented the Gulf in the material solidity that convey modernity—cars, paved streets, high-rise buildings, etc.

The linguistic, cultural, and material contexts of photographic technology have attracted attention in recent times. The possibilities in photography beyond documentation, evident since at least the 1970s, has made us turn to the specific forms of representation that photography affords in specific cultures.[8] The study of visuality now involves what gets represented and how, as well as its trajectories of circulation and modes of consumption.[9] It requires us to explore 'the forces that construct [photographs] into this rather than that ... [the] change through time, through political position, through culture, through class ...', its entanglement 'in different systems'.[10]

The revolutionary feature of photography is its indexicality—it captures what is put in front of it. This indexicality of photograph allows it to exceed the human design as well as transcend the inherent human limitations. In Walter Benjamin's assessment of photography, the technology effects a paradigm shift from the distancing aura to a congealing of potentialities that transcend the potentialities of the here and now. 'We are compelled to find the inconspicuous place in which, in the essence of

---

[7] Sujith Parayil, *Photography in 20th Century Kerala*, Unpublished PhD Diss., Manipal University, Manipal, 2007, 261.

[8] Elizabeth Edwards, 'Beyond the Boundary: a consideration of the expressive in photography and anthropology', in *Rethinking Visual Anthropology*. eds Marcus Banks and Howard Morphy (New Haven, CT and London: Yale University Press, 1997), 53–80.

[9] Deborah Poole studies photography in terms of visual economy—the individuals and technologies of its production, the technologies of its circulation, and 'the cultural and discursive systems through which the graphic images are appraised, interpreted, and assigned historical, scientific, and aesthetic worth'. See Deborah Poole, *Vision, Race, and Modernity: A Visual Economy of the Andean Image World* (Princeton, NJ: Princeton University Press, 1997), 10. For a discussion on studying the cultures of vision, see Marcus Banks and Howard Morphy (eds), *Rethinking Visual Anthropology* (New Haven, CT and London: Yale University Press, 1997).

[10] Christopher Pinney, *Camera Indica: The Social Life of Indian Photographs* (Chicago, IL: University of Chicago Press, 1997), 10.

that moment which passed long ago, the future nestles still today, so eloquently that we, looking back, are able to discover it.'[11] The indexicality of photograph not only effaces human intention, it effects 'misrecognition'[12] in terms of space and time too. That is, precisely because the photograph can capture what is before it irrespective of whether the profilmic adheres to 'reality', the photograph is a medium in which the space and time of the here and now can be replaced with alternative possibilities. This misrecognition by photography as a medium in its very ontology makes it a medium of imagining other space times—in providing alternative to homogenous empty time in imagining the nation,[13] in the heralding of individuals and their individuality for the lower classes while they could otherwise find their existence only as members of population groups,[14] in projections of oneself as part of national modernity,[15] in imagining alternative futures by marginalized populations,[16] etc.

In the context of migration, photography is shown to be a sign of one's death,[17] or to convey survival and well-being,[18] even in harsh conditions, such as labour camps in the Gulf.[19]

---

[11] Walter Benjamin, 'Small History of Photography (1931)', in *On Photography: Walter Benjamin*, ed. and trans. Esther Leslie (London: Reaktion Books, 2015), 66–67. For a discussion on the future-telling feature of photography, see Christopher Pinney, '"What Time is the Visual?" Photography and the History of the Future', *Visual Anthropology Review* (2023): 12, doi: 10.1111/var.12288.

[12] Pinney, '"What Time is the Visual?"'.

[13] Kajri Jain, *Gods in the Bazaar: The Economies of Indian Calendar Art* (Durham, NC and London: Duke University Press, 2007).

[14] Christopher Pinney, *The Coming of Photography in India* (London: British Library, 2008), 136–137.

[15] Karen Strassler, *Refracted Visions: Popular Photography and National Modernity in Java* (Durham, NC: Duke University Press, 2010).

[16] Thy Phu and Elspeth Brown, 'The cultural politics of aspiration: Family photography's mixed feelings', *Journal of Visual Culture* 17, no. 2 (2015), doi: 10.1177/14704192918782352.

[17] 'He carried with him, as was instructed, a spare set of clothes, a bag of flattened rice, a couple of lemons, some *nendran* banana, and glucose powder. He also took along a photo of himself wrapped in plastic—in case the worst occurred and the boat sank.' Mohamed Shafeeq Karinkurayil, 'A Strangeness One Can Occupy: Clothes and Their Codes in the Photographs of Gulf Migrants from Kerala', in *Migration in the Making of the Gulf Space: Social, Political, and Cultural Dimensions*, eds Antia Mato Bouzas and Lorenzo Casini (New York and Oxford: Berghahn Books, 2022), 120–121.

[18] Stuart Hall, 'Reconstruction Work: Images of Post-war Black Settlement', in *Writings on Media: History of the Present*, ed. Charlotte Brunsdon (New York: Duke University Press, 2021); Faime Alpagu, '"I am doing well in Austria": Biography, photography and migration memories of a 1970s guest worker', *Rassegna Italiana di Sociologia* (2019), doi: 10.1423/93559.

[19] Mohamed Shafeeq Karinkurayil, 'The days of plenty: images of first generation Malayali migrants in the Arabian Gulf', *South Asian Diaspora* 13, no. 1 (2021), doi: 10.1080/19438192.2020.1767895.

Ashish Rajadhyaksha points out that the paradigmatic Indian cinema combines the indexicality of photography with an established tradition of non-mechanical art form which combines illustration with story-telling. The paradigm was established in Raja Ravi Varma's paintings where the aesthetics of realism could combine with scenes from Hindu mythologies, thus displacing the interpreting eye with the receiving eye.[20] This receiving eye, far from being the scrutinizing eye, is one which can be overwhelmed by the image. The Gulf photographs in Kerala from the late 1970s onwards until the images of the Gulf became ubiquitous towards the late 1990s are to be read in this fusing together of indexicality and iconicity.[21] The indexical Gulf, of high-rise buildings or caravan housing, of the roads with streetlights or electronic gadgets in one's living space, all of them, while being indexical, also got made sense of in a discourse where 'Persia'[22] or 'Dubai' are, like in the *Thousand and One Nights*,[23] the lands of gold and riches beyond compare. The indexicality built into photographs made it, ironically, the space where one could see the fantastic and—in a world in which all ideas of future were associated with 'development' imagined after Western models—the future of oneself. Thus, the Gulf photographs become aspirational in a double sense—that the Gulf is established as an aspiration for oneself and one's land, but also, in the sense that the photograph has already, in its indexicality, made possible in the here and now of the Gulf migrant households that which is otherwise not available.[24]

---

[20] Ashish Rajadhyaksha, 'The Phalke era: Conflict of traditional form and modern technology', *Journal of Arts and Ideas* 14, no. 15 (1987).

[21] While indexicality refers to the photographic function of capturing what is placed in its field without value judgement and whose value is deferred to the interpretation of the beholder, iconicity is when the image comes with in-built message, i.e. when the image also directs the right way it is to be read. The iconicity of the image has been read as key to understanding popular politics in India. See Geeta Kapur, 'Mythic Material in Indian Cinema', *Journal of Arts and Ideas*, nos 14–15 (1987).

[22] 'Persia' used to be the more popular name for what we now call the (Arab) Gulf.

[23] While *Alif Laila wa Laila* (*Thousand Nights and One Night*) is known as *Arabian Tales* in English, in Malayalam it is called *The Thousand and One Nights* (*Aayirathonnu Raavukal*).

[24] This second sense of aspiration draws upon the usage by Christopher Pinney in *The Coming of Photography*: ' ... prophecy, as a tactic of enquiry and imagination' (139). For a discussion, see Mohamed Shafeeq Karinkurayil, 'Reading Aspiration in Kerala's Migrant Photography', *South Asia: Journal of South Asian Studies* 43, no. 4 (2020), doi: 10.1080/00856401.2020.1759000. Deirdre McKay points out, with examples of photographs by Filipino migrants in Hong Kong, that migrants use photographs to project desired future selves. See Deirdre McKay, 'Ghosts of Futures Present: Photographs in the Filipino Migrant Archive', *Visual Anthropology: Published in Cooperation with the Commission on Visual Anthropology* 21, 4 (2008), doi: 10.1080/08949460802156466.

The Order of the Eye

The system of visuality and the visible in the Mappila culture is part of the locally practised Islam (or equally, the locally practised Islam is also about how the system of visuality and visible is ordered locally). While the Mappilas belong to various schools of thought within Sunni Islam, most belong to what is locally known as 'Sunni' (henceforth, Kerala Sunni) distinct from the other major line of thought known as Salafi/Mujahid. What follows will mostly focus on the popular Kerala Sunni Islam, while in the next section we will see how technology and Salafism interact with this popular Islam.

The faculty of sight is a valued one in Islam. This is obvious from the positive use of sight as a metaphor for the believer, and in contrast to blindness. The Qur'an asks if the seeing and the blind are equal, in which the seeing is understood to be the positive quality. Seeing stands not only for the act of seeing, but also for reflecting and contemplating.[25] Two incidents involving sight are oft repeated around Prophet Muhammad's flight to Madina from Makkah, known as Hijra, the event which marks the beginning of the Islamic calendar. What prompts the flight is the decision by Prophet's enemies in Makkah to assassinate him. The group surrounds the Prophet's house in the night. At that point, the Prophet steps out, takes a fistful of sand, recites the first few verses of the chapter Ya-Sin from the Qur'an and blows it towards them upon which they could not see the Prophet leaving the house. The next instance regarding sight is during the flight, when, at one point, the pursuers are close behind and the Prophet and his companion Abu Baker decide to hide in a cave. Once they enter the cave, a spider weaves its web covering the entrance giving

---

[25] Three different terms are used in the Qur'an in relation to sight, with conceptual distinctions attributed to them. 'The terms *naẓar*, *basar*, and *ru'ya* are intertwined in meaning and conceptual scope. They are extensively used in the Quran, appearing in various derivations 129, 135, and 328 times respectively. The most repetitive use of *naẓar* is in the imperative form of *unẓur* (26 times), whereby God commands humans to look carefully and consider the meanings and/or consequences of certain things, events, or actions. The most repetitive use of *basar* is in the adjective form of basīr (36 times), which designates God's all-seeing attribute. Al-Basīr is one of God's ninety-nine most beautiful names (*al-asmā' al-husnā*). In contrast, the most repetitive uses of *ru'ya* are in two related verbal forms, *tarā* (thirty-six times) and *tara* (thirty-one times, as in *alam tara*, 'do you not see'), which prompts Muslims to see in order to discern the implied lessons and learn from them.' Samer Akkach, 'Naẓar: The Seen, the Unseen, and the Unseeable', in *Naẓar: Vision, Belief, and Perception in Islamic Cultures*, ed. Samer Akkach (Leiden and Boston, MA: Brill, 2022), 13–14.

the impression that the cave opening has not been disturbed for a long time, and therefore no one could be hiding inside.[26] The pursuers are deceived by their sight.

Show is an aspect which is regulated in local Islam. This regulation extends not just how much of one's body one can show, but also how much of one's emotions, wealth, etc. A prophet saying[27] reminds the faithful that a father should not display much affection for his children in public as it will make the orphans feel bad. Similarly, one is instructed to dress neatly but modestly. The same rule of modesty applies to the display of one's wealth. One is not to make a show of one's prosperity for it might attract the attention of the black eye too. The black eye is also referred to as the black tongue, and both bring destruction on the remarked upon.[28] A similar look of destruction is one caused by envy. This emotion is understood to be potent as God asks the Prophet (and by extension the believers) to seek refuge in Him against the envious. Envy is understood to be so powerful that it can obscure the obvious for the envious. It brings destruction not just to others but also to oneself.[29]

Dreams are another realm of sight which can have effect on the world. Dreams are understood to be messages from another dimension. Dream interpretation is a sensitive affair. There are cheap guide books available to know the language of dreams. In such books, dreams are treated as messages with fixed codes. Snakes stand for enemies, while flying people

---

[26] In an apocryphal version of this incident, as the pursuers stand at the opening of the cave remarking that no one could have entered the cave given the stability of the spider web, a lizard perched on the rock of the cave clicked. The clicking of lizard is taken to be a sign of truth being uttered in popular belief (but, thanks to popular films, usually referred to in an ironic mode). I heard this apocryphal story when I was eleven (a student of fifth standard), from a non-Muslim male teacher in an Islamic school. I have not come across this version anywhere else.

[27] Direct quotes are avoided because it is the understood message rather than the actual prophetic saying which is popularly known.

[28] To narrate a funny story told to me by my maternal grandmother: there used to be a Mama (a very old woman) in our village. She was notorious for her black eye. One positive remark from her on anything, and the thing is destroyed forever. A man had recently bought some land. After the intensive planting, all that grew were some odd stalks of paddy. He realized that his new land is not going to yield rice as it is mostly rocks underneath. He happened to hear of the Mama and thought of taking her to the land. She would remark on how obstinate the rocks are, and lo and behold the rocks would melt to water and make it a wet field! Or so he thought. On the day, the man accompanied Mama to the land. The Mama, already very old, took a look around. 'Hmmm, it's all rocks. But the odd paddy that grows, they are gritty!' Whatever few paddy stalks were around burned down to the ground that very moment.

[29] One can turn every enemy into a friend, except those who are an enemy out of envy, goes a prophetic saying.

stands for imminent death, etc. The sensitivity of dreams, however, comes from the potency of dream interpretation itself. It is understood, by way of Prophet Yusuf's story narrated in the Qur'an, that the meaning of a dream is what it is interpreted as, and such an interpretation is binding on the world.[30] It is therefore advised that one shares one's dream only with the most trusted and well-wishing, for the meaning of the dream is dependent on how they are put into words by the interpreter.

The laws of modesty, the fear of black eye and envy, and the confidence in the interlocutor are crucial in the order of visuality in the local Islam, and have a bearing on the see ability of Gulf photographs in this milieu. To be surrounded by wealth meant to be in a good state. While the Gulf photographs depicted immense wealth one is surrounded by, this sight was to be guarded from being a display of arrogance and from the evil eye it could attract. The selective vision of the Gulf, that sight itself could be subject to anticipations and apprehensions, in itself made the Gulf an object of fantasy.

A New Way of Looking

Two important functions of photography prior to its popularization via the Gulf were its use as portraits and for documenting public occasions. Portraits played an important role in the households of various communities or ideological formations in Kerala. The Communists would use the icons of Marx, Engels, Lenin, and Che Guevara in their public messaging. Homes of many Communist Party members featured hung portraits of these and local leaders such as P. Krishnapilla, or A. K. Gopalan (popularly known as AKG) on the walls of their houses.[31] Besides, the portraits of elders, both alive and deceased, are hung on the walls to

---

[30] When Prophet Yusuf was a prisoner, he used to share the cell with two others. Both of them had a dream one night and narrated it to Yusuf asking him for their meaning. One of them saw himself pressing wine, while the other saw birds feeding off his head. To the first Yusuf said that he will be freed and be reinstated to his palace duties, and to the other that he will be executed. On hearing this, the latter asked if the interpretation can be changed, to which Yusuf replied, 'it has been pronounced'. Do note that I am referring to popular discourse which might be at variance with scholarly interpretations of the Qur'an.

[31] Anagha Anil, 'Portrait Populism: On Communist Iconography of Kerala', in *Populist Mediations: Aesthetics and the Politics of Affect in (Digital) Media*, eds Catherine Bublatzky and Simone Pfeifer (forthcoming).

suggest family lineage and serve as codings of inclusion and exclusion of particular individuals from the family genealogy.[32] At times the portraits of family elders are hung with the portraits of political leaders to indicate the ideological moorings of the elder as well as the household in general.[33] In popular Hindu religious practice, the walls of the *kolaya* (foyer) is also where the chromolithographs of gods are hung and worshipped.

Before the 1980s, many relatively affluent Muslim households did have wall photography. Some of these featured the family members who had achieved aspirational heights in their professional lives. For example, that of the man of the house in his professional uniform—that of the police, a feared, respected, and influential job, when most Muslims were peasantry or small traders, and without a hold in bureaucracy. Other photographs featured members of the family. An important difference here between the wall photographs in Muslim households is that they were of family members who were alive. The dead elders did not feature on the walls because of its resonance with idolatry.

Another kind of photograph which was hung on the wall were occasional group photographs. This could be passing-out-of-school pictures, retirement pictures, etc. As can be understood, these photographs suggest a link to modernity, such as modern education, modern professions, the idea of modern saree-wearing women, etc. What is interesting here is the presence of post-puberty women in these photographs adorning the *kolaya* (foyer) of the house at a time when women did not have access to *kolaya* in the presence of men not belonging to the house, and women and men had separate doors to enter the house.[34] Photography itself was a signifier of the modern, and to hang a photograph suggested an amicable relationship with modernity.[35]

---

[32] Pooja Sagar, 'Images of Deaths and Marriages: Syrian Christian Family Albums and Oral Histories in Kerala', in *Photography in India: From Archives to Contemporary Practice*, eds Aileen Blaney and Chinar Shah (London: Bloomsbury, 2018).

[33] Sujith Parayil, 'Family Photographs: Visual Mediation of the Social', *Critical Quarterly* 58, 3 (2014).

[34] This practice continued well into the 1990s.

[35] This suggests a gesture of distinction as a section of Mappilas looked at modernity, insofar as it was identified as such and associated with the colonial powers, with disdain or hostility. Referred to as *parishkaaram* (revision), modernity had a range of negative associations, such as haughtiness, arrogance, corruption, or even *jahiliyyat* (ignorance; used to refer to the Arabia before the Prophet), thereby making modernity sound more like primitive barbarism. Another section, on the other hand, imbibed modernity as a neutral ethic (often understood to be rooted in Islamic history) and not particularly associated with the British.

At the same time, the general Muslim attitude towards photography was ambiguous. The popular Kerala Sunni Muslim belief at the time shunned making human or living likenesses as that would be arrogating the role of God. The one who creates a likeness will be asked to bring it to life on the day of judgement.[36] As these are not codified rules but popular beliefs, how much of it was applicable to photography often depended on individual dispositions. The important factor however was that prior to the Gulf migration, photography was not accessible to most of the mostly poor south Malabar Muslim households.

This economic situation of the Muslims began to change with the large-scale labour migration to the countries of the Arab Gulf. Despite gaining considerable mobility in the 1980s, when it comes to photographic practice, we do not see an imitation of the established elite by the newly mobile migrants. Hanging of portraiture of respectable elders and frames of solemn occasions did not become a general practice among Muslims even though they could now afford photographs. While there are pragmatic reasons for this,[37] the culture of hanging photographs even among the affluent Muslim households more or less came to an end in the 1980s.[38] The answer also lies in how religion—Islam—itself was undergoing a change in the period.

The affluence achieved by Gulf migration refracted itself into religion. As Osella and Osella have noted, this is the time in which the migrants, who hailed from subaltern backgrounds, were now making their way into social institutions through redefining their social status.[39] Religion was one of the avenues through which one's social status could be improved.

In the ASJ houses, one can see *lauh* (lit. plate, but is usually paper posters) featuring the ninety-nine beautiful names (*asma-ul-husna*) of Allah and/or various chapters from the Qur'an (such as Fatihah, the four chapters starting with 'qul' towards the end of the Qur'an, Ya-sin, or the 255th verse (*aayat*) known as Aayat-ul-Kursi (the Verse of the Throne) of Chapter 2 of Qur'an), the names of the martyrs at the battle of Badr, with some of them featuring the equine of heavenly ascendance, Buraq.

[36] Children are often told that illustrations of likenesses to living things come to life in the night.

[37] An obvious explanation is that such photographs did not exist.

[38] This too has pragmatic dimensions—the discomfort with hammering nails into the walls in the newly constructed/renovated houses (thanks to the Gulf), and stories of small venomous snakes getting cosy in the gap between the wall and the photo, in those instances where the photo was hung slanting at an angle.

[39] Filippo Osella and Caroline Osella, *Social Mobility in Kerala: Modernity and Identity in Conflict* (London: Pluto Press, 2001).

There was a new-found insistence and even invention of rituals by the migrants at the time.[40] In the Muslim community, Gulf money made many community endeavours of 'common good' possible.[41] This includes building new schools, colleges, and mosques.[42] These endeavours were by specific factions within the community. These factions had been contesting each other both ideologically and materially, especially over establishing and controlling new institutions. The Gulf money, channelled by direct contribution by individual Arabs, various foundations in the Gulf, and sourced from crowd-funding among Malayali Muslim migrants in the Gulf, lent ammunition to the debates that were going on within the community. The debates were mainly between the Kerala Sunni, and the Salafis/Mujahids.[43] The debates centred around theological and jurisprudential issues which should not concern us here. However, a central theological concern, relevant to the topic at hand, is about the role of the elders in religious stature and by extension, in setting the model for one's life. It is a common practice among the Kerala Sunni to invoke the Prophet, his companions, his family members and lineage, and the martyrs in the cause of Islam, to intercede on behalf of the worshipper. Moreover, visiting graves (*qabr ziyarat*) of deceased family members and saints was an important aspect of Kerala Sunni practice. The Salafis opposed this vehemently likening it to polytheism. According to Kerala Sunni, the Salafis are deviating from the path shown by the elders (the followers of the Prophet, and the followers of the followers) and setting up new precedents (*bid'at*). The Salafis/Mujahids on the other hand claimed that theirs is the way shown by the Prophet, and the local traditionally practised Islam has a lot of non-Islamic influences. The story of

---

[40] Osella and Osella, *Social Mobility in Kerala*.

[41] Filippo Osella and Caroline Osella, 'Muslim entrepreneurs in public life between India and the Gulf: making good and doing good', *Journal of the Royal Anthropological Institute* 15, s1 (2009).

[42] Mohamed Shafeeq Karinkurayil, 'On Stale Images: A Photo Essay', *Dastavezi: The Audio-Visual South Asia*, 3 (2021), doi: 10.11588/dasta.2021.1.15080.

[43] An ideologically third faction is *Jamaat-e-Islami* which concerns itself with religion in its interaction with the state, but aligns mostly with the Salafi/Mujahid faction in theological aspects while leaving matters of Islamic jurisprudence (*fiqh*) to the principle of community consensus and avoidance of disruption within the community. For a discussion on the different ideological positions within the contemporary Mappila community, see R. Santhosh, 'Contextualising Islamic Contestations: Reformism, Traditionalism and Modernity among Muslims of Kerala', *Indian Anthropologist* 43, 2 (2013); Filippo Osella and Caroline Osella, 'Islamism and Social Reform in Kerala, South India', *Modern Asian Studies* 42, 2/3 (2008).

the Prophet Ibrahim, who defied his father and destroyed the idols, becomes an oft-repeated one in this context. The story suggested distancing
and defying one's elders, if need be, in the path of true faith. Over the
course of the long formal and informal debates between the adherents
of the factions, the absolute veneration of elders as a value came under
scrutiny, forcing an acknowledgement from all sides that it is done for the
right reasons.

The religious establishment plays a role in delimiting the zones of technology too. From time to time and place to place, the *mahal* (parish)
committees instruct their members regarding injunctions in the use of
photography and videography. Some committees disallow the use of
cameras in mosques while some don't. Some disallow videography at
weddings while some don't. This extremely local nature of Islam in Kerala
with regard to many daily practices on which there is no categorical
Prophetic tradition is to be accounted for while discussing the relation
between the community and technology. Thus, to be clear, the religious
debate has nothing to do with photography as such. There isn't any injunction by any Muslim organization against the use of photography or
about hanging pictures of elders. As an indexical medium, photographs
were used as a device of documentation. On the other hand, performative
arts which involved impersonation was frowned upon, and this includes
photography when used in such a mode.[44] Nevertheless, the displacement of the wall portraiture can be inferred to be an indirect result of the
convolutions around the figure of the elders at the time. It is a displacement rather than disappearance because, there was now the arrival of a
new apparatus of photography.

The coming of cheap cameras and the photo albums in the 1980s set
in a new disposition towards photographs in general. Photographs were
not rare any more. In the albums, the photographs are characterized by
their multitude in numbers as opposed to the rare and imposing ones

---

[44] Mahmood Kooria notes that the injunctions against cinema among ASJ were based
on three reasons: that films may be considered image-making, which is forbidden, the
public presence of female body, and imposturing. See Mahmood Kooria, 'Pothumandalam,
Drishyamadhyamangal, Matham: Oramukham' ('Public sphere, visual media, religion: an introduction'), in *Matham Drisyabhashayil: Keraliya Pothumandalathil Islam Thedunna
Puthuvazhikal (Religion in Visual Language: Recent Islamic Trends in Kerala's Public Sphere)* ed.
Mahmood Kooria (Kozhikode: Islamic Sahitya Academy, 2011), 35. The breach of privacy of the
women's quarters is an oft-cited reason to dissuade videography during weddings.

from earlier times. While photographs were earlier objects of worshipful or reverential eyes and was as much about being placed in front of the picture as the picture is in front of oneself, the coming of the photo albums altered the corpothetic[45] conditions which occasioned the viewing of photographs. The albums are held in hands and looked down into, usually by a group of viewers. The portraits do not preside over the public space of domesticity anymore. Even as the portraits moved to the albums, they were moved from their stature too. The playfulness of the photographs is thus the displacement of the medium of photograph itself from a position of reverentiality and publicness,[46] to one of selective viewership and controlled appreciation. The albums are accessed by the household members, thus exercising within limits the power to ward off envy and black eye.

Another factor that changes the order of seeing at the time is the greater prevalence of television in the 1980s. The emphasis turned to policing vision, and its ethic was to reign in the power of the images over oneself. Rather than using visuals as a means of religious communication, the fact that the visuals were not in one's control made the consciousness of the viewer the prime object of training in religious discourse. Thus, the injunction to turn away from obscenities, an injunction which was shrill with the coming of videography and the voyeurism it made possible at a new domestic scale, is about maintaining a distance between the viewer and the viewed. The Islamic regulation on images, such as the instruction on modesty on the part of all genders, is also meant to make the viewer conscious of the act of viewing. As a testament to the artifice of photographic technology, photographs now become a means for coding

---

[45] Pinney defines 'corpothetics' as 'embodied, corporeal aesthetics' (9), 'synaesthetic, mobilizing all the senses simultaneously' (19). See, Christopher Pinney, 'Photos of the Gods': The Printed Image and Political Struggle in India (London: Reaktion Books, 2004).

[46] It is significant to note that this changed attitude towards portraiture on the walls is a photographic practice without currency in other aspects of life. Even though the role of ancestors in religious matters was challenged by one faction of Islamic thought, there is now (2000s) an increasing tendency to situate oneself in terms of a genealogy, aided by the mobility granted by Gulf money. The post-Gulf migration period among Muslims is noted by various attempts to trace, establish, and invent lineages. Such enterprises were channelled through newly minted family trees, family meetings, lores of ancestors, etc. P. C. Saidalavi, who has worked on the status claims among Muslims in Kerala, shows examples of how families often tend to trace their lineage to the earliest Arab Muslims who had settled in Kerala and in the process, invisibilize their earlier lower-caste status in the wake of the new mobility. See P. C. Saidalavi, 'Status claims among Muslims in Malabar, South India', Anthropological Notebooks 23, no. 2 (2017).

of aspirations and imposturing. It becomes a document of the youth culture of a time in which localities are opening up to global forces. The new social churning in India in the early 1990s was primarily expressed as a bodily disposition,[47] and photographs were the means to declare this new disposition.

Any account of the systems of the visible has to take into account the value of visuality, the conditions of its production, the media of its manifestation, as well as its resources of expressivity. While this chapter has already covered some of this ground, in the next section I read a migrant photograph placed in an album along the axis of expressivity, and see the role of migrant photographs in the affective pull of Gulf migration.

The Leisurely Migrant

In this photograph (Fig. 1.1) taken in Abu Dhabi in 1981, we see two men shaking hands with each other. The distance between them and the stretch of the hands suggest that they are unknown to each other. These are two strangers meeting in the city. Behind them the Abu Dhabi Corniche, constructed in the 1970s, stretches to infinity. The broad walkway by the sea lined by streetlights clearly convey that this place belongs to the city and the developed world. It is a deep composition. While the two men occupy the space closer to the foreground, a lonely figure in white is visible towards the background; the bright sea, the shaded Corniche, and the dark undefined boulders meet at the vanishing point where the walkway meanders to the right. The two men are dressed impeccably. They are wearing shiny black shoes. Their shirts are in vogue.

What could this photograph, of a real space rendered fantastic, tell us about migrant self-representations? The reading of this photograph requires us to see it for its intermediality. The photograph is caught with movement that it is rightly to be considered a freeze frame. In its form, the shot of the photograph is closer to Malayalam film's depiction of the city as a space of crime, thrills, and adventure. The beginning of the 1980s

---

[47] Vivek Dhareshwar and Tejaswini Niranjana, 'Kaadalan and the Politics of Resignification', in *Making Meaning in Indian Cinema*, ed. Ravi Vasudevan (New Delhi: Oxford University Press, 2000).

Fig. 1.1 By the Corniche. Photo as placed in the photo album. Reproduced with permission from K. K. Abdul Razaq.

saw a few Malayalam movies that were set in foreign locales—*Ezham Kadalinakkare* (*Beyond the Seventh Sea*) (I. V. Sasi, 1979); *Vilkkanundu Swapnangal* (Azad, 1980); *Love in Singapore* (Baby, 1980); *America America* (I. V. Sasi, 1983); *Mandanmmar Londanil* (*Fools in London*) (Sathyan Anthikad, 1983); and *Iniyenkilum* (*At Least from Now*) (I.

V. Sasi, 1985). *Ezham Kadalinakkare* begins with the premise of two migrant labourers to the US, one a driver, and the other a nurse, but soon turns into a narrative of casinos and chases and killings, and aligns with the gangster film genre, with a considerable chunk of the screen time dedicated to the wonders of the first world. *America America*, screenwritten by T. Damodaran, directed by I. V. Sasi, and stars Mammootty and Seema, is set completely in the US, shot mainly in Florida. The film is a whodunit around the murder of the captain of a ship, and, like *Ezham Kadalinakkare*, it is a veritable procession of the marvels of the first world—high rises, digital hoardings, long glitzy cars, sea planes, disco bars, skimpily dressed women, and an Afro-American muscleman whose signature stunt move reminds one of Muhammad Ali. According to *Encyclopaedia of Indian Cinema*, 'this definitive Malayalam hit established the combination of star Mammootty and director Sasi'.[48] *Love in Singapore*, shot mostly in Singapore, shares the same grammar as these other movies, with its high rises, rooftops with views, shopping malls, women in Western wear, etc. The plot follows the investigation around a relic stolen from Kerala and taken to Singapore. The investigating officer from Kerala meets his long-lost brother in Singapore. Starring Prem Nazir and Jayan as the two brothers having to deal with crime in Singapore in their own ways, *Love in Singapore*, again, shows the foreign to be a location of thrills and adventure. The easy-going, matter-of-fact nature of the romantic relationships of the brothers is striking and can only be attributed to the exotic location.[49] The foreign locale in these films is a place of crime as well as romantic relations that do not involve the pedigrees of the characters.[50] *Iniyenkilum* was shot partially in Tokyo. The plot is that a group of performers who have left for Tokyo are stranded there when their host disappears. This film, too, presents the foreign locale as a place

---

[48] Ashish Rajadhyaksha and Paul Willemen, *Encyclopaedia of Indian Cinema* (New Delhi: British Film Institute and Oxford University Press, 1994), 458.

[49] Ratheesh Radhakrishnan notes that with respect to the Malayalam films of the 1970s that the space of the city outside Kerala allowed the films to sidestep the inner–outer binary of city and domesticity and allowed one to be contiguous with the other. See Ratheesh Radhakrishnan, 'Aesthetic dislocations: A re-take on Malayalam cinema of the 1970s', *South Asian Popular Culture* 10, no. 1 (2012), doi: 10.1080/14746689.2012.655111.

[50] *Love in Singapore* is a reiteration of a plot familiar to Malayalam cinema by then, and is most evocative of *Love in Kerala* (Sasikumar, 1968) which too starred Prem Nazir, and dealt with estranged brothers and foreign crime networks, but was set in Kerala.

of high rises, glistening cars, high density of vehicular traffic, and a place of shootouts and thrills.

The affinity of the photograph (Fig. 1.1) with these movies of thrills and adventures is hard to miss. The handshakes between strangers are a staple of these films. When new associations are made in the city whether for nefarious reasons or for the noble reason of fighting the bad guys, this is how the interested parties meet, with their hands stretched out, as in a business meeting.[51] It is suggestive of a modern association. It is very different from greetings which do not touch each other. Or those that involve bodies which are in closer proximity to each other. The shaking of hands is when people meet in a city for there are things to be done, deals to be fixed. These are men on a mission. Listen to the picture, and you can even hear English—'how do you do!'

The two people we see in the picture are, as we might have expected by now, quite known to each other. They are flatmates, and so is the one taking the photograph. The three have set out one Friday, being a holiday, to photograph themselves against the wonders of the new place that they are now in. What we have in the photograph is an instance of imposturing. It is one of those instances when the photograph is relieved of its task to be an indexical document and is made to picture a fantastic situation.

The impact of James Bond films is discernible in these films. However, these are not films which involve international relations, but a bid to reproduce the attractions of the thrillers within the affordances of the vernacular. In her study of 'transnational imagination in action cinema', with reference to action cinema not made under the auspices of the big studios, Meaghan Morris observes that 'the pitch of these films is broadly to a mobile and self-selecting "community" rather than state based modes of affective mobilization'.[52] The photograph, whose debt to transnational action cinema is already indicated, is the staging of this self-selection of a

---

[51] David Howes and Constance Classen invite our attention to a range of meanings that can accrue in handshakes as an example of the need to pay attention to the full range of sensory experience and expression for their role in meaning making. See David Howes and Constance Classen, *Ways of Sensing: Understanding the Senses in Society* (Oxford and New York: Routledge, 2014), 4.

[52] Maeghan Morris, 'Transnational Imagination in Action Cinema: Hong Kong and the Making of a Global Popular Culture', *Inter-Asia Cultural Studies* 5, no. 2 (2004): 191, doi: 10.4324/9780203960981-31.

community. In the feigned encounter that is the handshake in the photograph, the migrant conjures the meeting of two people, an affiliation that
now strives to go beyond filiation, even as kinship networks play a major
role in the migration process and the condition of possibility of this very
photograph. The close friends who are also flatmates become strangers
in the photograph; the elder sibling who photographs becomes invisible. The personal is sundered for it to be open to receive the affinities
and affiliations the world can bring. These are quite meaningless photos,
which thereby brings their meaninglessness to the fore. These are acts of
mimicry.

What does this performativity, this excess, do? If anything, the
interocularity serves to construct the Gulf as a place which is like
Manhattan. When a photograph becomes a still from an unfolding action, the being-there, the place of the action in its continuous present
tense is an evolving possibility rather than the given of a there–then.[53]
The migrant labourer thus constructs the city in their leisure as much as
in their labour. The Gulf becomes the *terra nova* of new relations, new
settlements, new possibilities, new futures.

What is evident in these photographs is the 'capacity to aspire', and
aspirations are fashioned by the possibilities obtained in a given historical situation.[54] The migrant's body was his potential, and as much as this
might be a precarious state to be in, it was still a possibility to be free
from the deterrents of a traditional society that make some bodies dis-
qualified bodies. The body with traces of history is left behind for a body
which can shed one skin for another in its very nature. Impersonation
becomes a migrant reality as much as it is a photographic reordering. This
photograph is hardly even personal, it partakes of a language which belongs to the public space of the cinema hall. Ordered thus, it brings in the
public to the personal; it stages the personal as public, operative in public
knowledge.

---

[53] Roland Barthes attributes to photography a new type of consciousness, that of spatial im-
mediacy and temporal anteriority—the here-now and the there-then. In contrast, he says that
cinematic consciousness is marked by being-there. See Roland Barthes, *Image, Music, Text*,
trans. Stephen Heath (London: Fontana Press, 1977), 44.

[54] Arjun Appadurai, 'Archive and Aspiration', in *Information is Alive: Art and Theory
on Archiving and Retrieving Data*, eds Arjen Mulder and Joke Brouwer (Rotterdam: NAI
Publishers, 2003).

The performativity, the very nature of its excess gives its reader a privileged access as the one who is capable of reading and interpreting the situation. In the photograph we apprehend the noirish scantiness of an evening of new deals. The camera is placed at a high angle. This is a shot which is not supposed to foster identification with the characters. The high angle of the shot suggests conveying objective and authoritative knowledge. Even as the meeting of two strangers is staged, it is staged as if it is a clandestine affair. The meeting is enacted as being away from the public gaze. In this the camera frees itself from the artist and re-enacts the transparent medium that it is supposed to be, and the migrant photographer manipulates this transparent being of the camera to *reveal* a secret, one that shares its grammar with the glamour of cinema and its space with the glitz of wondrous urbanity. The noirish sparseness of the location gives it an edgy freeze. One is standing at the tip of an action about to unfold. The photograph is the staging of a pleasure, that of belonging to the new world, but one that is articulated in the thrill of a secret. It is the disavowed display of a private world; like cinema, in its very staging it seeks transparency.[55]

The gaze of the camera intersects with that of the viewer of the photograph. The affinity with transnational cinema effects that though it is the revealing of a secret, the camera threatens to slip away from a position of neutrality. There is an intimation of a gaze involved, as if someone else is looking, someone not seen by those in the picture. The scene is suddenly one of being exposed. We feel another body. But because the gaze of that third person coincides with our own, we are turned into the voyeur existing within the diegetic space of the photograph.[56] The chill and thrill now is because of an intimate foreboding that this body whose vision I share might be up to something I do not approve of. We are now beside ourselves, both ourselves and not ourselves, existing within and without.

[55] See Christian Metz's formulation of cinema as that which needs to appear transparent because it does not have a narrator. See Christian Metz, 'Story/Discourse (A Note on Two Kinds of Voyeurism)', in *Psychoanalysis and Cinema: The Imaginary Signifier* (London: Macmillan Press, 1982), 89–97.

[56] Laura Mulvey identifies three looks in cinema—that of the camera looking at the pro-filmic event, the audience looking at the screen, and the characters looking in the film. See Mulvey 'Visual Pleasure and Narrative Cinema', in *Film Theory and Criticism: Introductory Readings*, eds Gerald Mast, Marshall Cohen, and Leo Braudy (New Delhi: Oxford University Press, 1992). The tension here, because the photo participated in an action genre with a noir feel, is between the second and the third looks.

The pleasure of the photograph is in communicating, stealthily, of a third gaze, and in that frozen moment the viewer, if in the know, is caught between the third gaze and herself.

That is to say, the photograph, while an indexical medium, is also in its performativity a calling out to the subject in the know. In the interocularity with the transnational action film, it calls forth a subject who is instantly presented a place within. There is, this is, an invitation, if only one knows it. It is the excess itself which serves to produce a distinction, and thereby produce a knowing subject, the citizen, one who is able to read beyond their confines. The one who can be beside oneself. It is this intimacy, whose basis is the indulgence in a public speech, this possibility of belonging as an excess, that the Gulf invites you to. This performativity is also the carving out of a seemingly transparent medium such as a photograph, an enjoyment available only to some. The lure of the Gulf is also the chance to partake in this community of enjoyment, in alienation.

To belong to a community of Gulf migrants then, is to belong to it in this order of personal distinction. As an excess that one can feel about oneself. To belong to a community of migrants is to begin to experience the world as a personal invitation and a distinct experience. The lure of the Gulf is the lure to be beside oneself. The invitation is one to enjoy being uncertain of what the body whose vision we share is up to. To experience the world ironically, in doubling of selves, as an excess.

A Private Modernity

It was from the second half of the 1970s that outmigration from India to the Gulf began to be regulated. The migrants before that were mostly undocumented. The Gulf itself settled into its present political contours mostly in the 1970s. The state's relation to the Gulf migrants were mostly one of tutelage and guardianship. Such a relation has a longer history in India. The Gandhian model of struggle, known as *satyagraha*, schematized training of the majority by a small number of core *satyagrahis*. The Nehruvian state's developmental model also imputed a major role to cultural pedagogy in its bid to attain a developed status for India. The vast population of India was understood to require training in modernity, down to the level of personal hygiene. As a corollary of the need to train and bring into being its citizens, the Nehruvian state understood statecraft to be about rational allocation of resources controlled by technocrats and away from politics. The state-driven development and modernity was constrained by the resources at hand.

What the Gulf presented was another route to modernity. The riches that the Gulf photographs present—the shiny shoes, the fashionable clothing, etc., do not just represent material riches, but also symbols that are mobilized towards a cultural claim, that of having embraced modernity. The creative skills displayed in the composition of the photograph declared the arrival of a modern subject. Popular cinema in India is understood to be a pedagogic exercise aimed at the culturally backward spectator. On top of it, Hollywood has been an object of Indian postcolonial desire.[57] To imitate Hollywood, therefore, is already a statement of one's cultural capacity for modernity, and thereby an assertion of one's deliberative capacities of citizenship. Through living a freeze frame, the subjects of the photograph as well as the photographer also declare their cultural belonging as one which belongs to the order of individualism and agency, and having outgrown the need for paternal care of the state. By crystallizing life in the order of transnational action film in which individuals play out the struggle for their nation states, these protagonists already declare themselves to be representing rather than be represented by the state.

These images also transformed the image of labour into that of a consumer at a time (the 1980s) when national modernity was beginning to be redefined in terms of consumption rather than production. This was, among other factors such as the rise of small-scale industries and the increase in the disposable income of the white-collar salaried class, connected to the rise of an informal economy which owed itself to remittances from the Gulf.[58] There was a move from a consensus based on deliberation, which marked the earlier self-representation of the polity, to one that was based on desire. It was the coming of commercial

---

[57] For a discussion, see M. Madhava Prasad, 'From Cultural Backwardness to the Age of Imitation: An essay on film history', in *Routledge Handbook of Indian Cinemas*, eds K. Moti Gokulsing and Wimal Dissanayake (Oxford and New York: Routledge, 2013), 7–18.

[58] William Mazzarella, *Shoveling Smoke: Advertising and Globalization in Contemporary India* (Delhi: Oxford University Press, 2003), 72.

colour television in 1982 accompanied by the spectacle of Asiad (the Asian Games), which signified and articulated the new move towards consumerism.[59] The turn to consumerism was a necessary acknowledgement of the limits of state-induced production-based articulation of modernity. Instead, the state now reinvented itself as the protector of consumers.

However, the consumerist modernity was resisted in Kerala with its own version of modernity that insisted on a 'common minimum'. This was a modernity based on articulating identities on the basis of a minimal commonness that all communities can agree to. The meta-narrative of modern Kerala begins with the adoption of Malayalam as a common language by the different communities. Similarly, the white *mundu* (a wraparound cloth for the lower body) and white shirt represented the sartorial modernity in Kerala,[60] while vegetarian *sadya* represented its common food. Such a modernity viewed individuality as expressed in liberal consumerism as opposed to the values of public life it professes.

At the same time, the image of national modernity itself was unravelling. From the 1970s, the various community and caste factions began to put pressure on the central allocation of resources, thus pushing politics into what was planned to be a purely technocratic affair. Rather than being universalized, the version of Indian modernity was felt to be the characteristic of particularity of the Indian ruling elite.

The 1970s and the subsequent period is therefore characterized by the contradictory pulls of a consumerist individualism and aspirational national modernity, the austere Kerala modernity insisting on collective values, and ethnic/caste/community[61] assertion. The second half of 1970s marks a new-found assertion and confidence among the Mappilas. One can see numerous efforts to mark the community in the history and contemporaneity of the state as one of its major players. Roland Miller's classical book on the Mappilas came out in 1976; *Mahattaya Mappila Sahitya*

---

[59] Mazzarella, *Shoveling Smoke*, 72.

[60] For a discussion, see Karinkurayil, 'A Strangeness'.

[61] My choice of the word 'community' rather than 'communal' is deliberate and is used to mark the distinction between two terms in Malayalam—*saamudayikatha* (community), which marks a positive engagement with matters related to community development, and *vargeeyatha* (communal), which marks a negative engagement with other communities.

Paramparyam (The Great Mappila Literary Heritage)[62] by C. N. Ahmad Moulavi and K. K. Mohammad Abdul Kareem came out in 1978 and is considered a benchmark, the debates over exclusions and inclusions in which is yet to die down. P. K. Muhammad Kunhi's *Muslimkalum Kerala Samskaravum (Muslims and the Culture of Kerala)*[63] was published by the Kerala Sahithya Akademi[64] in 1980, thus giving Muslim culture in Kerala the imprimatur of secular recognition. R. E. Asher's translation of works by Vaikom Muhammad Basheer,[65] published by Edinburgh University Press in 1980, and the publication of *Islamic Society on the South Asian Frontier*[66] by Stephen Dale in 1980 locating the community as part of the global Islamic community, all gave a fillip to the self-assertion at the time. In the political sphere, the Indian Union Muslim League, the bulk of whose following came from the Mappilas of south Malabar, had successfully overcome the distance that other parties maintained from them in the aftermath of the partition of India[67] and had become part of the Kerala government in 1967. The symbolic high point of the party was when its leader C. H. Mohammed Koya became the Chief Minister of the state, albeit for a very brief period of fifty days in 1979.[68] With the stabilization of the broad contours of the coalition politics in Kerala from 1980,

---

[62] C. N. Ahmad Moulavi and K. K. Mohammad Abdul Kareem, *Mahattaya Mappila Sahitya Paramparyam* (Kozhikode: Azad Book Stall, 1978).

[63] P. K. Muhammad Kunhi, *Muslimkalum Kerala Samskaravum* (Thrissur: Kerala Sahithya Akademi, 1980).

[64] Kerala Sahithya Akademi was formed by the government of Travancore-Kochi in 1956, predating the formation of Kerala. It is an autonomous body with state patronage, with a view to promoting Malayalam language and literature.

[65] Vaikom Muhammad Basheer, *'Me Grandad 'ad an Elephant!': Three Stories of Muslim Lives in South India*, trans. R. E. Asher and Achamma Coilparambil Chandrasekharan (Edinburgh: Edinburgh University Press, 1980).

[66] Stephen Frederic Dale, *Islamic Society on the South Asian Frontier: The Mappilas of Malabar, 1498–1922* (Oxford: Clarendon Press, 1980).

[67] The partition of India was and continues to be attributed to the machinations of the Jinnah-led All India Muslim League (AIML). The Indian Union Muslim League was formed in 1948 as a new party by the Madras Presidency leadership of the erstwhile AIML.

[68] From 12 October to 1 December 1979. The symbolic importance of the event (other than the sheer fact that Chief Minister is the leader of the government), counted as the achievement of the Muslim League to this day in the assertion of the identity of the community in Kerala, was that Koya could wear his (black) cap (suggesting Muslimness) and still become the Chief Minister, while at an earlier time (1961), he was asked to remove his cap if he was to serve as Speaker of the Kerala Legislative Assembly. For a discussion on Koya and Indian Union Muslim League, see, Mohamed Shafeeq Karinkurayil, 'The Political Language of Minority Islam in the Indian State of Kerala: The Works of C. H. Mohammed Koya', *Journal of Muslim Minority Affairs* 41, no. 4 (2021), doi: 10.1080/13602004.2022.2028461.

the party has not just been part of governments, but has also extended its pockets of influence.

While the popular beliefs in black eye and envy necessarily regulated how much of one's well-being can be shown outside a circle of confidantes, given the power of vision to cause destruction,[69] those are not the only reasons for the Gulf to be a private experience. The photo albums are themselves a private record and not an object of unintended vision.[70] It is restricted to those who enter the house, and not open to the public gaze, unlike the portraits or calendar art that usually adorn the *kolaya*. However, equally, if not more, important is the fact that the available language in which the Gulf can be translated to a public experience was that framed by individuality—the very frame in which the Gulf is translated in the photographs.

The network was lost in the discourse of individualism. Even as the Gulf migrants or their dependents were conspicuous in their consumption, or when old thatched stone-mud-and-palm frond houses were transformed into concrete houses, these were framed as individual achievements. The *Gulfkaran* (the Gulf man) was always an individual, and his spending practices were framed in a moral language of individualism in which there were good or bad ways to spend money. His mobility was translated to one of personal growth, and was framed in terms of how close he remains to his roots. These were tropes repeated in films and literature, as we shall see in the coming chapters.

The public representation of the community was framed, however, in terms of the religious and community identity. This self-representation of the community was that of having resisted a long line of colonizers, starting from the Portuguese to the British. The peasant rebellions of the nineteenth century extending to the cataclysm of 1921 continue to exert a major pull in the self-assessment of the community.[71] This

---

[69] As mentioned earlier, the belief in the existence of black eye is particular to the numerically far superior ASJ, and not uniform to the Muslim community in Kerala.

[70] This private nature of the photo album is in force for the researcher too, thus making research into private albums bound by bonds of often unspoken trust regarding the citability and reiterability of its contents.

[71] One of the slogans still in use in demonstrations by the Indian Union Muslim League is, after raising a demand, the following refrain: '*parayuvathaarennariyille/vellakkaraude thokkin munnil/nenchu virichoru Mappila makkal*' (don't you know who is saying this [making this demand]/the Mappila sons who bared their chests/against the white men's guns). The slogan implies the courage and determination of the Mappilas. A point of interest here is that the Muslim

self-understanding of the community had oriented its public discourse as opposed to the colonizer's modernity. Such an imagination of the community did not know how to place the Gulf experience, experienced as it was as an individual sojourn through the thrills of modernity. Crucially, even this modernity was suspect, as modernity in Kerala was defined in starkly different terms. Kerala modernity, in its bid to construct a regional identity, opted for the austerity away from consumption, meant to impart the rationality and associated sobriety that modernity is supposed to usher in, thereby turning the Gulf modernity into a vacuous expression of thoughtless consumerism. Kerala modernity insisted on uniformity (such as in the white *mundu*), and overt expressions of individuality in terms of appearance could only suggest corruption of its progressive values.

Thus, even when in the 1980s the Gulf migration had already acquired its networked character, with migration becoming even more large-scale through kinship and neighbourhood networks, this collective experience of the Gulf could not be translated to the public life of Kerala because the language of collective bargaining was already split into that of work place or of identity, in which the citizen-worker nexus of class imagination invisibilized the migrant labourer, and the community identity did not have a space to express the transformation that the Gulf had brought about.

League did not exist at the time of the peasant rebellions, and the slogan does not refer to the party either but to the Mappila community.

2

The Gulf in Malayalam Cinema

In Malayalam films, when migrant labourers discuss life in the Gulf, they say that people in Kerala do not know the real plight in the Gulf. One can hear such a statement in *Vilkkanundu Swapnangal* (*Dreams for Sale*) (Azad, 1980) as well as in *Pathemari* (*Dhow*) (Salim Ahamed, 2015), no matter that the two films have three and half decades between them.[1] Once stated thus, it becomes the task of the film to depict the real Gulf for its audience. This chapter focuses on this question of knowledge/ignorance, this epistemic border which is not only thematized in movies, but is also an ideology which conditions the Gulf question in Malayalam cinema.

This chapter takes as its premise that the Gulf was a presence in Malayalam cinema, whether acknowledged or otherwise, since the 1980s. The question, rather, is of the function of the inscribed knowledge or ignorance regarding the Gulf in Malayalam cinema. Such a knowledge/ignorance of the 'reality' of the Gulf, this chapter illustrates, is also the performance of a border which makes possible ways of belonging, zones of pleasure, and modes of enjoyment.

The Prodigal Migrant

Vilkkanundu Swapnangal, written by M. T. Vasudevan Nair, directed by Azad, shot partially in Sharjah and Dubai, was the first Malayalam film to be shot on location in the Gulf. The film begins with the protagonist

---

[1] I have detailed the continuities between the two films elsewhere. See Mohamed Shafeeq Karinkurayil, ' "Dubai" as a Place of Memory in Malayalam Cinema', *International Journal of Politics, Culture, and Society* 36 (2023), doi: 10.1007/s10767-022-09422-1.

The Gulf Migrant Archives in Kerala. Mohamed Shafeeq Karinkurayil, Oxford University Press. © Mohamed Shafeeq Karinkurayil 2024. DOI: 10.1093/9780198910619.003.0003

Rajan (played by Sukumaran) making his way to the Gulf through un-documented means, in a dhow. He is accompanied by many others, and not all of them make it to the fabled land of gold. The voiceover at the beginning of the film introduces the movie to be the story of young men who left for the western shores of the Arabian Sea.

> We were always attracted to the idea of a place which yielded gold. Once upon a time it was Ceylon; then Malaya. In the last decade there were rumours going round the western shores, of a land, where, if you could somehow reach there even if you had to sell off your house, you would be rescued (you would prosper). For thousands of youth there was now a dream to nurture—Dubai! [2]

The protagonist Rajan, in his initial days in Dubai, is told that the Gulf has its own share of problems, like unemployment, and is quite similar to Kerala in that manner. 'When we land up at home with all our boxes of goodies, people think we lead such luxurious lives here', says one of the characters early in the film, contrasting it with what he sees around him, their packed dorms and frugal ways. Even so, the film depicts the life of the protagonist to be a constant movement towards greater heights of riches and opulence. It is a tale of upward mobility for him. The sparse and oppressive landscapes which greet us early in the film grades up into high rises and spacious living rooms. We see that the landscape of the Gulf changes along with the changes in the protagonist's station in life. The glitzy cityscape of the Gulf is produced along the progress of the mi-grant labouring body. Rajan, who had come to the Gulf unable to bear the insults he was heaped with back home, including the accusation of being a thief, is now able to build a spacious house for himself in Kerala exactly where their former wretched house stood. While he enjoys his new-found respect at home, the movie ends with him having to return to the Gulf, unable to belong to his village.

Vilkkanundu Swapnangal thematizes many of the social fantasies in Kerala around Gulf migration. The space of the Gulf is presented as a space of strife but also that of fantastic mobility for those who didn't

---

[2] Translation mine.

have any means to go on in Kerala. M. T. Vasudevan Nair, a formidable
name in Malayalam literature known for his novels such as *Naalukettu*[3]
and *Asuravithu* (*Demon Seed*)[4] which thematizes the fall of the former
landlords,[5] combines the tragedy of the fall of the former order with the
rise of a new breed of rich men who have made their money outside one's
view, who have access to illicit comforts in that strange land, and who are
disrespectful of the social custom. In the movie one also hears about the
newly mobile Mappilas preying on the fallen times of the former landlords and are buying up the land at bargain rates. The space of Kerala after
the migration is a space of social churning. The rise of the migrant in this
social–realistic space of strife both at home and away imbues it with a
greater force of fantasy.

By the 1980s the Gulf had become a prime source of funding for
Malayalam movies. As the *Encyclopaedia of Indian Cinema* notes, 'The 80s
is Kerala are marked by the "Gulf money" remitted by expatriate workers,
spawning a "newly rich" consumerist sector and fostering a lumpenised
urban mass culture'.[6] Ratheesh Radhakrishnan draws a link between the
sudden astronomic spurt in the number of Malayalam movies produced
from the mid-1970s (to mid-1980s) and the influx of Gulf money.[7]

Though this be the case, after *Vilkkanundu Swapnangal*, the Gulf as
a diegetic space was absent in Malayalam cinema until the late 1990s,
though references to the Gulf, verbal as well as in terms of props, abound
in Malayalam cinema of the period. As Radhakrishnan notes, it was in the
formal features rather than in the thematic space that the Gulf made an
appearance. On the one hand the influence of the Gulf was evident in the
rich sets which marked the commercial Malayalam cinema of the time.
'The new economy was marked using objects that clearly had a semiotic
link with the Gulf, including clothing of the latest fashion, fancy watches,
transistor radios, sunglasses, suitcases, gold bars which were called "gold

[3] M. T. Vasudevan Nair, *Naalukettu* (Kozhikode: Current Books, 1958).

[4] M. T. Vasudevan Nair, *Asuravithu* (Kottayam: DC Books, 1962).

[5] For a discussion, see M. T. Ansari, 'Within/Without the Naalukettu: More on the Muslim in Malayalam Literature', *Humanities Circle* 2, no. 1 (2014).

[6] Ashish Rajadhyaksha and Paul Willemen, *Encyclopaedia of Indian Cinema* (New Delhi: British Film Institute and Oxford University Press, 1994), 143.

[7] Ratheesh Radhakrishnan, 'The Gulf in the Imagination: Migration, Malayalam Cinema, and Regional Identity', *Contributions to Indian Sociology* 23, no. 2 (2009): 219., doi: 10.1177/006996670904300202.

biscuits" and through narratives of mobility.'[8] A condensed rendering of this can be seen in *Visa* (Balu Kiriyath, 1983) where the migrant who has returned from the Gulf is shown surrounded by such riches—wrist watch, perfumes, gold—that can only be termed consumerist fantasy at a time when India had a state-regulated market with heavy import duties. [9] On the other, the art cinema (understood to be the Other of commercial cinema) produced the Gulf as an illegitimate source of wealth. The sea and its shores were the arenas of smuggling, and as the moral of the movie would have it, crime never pays.

The 1980s saw the struggle over the definition of Malayalam cinema and a new aesthetic of cinema, called the 'middlebrow' or 'middle cinema' (*madhyavarthi*) assuming hegemony. 'The genre of movies called madhyavarthi cinema was ubiquitously staged as a genre of quality, in-between films which defied some of the cinematic conventions of both Malayalam kachavada (commercial) and kala (art) cinemas and self-consciously indulged in new film practices, carefully developed through principles of adaptation and refusal.'[10] The middle cinema of the 1980s and early 1990s, in its bid to formulate an aesthetic which was opposed to commercial cinema and its gaudiness, shaped an austere look which while deploying star bodies and songs—two staples of commercial cinema—moulded these to fit its understating style. This bid to create a regional-specific genre of cinema derided the migrant as a threat to this universe. In these films, the migrant and his new-found wealth threatened

---

[8] Radhakrishnan, 'The Gulf in the Imagination', 220–221.

[9] *Visa* is about a group of youngsters who are stuck in Bombay because the agent who was supposed to arrange their travel to the Gulf cheated them. *Visa* is one of those movies of the early 1980s which feature both Mammootty and Mohanlal, the two fledgling actors whose reign over the Malayalam screens was just around the corner. Notably, both Mohanlal and Mammootty occupy less screen time than the other male characters in the movie. Mammootty's character is, however, central to the plot. As the Gulf man, he is the one around whom the aspirations of the other characters are built. Produced by N. P. Abu, the movie is a rare instance in Malayalam cinema in which the rich migrant is also the source of solace for those around him. Contrast this with another film from the time with Mohanlal and Mammootty in guest roles, *Akkare* (*On the Other Shore*) (K. N. Sasidharan, 1984), which is about a low-level government functionary, a Tahsildar, losing everything—his respectability, marital stability, job, and his self-respect—lured by the riches of the Gulf migrants, none of whom are a match to him in terms of education or pedigree.

[10] Bindu Menon, 'Malayalam Middle Cinema and the Category of Woman', in *Women in Malayalam Cinema: Naturalising Gender Heirarchies*, ed. Meena T. Pillai (Hyderabad: Orient Blackswan, 2010), 105.

to destabilize families, buy out their land, dissolve their families, and occupy spaces they weren't meant to.[11]

After *Vilkkanundu Swapnangal*, the Gulf would start appearing as a diegetic space in Malayalam cinema only towards the late 1990s. As multiple crises beset the Malayalam film industry, the 1980s would be recalled as the golden era of Malayalam cinema. A marginal film movement, associated with the name of Salam Kodiyathur, would ride on the back of the digital technological leap of the late 1990s to attempt a reconciliation between the 1980s film ethic and a Gulf migrant point of view. It is to this moment that we turn in the next section.[12]

The Migrant Look

I met Salam Kodiyathur for the first time in a small hotel room in Kozhikode in one of the closing days of 2017. Me being a stranger, he did not close the door but left it half open. This is a gesture which suggests to the outside world that there is nothing spurious going on inside. To those who are in the room, it gives different kinds of guarantees. To the one who has just come in, it suggests that s/he is free to leave any time. For the one who is the host, it offers a thin guarantee that s/he wouldn't be accused of ill intentions and improprieties. In short, it is a gesture which affirms the public nature of the private itself; that the private sphere is, even as private, subjected to the terms set by the public.

The importance of Salam Kodiyathur is in his realizing the affordances of the newly arrived CD technology in developing a vernacular style of films and film-making in Kerala. The first impact of the relatively easy accessibility of digital cinema in terms of production as well as distribution was felt in the northern districts of Kerala (usually called Malabar)

---

[11] A famous example is from the 1993 movie *Devasuram* (*Of God and Demon*) (I. V. Sasi, 1993), in which the newly rich Mappila who made his money in the Gulf is humiliated out of the premises of a decaying feudal household by its heir, who reminds the migrant that the latter's father wouldn't have dared to step in that premises thanks to their lowly station. Interestingly, just before the entrance of the migrant in the scene, the feudal heir and his minions were exclaiming the greatness of their vintage car because it has come across the seas, from England.

[12] The next section adapts my essay 'The Islamic Subject of Home Cinema of Kerala', *BioScope: South Asian Screen Studies* 10, no. 1 (2019). Reproduced by permission of Sage Publications India Private Limited.

in the late 1990s. Television, among others, has been a major avenue of consumption, of films and otherwise, in the aftermath of the mobility achieved by migration.[13] Digital consumption has also been about production at the local levels. The late 1990s and the early 2000s saw the mushrooming of local channels, run by locals of the small rurban localities of Kerala, and finding a slot on the local cable network. Often these channels allocated a huge chunk of their time to songs which had by now become an independent commodity in a protracted change of form effected by MTVization of Indian television. Many of these local channels had a second channel which was just a jukebox where one could dial a phone number displayed on the screen, and once connected, pick songs from a wide range of categories based on language, genre, etc. That there was a perceptible demand for 'Muslim' songs in north Malabar channels was discernible in that the channels used to broadcast even foreign Muslim songs, such as those from Indonesia, which were until then at a remove from the public imagination. One of the categories in the jukebox and a major component of the parent channel was the genre of Mappila songs which gained momentum when the song 'Fathima' produced by East Coast became a tremendous hit. Soon the Mappila songs moved away from the community song and dance forms of Oppana and Kolkkali and began a genre of romantic songs, some of which, like 'Qalbanu Fathima' (Millennium Videos), 'Monjulla Penalle' (Essem Creations), though produced by small-scale production houses, caught the imagination to spur numerous productions of video songs at the local level. These songs, cinematic in their visual form, typically narrated a love story between a Muslim boy and girl, and the sartorial as well as décor of the scenes suggest an aspiration as yet to become reality, but very much on the horizon of plausibility of an upwardly mobile community. Thus T-shirt, jeans, sunglasses, etc. were plausible for both men and women—choices which were as yet removed from lived experience of Kerala (and not just for Muslims).[14] What typically made these songs 'Mappila' was

---

[13] Ritty A. Lukose, *Liberalization's Children: Gender, Youth and Consumer Citizenship in Globalizing India.* (Durham, NC: Duke University Press, 2009).

[14] Caroline Osella has characterized the Kerala Muslim sartorial style as 'glamorous modesty' (123), a style which is characterized by flashy aesthetics as well as Islamic modesty. See Caroline Osella, 'Memories of Luxury, Aspirations towards Glamour, and Cultivations of Morality: How south Indian Muslim women craft their style', in *Fashion India: Spectacular Capitalism*, ed. Tereza Kuldova (Oslo: Akademia, 2013).

the lexical choice of the songs and gestural references such as the casually worn piece of cloth on the female's head. However, these songs weren't shy of jettisoning such Islamic symbols even as the auratic, signalled by the choice of vocabulary of the lyrics as well as the tune of the songs, labelled them as clearly Mappila.[15]

In this digitally invigorated climate, Salam Kodiyathur, a schoolteacher by profession, made his name in the 2000s for a distinct kind of cinema. Variously referred to as *Home Cinema*, or *Home Films*, or *Home Video*, it originally meant a business model but has come to acquire formal properties, and could therefore be called a distinct genre of cinema. Kodiyathur began his movie career in the year 2000 when he brought out *Ningalenne Branthanakki* (*You Made Me a Lunatic*). Originally a play, with the title a take on the famous Malayalam drama *Ningalenne Communistakki* (*You Made Me a Communist*),[16] the script was adapted for a film with a meagre budget of rupees one lakh.

The distinct model that Kodiyathur developed was to rope in local talents at all levels of production, and to market the movie directly to the video rental shops, avoiding theatrical release completely. His first two movies were made on video, and could be treated essentially as a local variant of video culture that had sprouted in various parts of India. Shortly the Compact Disc (CD) entered the Kerala markets, replacing video cassettes. By 2004, when Kodiyathur was making his third movie, *Parethan Thirichu Varunnu* (*Revenant*) (2004), he made it entirely as CD prints.

A considerable part of *Parethan Thirichu Varunnu* was shot in Qatar. Considering that very few mainstream Malayalam films had ever been shot in the Gulf until that point, it was a considerable achievement for a movie which had the hallmark of 'poor image'[17] about it. The images

---

The dressing style in the Mappila songs under discussion do communicate an embodied Muslimness even if they do not strictly adhere to a pardha–mafta (black overcoat combined with headscarf) modesty. The point I want to emphasize, however, is that the sartorial choices were aspirational not only for Muslims, but the Kerala public sphere itself. Looking back today, when denim has become ubiquitous, the aspired middle-class position looks tacky. Two decades since, these songs have already become signs of a past time.

[15] Certain words like *qalb* (heart), *ruh* (soul), *monju* (beauty), etc. as well as the use of Muslim proper names are some of the signals of a Mappila song.

[16] Authored by Thoppil Bhasi and first performed in 1952.

[17] Hito Steyerl, 'In Defense of the Poor Image', in *The Wretched of the Screen* (Berlin: Sternberg Press, 2012), 31–45.

were pixelated, the lighting was simply plain, the performances mostly wanting, and the scripts took after the plot structures of morality tales. Despite this, as Bindu Menon and T. T. Sreekumar notes, 'the home films have grown into a wide network of circulation in about four districts in Kerala, and six countries in the Middle East, with an average viewership of 500,000 people.'[18]

Parethan Thirichu Varunnu gained an immense level of popularity and established Kodiyathur as a household name. What explains this popularity of Home Cinema? In Salam Kodiyathur's opinion, it is because his films acted as the mediator between the migrants in the Gulf and their families back home. According to him, Home Cinema was noticed first by the migrants in the Gulf, and they sent CDs back home and urged their families to watch them.[19] Mainstream cinema had just begun to see the Gulf as something other than the fabled land of riches (more on this in the next section). *Parethan Thirichu Varunnu* speaks about the migrant labourers who are unable to come back home because of the unending demands put on them by their family members. The title of the movie refers to the central figure of the migrant who goes home to Kerala with the intention of finally retiring from the migrant life due to a serious medical condition he is suffering, but finds it impossible to settle there, thanks to the pestering of those around him (except his wife). In *Aliyanoru Free Visa (A Free Visa for the Brother-in-law)*, Kodiyathur's fourth film, shot partly in Kuwait, the migrant is similarly burdened by the demands of his family members, the most pressing of which is to arrange a free visa[20] for his sister's husband. The movie also thematizes the insecurities around the sexual fidelity of the left-behind wife. The figure of the left-behind wife is an easy target for the gossiping parasitic non-migrants who speculate on her marital fidelity, probe their own chances with her, and badmouthing her even if she refuses.

---

[18] Bindu Menon and T. T. Sreekumar, '"One More Dirham": Migration, Emotional Politics and Religion in the Home Films of Kerala', *Migration, Mobility, & Displacement* 2, no. 2 (2016): 6.

[19] Salam Kodiyathur, interviewed by the author, 30 December 2017.

[20] An underhand visa in which a *kafeel* issues a visa for a sum in which the visa is ostensibly to work for the *kafeel*, in effect the migrant is unemployed and is to look for a job himself. Though it has its attractions of searching for a job in the Gulf while already possessing a work visa there, the downside is that the migrant would have had to pay a hefty sum for the visa and is unemployed which adds to his/her desperation and makes him/her ready prey for extreme exploitation.

Though of extensive currency in the Muslim households, films and tele-vision in general were considered unIslamic by the established religious authorities, especially the organizations of the Ahl-ul-Sunnath-wa-al-Jamaath factions, which account for a major share of the Muslim popula-tion in Kerala.[21] Three questions were central to the objections: whether films can be considered as part of image-making, which was expressly forbidden, the public presence of the female body, and the question of acting. [22] Compounded with questions regarding the nature of cinema were the questions of consumer culture and attendant worries of profli-gacy, extravagance, and avarice, and anxieties about sexual discipline, es-pecially among the migrant labourers as well as their left-behind spouses. Injunctions against sumptuous food and supersized houses, and an in-sistence on hard work, labour, and education were a feature of the Islamic reformation in Malabar at this time.[23]

It is in this juncture compounded by consumer culture and the prolifer-ation of digital media that Home Cinema took shape. Salam Kodiyathur's movies share these anxieties about the erosion of 'traditional' values, and many of the vices of consumer culture—the 'use-and-throw away' culture, sexual and financial indiscipline—are central to the plotlines, with the wayward brought back to the right path of morality at the end of the movie, often through lessons learned the hard way. In an article propelled by the success of his initial experiments, Kodiyathur took a dig at the elements of the religious establishment who were still opposed to him. In the *Jamaat-e-Islami*-run weekly *Prabodhanam*, an establishment

---

[21] For more on different factions within Kerala Muslims, see Chapter 1 of this volume.

[22] Mahmood Kooria, 'Pothumandalam, Drishyamadhyamangal, Matham: Oramukham' ('Public sphere, visual media, religion: an introduction'), in *Matham Drisyabhashayil: Keraliya Pothumandalathil Islam Thedunna Puthuvazhikal (Religion in Visual Language: Recent Islamic Trends in Kerala's Public Sphere)* ed. Mahmood Kooria (Kozhikode: Islamic Sahitya Academy, 2011), 35.

There has been a gradual acceptance of the visual medium by the various Muslim factions. The launch of the Malayalam television channel Indiavision, which was linked to the political organization Indian Union Muslim League in popular perception (M. K. Muneer, the Muslim League leader who has occupied ministerial berths in Kerala, was its first chairperson) is a major event in this regard. The launch of Darshana TV in 2012, a channel which is widely perceived (though not officially linked) as closely connected with a faction within the Kerala Sunnis is an indicator of the sea change in the 'orthodox' position regarding the visual medium.

[23] Filippo Osella and Caroline Osella, 'Migration, Neoliberal Capitalism, and Islamic Reform in Kozhikode (Calicut), South India', *International Labour and Working-Class History* 79, Labour Migration to the Middle East (2011); Filippo Osella and Caroline Osella, 'Islamism and Social Reform in Kerala, South India', *Modern Asian Studies* 42, 2/3 (2008).

sympathetic to his projects, he mocked that those who oppose Home Cinema are like the caretaker of a mosque who, when the mosque had caught fire, was more concerned if the water in the fire engine which had rushed in was ritually clean. [24] Kodiyathur, while reiterating the argument that the youth are corrupted by the titillations of existing cinema and other sensory pollutants in television channels, defined his cinema as a counteracting force. One could thus, in his words, identify two trends which Kodiyathur aspires to combat through his movies, both of which discursively produce a youth under attack. One is consumerism (fuelled majorly by the Gulf remittances) and its attendant decadence. The other is the corrupting influence of the dominant visual culture which was considered an avenue for obscenities meant to corrupt the younger generation.

By no means were these a worry limited to the religious establishment alone but were widely shared in the public sphere, and coded as the erosion of traditional values. These anxieties overlapped with the anxieties about Malayalam cinema of the same time.[25] The Malayalam movie industry went through a phase of multiple crises towards the end of the 1990s and the beginning of 2000s. The crisis had its industrial as well as aesthetic dimensions. The availability of new digital technology leading to widespread piracy; the influx of high budget, larger-than-life films from Tamil, Telugu, and Hollywood making Malayalam cinema not worth watching in theatres; the rise of television and its discouraging effect on families visiting theatre; the obsolete nature of Kerala's theatres in the face of new technology and viewing practices such as multiplexes; the soaring fees of the superstars, etc. were some of the issues. Two new trends in Malayalam cinema also presented a national–ethical crisis— one was what was called the Shakeela phenomenon and referred to the prolific output of soft-porn movies.[26] These movies were of very low

---

[24] Salam Kodiyathur, '*Puzhuvarikkatha Drshyamadhyamangal* (Worm-free Media),' *Prabodhanam* (25 August 2007).

[25] On the latter, see Ratheesh Radhakrishnan, 'What is Left of Malayalam Cinema?', in *Cinemas of South India: Culture, Resistance, Ideology*, eds Sowmya Dechamma C. C. and Elavarthi Sathya Prakash (New Delhi: Oxford University Press, 2010).

[26] For a discussion on the genre in Malayalam see Ratheesh Radhakrishnan, 'Soft Porn and the Anxieties of the Family', *Women in Malayalam Cinema: Naturalising Gender Hierarchies*, ed. Meena T. Pillai (Hyderabad: Orient Blackswan, 2010); Darshana Sreedhar Mini, 'The Spectral Duration of Malayalam Soft-porn: Disappearance, Desire, and Haunting', *BioScope* 7, no. 2 (2016).

budget which made them more stable financial options in a crisis-hit industry. The second phenomenon was the rise of superstar movies which centred on the macho performances of a male superstar and was derided as the evil influence of the other southern industries, notably Tamil. The superstar trend reeked of star-worship and was deemed antithetic to the progressive values of Kerala. There was a long and heated exchange on the morality and immorality of superstars in the Kerala intellectual scene, when in 2001 SukumarAzhikode (1926–2012), a leading public intellectual in Kerala, accused Mohanlal of encouraging vices among the youth.[27] Thus, there was a general anxiety in the public sphere of the evil influence of the prevalent visual culture. In this crucial historical juncture, the middle-brow tradition which sought to calibrate a Malayali aesthetic, and had enjoyed its heyday in the 1980s, was hailed as the golden age of Malayalam cinema, a wish to return to which was sorely voiced.[28]

The middle brow's self-definition as *the* Malayali cinema, its oppositional nature to the gaudiness of the superhuman superstar movies, [29] the accessibility of its language, its low-budget nature, as well as the consecration of the middle brow towards the end of the 1990s, made this form an easily available register for a low-budget amateur filmmaker who set out to narrate the rural–vernacular.

A distant viewing of Salam Kodiyathur's films suggests an instantly recognizable affinity with the visual features of the middle brow. This includes stories set in rural milieux, long shots of paddy fields, the village marketplace populated by the male protagonist and his male friends, sites of homosociality like the local teashops, etc. In short, the project of Islamic cinema as a counter to the mainstream, in the absence of an established tradition and defined in opposition to the established mainstream as well as the emergent visual culture from the Muslim community, had to rely on the mainstream itself to provide it with a voice. [30]

---

[27] Ratheesh Radhakrishnan, '"Looking" at Mohanlal: Spectatorial Ordering and the Emergence of the "Fan" in Malayalam Cinema', *Deep Focus* (December 2002).

[28] Radhakrishnan, 'What is Left'.

[29] Even as Mammootty or Mohanlal were 'superstar' or 'megastars', they routinely played roles in non-star films, that is, films which did not need to employ cinematic devices associated with stars. This could work for low-budget films until the time the fees of these stars and the general budgeting of films themselves underwent an overhaul in the 2000s.

[30] This is not to imply that there haven't been Muslim socials in Malayalam cinema, however few and far between. Some examples are *Kuttikkuppayam* (*Baby Dress*) (M. Krishnan Nair, 1964), *Maniyara* (*Nuptial Bedroom*) (M. Krishnan Nair, 1983), *Manithali* (*Bridal Necklace*) (M. Krishnan Nair, 1984), *Ghazal* (Kamal, 1993), *Samantharangal* (*Parallels*) (Balachandra Menon,

However, the very features which make the middle brow an easy choice, namely its visual moderation as well as its doxa of simplicity, rural life, and its everyday, its rejection of consumerism etc. comes at a cost in Home Cinema's depiction of the migrant subject. The *Gulf-karan*, as the Gulf migrant was known, becomes a source of tension in the mainstream Malayalam cinema as the personification of consumerism and the erosion of traditional (a coding for feudal) values. The question then is how to reconcile the figure of the migrant, who is derided for his consumerism, as the protagonist of Home Cinema, while also providing room for a middle brow language. Which then translates into how to represent mobility sans consumerism.

It is in line with the mainstream anxiety that often in Kodiyathur's films one witnesses the migrant who forgets his roots. In the absence of any merit that can accompany spectacular economic growth, religion becomes the sole channel through which wealth can be socially acceptable. At the thematic level, thus, the Islamic injunctions on *zakat* and other means of redistribution of wealth become the means to guard oneself against the corrupting influence of money. Rather than celebrate the consumerist nature of Gulf migration as acts through which social boundaries were challenged in a society in which the access to seemingly secular objects were markers of hierarchical order, Home Cinema, under moral pressures of its own, toes the middle-brow line of deriding consumerism and social destabilization of the existing social order. Home Cinema does this by representing the migrant whose life is always in penury and who is alienated from his own community. The upper caste protagonist of the middlebrow cinema who is left behind by the Gulf phenomenon, gets replicated in Home Cinema in the migrant himself as the one who is left out of a consumerist society and sentenced to a lifetime of misery. On the other hand, the bombastic, unscrupulous, and philistine migrant gets displaced and reproduced as the dependents of the migrants.[31] The

---

1998), *Paadam Onnu: Oru Vilapam* (*Lesson One: A Wail*) (T. V. Chandran, 2003), etc. However, there is a sharp difference between Muslim socials and 'Islamic' cinema, the latter primarily being a self-definition and influenced much by the global success of Iranian cinema which operationalizes the logic of modesty.

[31] In other words, the two possibilities of *pavam* and *kallan*—identified by Filippo Osella and Caroline Osella as the possible resolutions of the subjectivity of the immature and unmarried Gulf returnee in his process of reintegration in his home community—is split into two different

mechanics of this replication and doubling is through the creation of two intimate publics within the diegesis of home cinema. Both the alienation of the migrant as well as the articulation of the two intimate publics, one, the migrant workers in the Gulf, and two, that of their dependents back home, are central to the articulating the Islamic project of Home Cinema.

In Kodiyathur's films, the migrant workers in the Gulf, the first of the two intimate publics, stay together in less than enviable conditions, they support each other emotionally and monetarily, they advise and admonish each other in coping with the distance from their loved ones at home, they are hardworking, etc. Often the newcomer to the Gulf is scorned in these movies for their snobbery, their queasiness about menial jobs, their airs about their own standards, etc. This public is ordered like a band of brothers, and it is within this intimate code that it functions. Thus, we have Baputty, the emigrant protagonist of *Aliyanoru Free Visa* reading out a letter from his father, a piece of personal correspondence, to those assembled there, without regard to what would be a question of propriety in a normative public sphere. In another telling scene from the same movie, we see Baputty narrating a cassette letter to the tape recorder. His Pakistani roommate, who comes in to this private space immediately withdraws as if to respect the transformation of the space into a very private one. It is made clear elsewhere in the movie that he does not understand Malayalam. The camera, after following the intruder on his way back, zooms in on the tape recorder. The scene then cuts to the face of Baputty's exploitative boss in the latter's shop, who is now shown in a sympathetic light, and then to the full profile of the Pakistani as he is lying down on a cot in the next room, zooming on to his face. The cassette letter continues to be narrated in the background, thus uniting in its subjective retelling of the migrant woes both the racial–national and the class other. In a rare instance of a subjective appropriation of the universal a community is imagined, with its differences intact, in spatial disjuncture, inaugurated by the truth of migrant experience rather than the tongue in which it is expressed.

agents in Kodiyathur cinema. *Pavam* denotes 'the innocent good guy generous to the point of self destruction' and *kallan* a self aggrandizing antisocial (117). See Filippo Osella and Caroline Osella, 'Migration, Money and Masculinity in Kerala', *The Journal of Royal Anthropological Institute* 6, no. 1 (2000). In Kodiyathur cinema the Gulf migrant is typically either still immature or is a *paavam*, while *kallan* is always a dependent who is in Kerala and not in the Gulf.

As opposed to this, the public at home is characterized by their alacrity to the unearned luxuries of life, like loitering around not having to work, and in such vices of the loafers such as gossip. They congregate for wasteful talk by the local teashop or coolbar. This public is engaged in schemes to usurp money, steal wives, etc. from the migrant. As opposed to the universality that the migrant finds elsewhere, here he is expelled from the local talk of the village. It is interesting to note that, the cassette letter which serves as the medium for universality in the first place becomes an instance of incommunicability when it reaches its destination, precisely due to the transparency of its language. The elderly father and mother happen to put on the wrong side of the cassette which was meant only for the ears of their son's wife. They get to hear the deep woes their son has been hiding, out of concern for them. What they hear shocks and hurts them. But rather than occasion any action, what it leads to is the silence it bestows. The privacy of the conjugal relationship, when breached, fails to constitute an engaging relationship at home.

Gossip plays a major role in constituting the intimate public in Kerala, which, in fact, due to this very nature, can only be constituted as a shady public. The sly efficacy of the opacity of this public is in contrast to the unyielding transparency of the migrant's speech. In the diegesis, it mobilizes sympathy for the migrant as the one wronged by the rural community. The rural community, who feeds off his labour, also otherizes him. As Michael Warner reminds us, '[i]ntensely personal measurements of group membership, relative standing, and trust are the constant and unavoidable pragmatic work of gossip'.[32]

While alienation ironically provides the shared ground of experience for an affective community elsewhere, this very construction of migration as alienating ails it in imagining a community back home. The deadlock is then sought to be resolved through a sublimation surpassing the class differences—that of religion, Islam, but now oriented towards a philosophy of personal conduct in public and private life. The figure of the local elder who is religious is the authority through which the ideal public-to-be is imagined.[33] This local figure exhorts the villagers,

---

[32] Warner, *Publics and Counterpublics* (New York: Zone Books, 2005), 79.
[33] It is interesting to note here that though this village elder is closely associated with the local mosque, he is not part of the clergy. This may suggest a dual strategy on the part of the filmmaker. One, a cleric would mean, precisely because a member of the clergy would necessarily be a part of a faction/school of thought within Muslims, taking sides one way or the other. Two,

understandably the work-shy beneficiaries of the Gulf remittances, to shun the life of opulence, to spend money wisely, not to fall into the trap of usury. Religion becomes a means of overcoming the traps of the globalized world, that of interest, speculation, wastefulness, promiscuity, and so on.

Precisely because the migrant has to be figured as the hapless and alienated, authority must be divested from him and placed on to the local elder. This then upsets the operation of the figure of the authority itself because the authority is now not derived from his starpower and its ready-made message but by its reliance on established religious edicts. When not mouthing these, the authority is just another human being. As the enunciator of the divinely ordained regulations, he is the symbolic through whom the protagonist's life acquires a new subjectivity. Having thus shown his hapless hands, the protagonist now is as bound as anyone else by the percepts of Islam, now available as a lifestyle. Devoid of the network of intimacy that produces the public in the Gulf or the public of the gossip, the new-found public is substantiated through an individuation rather than mobilization. What is gained is a new band of brothers called into being by the divine word. The Islamic public thus becomes the avenue of reintegration for the alienated migrant, while also curing the myriad ills of a remittance society.

A reason, perhaps the one which gained more attention in mainstream media, for Kodiyathur's popularity is his deployment of an Islamic aesthetics in his films, borrowed from Iranian movies. In this reformed aesthetics, the figure of the woman is a veiled (head-covered) subject, even if she is diegetically in her bedroom. Salam Kodiyathur, while maintaining that the aesthetic is drawn from Iranian cinema, also points to out that the aesthetic also involves avoiding physical contact between sexes on screen and also avoiding such situations in which the woman character will have to undergo uncontrollable emotions on screen.[34]

Veiling is a reconfiguration of the relation between the viewer and the diegetic world. While the Western realist cinema assumes an

---

this has to do with the organization of the mosques themselves, which are controlled by laymen rather than clergy. This might then suggest a local grounding of the religious resolution itself.

[34] Kodiyathur, interview.

unauthorized scopophilia,[35] that is a pleasure of looking that bypasses the conventions of the society, veiling foregrounds the public character of cinema itself. Veiling assumes a continuity between the world of the screen and the world of the viewers such that the character who is now diegetically in her bedroom is nevertheless understood to be an actress who is present before the public glare, and hence required to be modest. [36]

While Indian cinema too has been shown to defy unauthorized scopophilia and work with a communal gaze, the aesthetics of veiling is not just a cultural variation of the same communal authorization. Referring to the communal nature of gaze in Hindi films, M. Madhava Prasad points out that while a kiss between couples came under an unwritten prohibition, cabaret dances, or erotic display of female body, do not suffer from such a ban. [37] The question at the heart of the (informal) ban on kissing is therefore not obscenity but the question of the contract that exists between the viewer and the representation. While the kiss addresses the audience in their individuality by invoking the figure of a voyeur, the dance or the female body on display on the other hand is bound by a contract of performance which acknowledges the viewer and thereby sustains the space of performance as a public space. The film becomes a duplication of the theatrical space. Here, cinema is denied in its nature as the open edge of mass publicity in such a performance in the interest of upholding a stable performative dispensation.[38] The attempt is to control the very nature of cinema which always threatens to go beyond the policing of the semantic and visceral expanse in a given bounded space.

The aesthetic of veiling, on the other hand, is premised on the destruction of pleasure, i.e. scopophilia, rather than the participation in a communally authorized pleasure. For this reason, Negar Mottahedeh aligns the aesthetics of the veil with the call issued by Third Wave Feminism for the destruction of pleasure in cinema.[39] In Kodiyathur's cinema, the fact

[35] Unauthorized scopophilia refers to the condition wherein cinema does not acknowledge that it is meant to be seen by an audience, thus placing the audience in the position of a voyeur. See Metz, *Psychoanalysis and Cinema: The Imaginary Signifier* (London: Macmillan Press, 1982).

[36] Negar Mottehedeh, *Displaced Allegories: Post-Revolutionary Iranian Cinema* (Durham, NC and London: Duke University Press, 2008).

[37] M. Madhava Prasad, 'Guardians of the View: The Prohibition of the Private', in *Ideology of the Hindi Film: A Historical Construction* (New Delhi: Oxford University Press, 1998), 88–113.

[38] William Mazzarella, *Censorium: Cinema and the Open Edge of Mass Publicity* (Durham, NC and London: Duke University Press, 2013).

[39] Mottehedeh, *Displaced Allegories*.

of veiling, which is much more of an oddity given the prevalence of mainstream cinema in Kerala in which no such practice exists, becomes an act of the dissolution of the narrative. Ashish Rajadhyaksha argues that the narrative acquires a crucial function as the site which controls the gaze of the actual viewer in societies where cinema acquires a pedagogical function. [40] If one is to impose this logic on Kodiyathur's films, one sees that while the film claims to discipline its audience in what it calls Islamic aesthetics, the aesthetics undercut any indulging in the narration to the level of foregoing one's sovereign (the ability to be distracted, as opposed to disciplined) vision. [41] The odd figure of the veiled woman in her bedroom by her (fictional) husband brings the artifice to the fore, if it isn't already by the imperfection of the cinema itself. This then accentuates the consciousness of the viewer that what one is watching is, in fact, just a film and not reality. This, as Christian Metz puts it, makes the viewing self the locus of identification for the viewer, making them conscious that it is, in fact, for them that the movie was made, that it is they who make the movie meaningful.[42] Metz's argument draws attention to the agency involved in watching a movie, as opposed to those theories which views the viewer as hypnotized and rendered immobile by what he or she sees. In the case of veiling, the fact of a self-conscious gaze fuses with the consciousness of a masochistic gaze (as different from the power a voyeur enjoys), one which holds that gaze can be corrupting and therefore self-destructive.[43]

The lure of Kodiyathur's films then perhaps is in this mobilization of self-identification. This self is not the abstract self in Metz's theorization, but a particular self, understood to be Muslim, and in the environs of large-scale labour migration to the Gulf. The expunged emotionality of the women of the house keeps alive the opacity of the zone of the private, away from the prying eyes. Distinct from the mainstream films which thematized Muslim lives, Kodiyathur made the Islamic subject the bearer of the look as well as the one looked at. The religious gaze orders cinema

[40] Ashish Rajadhyaksha, 'Who's Looking? Viewership and Democracy in the Cinema', *Cultural Dynamics* 10, no. 2 (1998).

[41] Recall here how Walter Benjamin identified the distracted look to be the liberatory potential of cinema. See Walter Benjamin, 'The Work of Art in the Age of Mechanical Reproduction', in *Illuminations*, trans. Harry Zohn (New York: Schocken Books, 1968), 217–258.

[42] Metz, *Psychoanalysis and Cinema*, 45–49.

[43] For masochistic gaze, see Hamid Naficy, *A Social History of Iranian Cinema, Volume IV: The Globalizing Era, 1984–2010* (Durham, NC and London: Duke University Press, 2012), 107.

in an act of interpellation whose effectivity is the fact that one cannot but feel the failure of cinema.

The use of religion as both a formal device and the orientation of content in Salam Kodiyathur's films needs to be therefore understood as the resolution that is at the heart of a borderland. What is evident is the shift of cinematic populism from the question of representation to a staging of immanence. Rather than film as a text, the cinema as an institution is the new text in which one seeks representation.

Coming Out

'Who would have been the first Malayali to set foot on these shores?', asks Narayanan to Moideen on the eve of his final departure to Kerala from Dubai. 'Whoever it was', replies Moideen, 'it wouldn't have been as a tourist'.[44] This dialogue, from the 2015 movie *Pathemari*, written and directed by Salim Ahamed, is indicative of the changed attitude of cinema to the Gulf. While the Malayalam movie from 1980 onwards cast the Gulf as a space of unimaginable fortunes and overnight riches, the contemporary Malayalam movies' take on the Gulf is marked by its realistic approach to the Gulf as a space of toiling bodies and quotidian strife.

The Gulf began appearing in Malayalam films from the late 1990s onwards. Some of the films followed the trope of the Gulf as a space of thrills and adventure, and therefore interchangeable with any city, in some instances incorporating popular perceptions of Arabs such as the *kandoura* and sharialaw, thus making it more cultural-specific to the Gulf.[45] A few others took to the Gulf as primarily a space of thrills, crime, and adventure, and therefore in the mode of the tourist, but with some migrant labourer issues thrown in.[46] The definitive shift that began in the late 1990s was the reconfiguration of the Gulf as the realistic space of labour, deflating the fantasy that characterized this space earlier as a space of

---

[44] Translation mine.

[45] These include movies like *Ayal Kadha Ezhuthukayanu* (*He is Writing a Story*) (Kamal, 1998), *Sharja to Sharja* (Venugopan, 2001), and *Marubhoomiyile Aana* (*The Elephant in the Desert*) (2016).

[46] Examples include Mammootty-starring *Dubai* (Joshiy, 2001), the Mohanlal-starring *Oru Marubhoomikkadha* (*A Desert Tale*) (Priyadarshan, 2011), and *Diamond Necklace* (Lal Jose, 2012) which has the 'new generation' actor Fahadh Fasil playing the lead role.

unimaginable mobility. Two movies came out in the closing years of the last century signalled the shift even though their primary diegetic space remained Kerala: these were *Kallu Kondoru Pennu* (*A Woman of Stone*) (Shyamaprasad, 1998) which focused on a female domestic worker in Saudi Arabia; and *Garshom* (P. T. Kunju Muhammed, 1999) which thematized the perpetual exile that characterizes the Gulf migrant even when he is back home. The migrant protagonist of *Mampazhakkalam* (*The Mango Season*) (T. A. Shahid, 2004) and a movie set completely in Kerala makes the bold equivalence in those years of high patriotism following the Kargil war of 1999 between the migrant labourer who toils in the Gulf and the soldier who guards the territory of the homeland. *Khaddama* (*The Help*) (Kamal, 2011) was a searing take on the plight of the domestic labourers in the Gulf, and *Arabikkatha* (Arabian Tale) (Lal Jose, 2007) which took on the labour conditions in the Gulf in a partly comic mode, satirically crafting the two spaces of Kerala and the Gulf as spaces of labourless Communism and Communismless labour respectively.[47]

The new Malayalam cinema makes explicit its knowledge of the reality of the Gulf, but again in a mode of revelation. To take one instance, in *Shutter* (Joy Mathew, 2012), the protagonist who is a (Muslim) Gulf migrant has returned to Kerala briefly to get his young daughter married off. Having heard the enviable description of one of his friends' recent trysts with a sex worker, he wants to know the pleasure for himself and manages to get hold of a sex worker with the aid of another friend. He is to avail himself of the sex worker's services in his shuttered vacant shop space at night while his friend waits outside so that the shutter can be opened upon signal from the migrant inside. Things take a turn when because of unforeseen circumstances the migrant and the sex worker have to spend a whole day cooped up on the shop floor because the friend who was supposed to open the shutter for them has disappeared, and with him the key to the padlock of the shutter too.

The movie uses the shuttered-in condition as a plot device to expose the underbelly of the smooth society that the migrant thinks he is part

---

[47] For a detailed take on *Arabikkatha* as an example of the contribution of non-national resources (and geographies) towards imagining the region, usually subsumed within the discourse of the nation, see Ratheesh Radhakrishnan, 'The "Worlds" of the Region', *Positions: East Asia Cultures Critique* 24, no. 3 (2016).

of. This underbelly includes the sex worker who has to lie to her client that she is at the time in a five-star hotel in Mysore with another client; the petty fights that take place in the town; his friend who peeps on his wife and daughter knowing that he is away; and ultimately through the grime of all of this realizations, he also realizes the strength and understanding of the friendships of his young daughter in contrast to his own relationships.

One of the realizations that the migrant worker has is his real estimate in the eyes of his group of 'friends'. It is the next evening, and this group of drinking friends wait for the migrant to arrive, for he has brought expensive liquor from the Gulf, on the porch of the very shop in which the migrant is cooped up in, and ignorant of his plight. Of course, these are not friends the migrant could call out for help to get out of his situation, and so he has no choice but to sit quiet and overhear their conversation. As the friends' conversation turns to the migrant, one of them says that the migrant had told him that he would arrange for him to get to the Gulf but he did not want to go there because he is not interested in doing the work of a scavenger. At this another one from the group responds that the migrant has in fact not made his money in clean ways, but had cheated the Arab. After all the guy does not even know how to read and write. He then adds, in the tone of a rhetorical question, if they don't remember who the migrant's father was—a fish monger. Inside the shuttered space the sex worker smiles at the migrant, partly mocking and partly in sympathy that the life of her client, too, is built on lies just like hers, but at least she has more control over hers.

The conversation here needs more unpacking to feel the bleeding sharpness of the unasked-for sympathy. In the assessment of the group, which stands for the dominant consciousness of the mainstream of Kerala, the Gulf is a space where one has to labour in degrading conditions, in jobs that are considered to be that of a scavenger, that is an untouchable or an outcaste. Further, the migrant himself is discredited along casteist lines, that he is the son of a fish monger, and therefore a Muslim of low status.[48] Here, while verbally it is the Gulf which is being

---

[48] For a discussion on distinction within the Muslim community in Kerala, see P. C. Saidalavi, 'Status claims among Muslims in Malabar, South India', *Anthropological Notebooks* 23, no. 2 (2017).

subjected to gaze, it is also a reverse realization. It is for the migrant himself that the sheen of the Gulf is scrubbed away. While the discourse so far has been that the real Gulf is of plight and peril while the Gulf that is known in Kerala is that of glitz and glamour, the film slaps it on the migrant's face that Kerala always knew what the Gulf was, and that the fantasy space of the Gulf was, rather than anyone else's, the migrant's lone ideological crutch to keep living.

This truth-telling has become a formal feature of Gulf cinema in Malayalam. *Pathemari* (Salim Ahamed, 2015) is a moving statement on the changed attitude to the Gulf in the mainstream. The Gulf is not where you get fantastically rich anymore, in *Pathemari*. It is a place which turns you into a wreck. While the Gulf is indeed fantastic, it has now acquired a history of foresight and labour. Narrating the story of one of those migrants who made it to the Gulf in the 1960s undocumented on a dhow, the film looks at the Gulf migration of the past five decades in a mode of remembrance. Thematizing the constant wants that perpetuate the awayness of the migrant, the film renders the division between the migrant and those at home sharply, speaking in favour of the Gulf migrant and depicting those in Kerala as leeching on the labours of the migrant.

Those back at home only get to appreciate the migrant's effort when the migrant appears on television, speaking about his life. The film thus draws on its own mission, to echo Kodiyathur, of mediating between the labourers in the Gulf and their folks back home. Of the many facts of migrant life—narrated by the migrant in a TV interview in the closing minutes of the film—that comes as a 'revelation' to those at home:

When we sent home ten thousand rupees, those at home think we actually got twenty thousand, we have kept ten for ourselves and are sending them only ten; the fact is we got only seven thousand, and then we borrow three, so that we can send home ten thousand … When we see children here we always remember our children at home, how many children remember their father when they see a man of their father's age?[49]

---

[49] Translation mine.

I have read *Pathemari* elsewhere as the memorialization of the Gulf experience at a time when both Kerala and the Gulf are undergoing seismic changes.[50] While the Gulf may have an objective existence, it continues to be an object of revelation for the folks in the movie. At its heart, such a disjuncture is at the heart of the Gulf experience for the Keralan. The Gulf is a place of miracles, it is one of overnight transformations. It is like those structures which are claimed to have been constructed by the *jinns*—nothing less than mysticism can explain them. There is no rationality here. No known laws can explain it. At the same time, it is also a place of difficult living conditions. The conditions there are too real that its translation will also have to rely on mediations. The point is not that one reality trumps the other, but the confounding coexistence of both at the same time. The 'revelation' then is the necessary epistemic starting point not just as a border reinforcement, but also as the starting point of border struggles. However, any attempt at binarizing the migrants and the others, such as in *Pathemari* or *Shutter*, might offer sympathy for the migrant, but falls short of the labour of translation.

Assuming a strict separation between migrants and non-migrants in Kerala where large-scale migration has been an ongoing fact and has been fuelled especially through kinship migration is an ideological confirmation that the Gulf revolution in Kerala is well and truly over. While in the changed conditions, when the Gulf has ceased to be a catalyst for social churning, one could speak about the 'real' conditions of the Gulf, it would be naïve to assume that these hardships of the Gulf were unknown to the generations before. If anything, we have the 'real' conditions on screen in 1980. Instead, if the Gulf still requires revelatory voice-overs, one has to place it in the singularity—as that untranslatable that demands a translation—that the Gulf as an experience was in the 1980s when the social revolution that was being unleashed by the Gulf was felt in Kerala, one that is only now beginning to be assessed, and mostly in the nostalgic mode as a memoir of personal distinction. Right now, it is the failed promise of a revolution. The past continues to stick, as the migrant in *Shutter* is made to realize.[51]

---

[50] Karinkurayil, ' "Dubai" as a place of memory.'

[51] In recent years, the Gulf has become slightly more prevalent and versatile as diegetic space. *Neeyum Njanum* (*You and I*) (A. K. Sajan, 2019), partly shot in Dubai, thematized the darker side of an idyllic Kerala village which includes among others the intense moralist gaze of the society on the left-behind wives. *C U Soon* (Mahesh Narayanan, 2020) dealt with the plight of

But when revolutions are underway, they question the very ground on which it stands. Like in the 1980s, in cinema this ground is the gaze that makes a unitary narrative out of the play of individual images. It is in a hugely successful genre of Malayalam films from the second half of 1980s to the mid-1990s—the laughter-films—that one can discern this shaky ground of identification mostly clearly.

A Revaluation of Laughter Films in View of the Gulf

In the film *Akkare Ninnoru Maaran* (*A Groom from the Other Shore*) (Girish, 1985), a young Nair man, played by Maniyanpilla Raju, is in love with his fiancé and is about to lose her. The woman's father, his uncle,[52] an assertive parsimonious patriarch, however insists that he would get his daughter married off only to someone who works in the Gulf, obviously because of the prosperity that the Gulf promises. Our protagonist on the other hand is an educated but unemployed youth who finds the system tilted against him and has to make his way through crooked means. His friends, too, are a bunch of unemployed youths who make their way indulging in petty fraudulences. Desperate to win his woman, the protagonist disappears from the village in the pretext of leaving for the Gulf, while he is in actuality living in hiding in a nearby village with the connivance of his friends.

After a few months he, in order to impress his merit upon his uncle gets one of his friends to dress up as an Arab, in long white *kandura* with white *ghutra* and *iqal*, [53]and go visit his uncle. This friend is the owner of the lodge in which the pretend-migrant has been living in hiding. He is not from the latter's village, and therefore there is little chance of someone recognizing him there. He is to pretend to be the Arab employer of the

---

female workers in the Gulf who were cheated by their agents into sex work. *Meow* (Lal Jose, 2021) narrates the everyday travails of a convenience-store keeper who finds himself having to take responsibility for an undocumented Central Asian migrant; *Momo in Dubai* (Ameen Aslam, 2023) thematizes the stark contrast between the luxurious, futuristic Dubai in Kerala's imagination and the reality of migrant life there.

[52] The fiancé is called *murapennu* in Malayalam or the woman who is one's fiancé according to custom, which, in the case of Nairs, is one's maternal uncle's daughter.

[53] *Ghutra* is the cloth on one's head held in place by black double cord, or *iqal*,

supposed migrant. The entire episode is facilitated by another friend, played by Mukesh, who would act as the interpreter between Malayalam and Arabic. What follows is one of the most hilarious sequences in Malayalam cinema. The fake Arab speaks an Arabic which is notably just guttural nonsense and once in a while his tongue slips to Malayalam, which is his language anyway. The cover-up for these slips provides for more laughter. The Arab tells the uncle that the latter's nephew is going to take over as the manager of all his business interests. The mimicry of an impossible Arabic, the crestfallen uncle, his attempts to impress the fake Arab, the bending of this patriarchal authority over the possibility of the Arab money, all of these provide for the wild laughter.

The movie, released in 1985, is one the early full-length comedy films in Malayalam, a genre that would subsequently dominate till the mid-1990s. The lead actors in many of these movies were those considered to be second-rung actors at the time. In the sequence just described, the fake Arab is played by Sreenivasan, an actor who is by convention considered too short and dark to play leading roles. That he can pass off as an Arab—stereotypically understood to be fair and tall—before this countryside patriarch is a joke on the navel-gazing of dominant traditional Malayali authorities. Sreenivasan is also the screenwriter of this movie, and the most successful screenwriter of the genre. The patriarch uncle is played by Nedumudi Venu, whose career was at a turning point at the time between playing comic roles and those of a patriarch. He would eventually settle for the patriarch who, in some films, is also comical. Looking at this sequence, Ratheesh Radhakrishnan takes the movie as exemplifying how the sensations and orientations of the austere Kerala patriarchal world was shaken by the presence of the foreign—the *kandura* denoting the full-length manifestation of that strangeness.[54]

In this section I am interested in exploring the staging of epistemic boundaries in the organization of gaze in the full-length comedy film, or 'laughter films' or 'comic' films, as they are called variously. Studies on this genre[55] frame their study within the socio-economic aspects within

[54] Ratheesh Radhakrishnan, 'Habits and Worlds: Malayalam cinema's travels with the Gulf', in *Industrial Networks and Cinemas of India: Shooting Stars, Shifting Geographies, and Multiplying Media*, eds Monika Mehta and Madhuja Mukherjee (London and New York: Routledge, 2021).

[55] These are Jenny Rowena, 'The "Laughter-Films" and the Reconfiguration of Masculinities', in *Women in Malayalam Cinema: Naturalising Gender Hierarchies*, ed. Meena T. Pillai

the state of Kerala, such as the rising unemployment, or the increasing visibility of women and consequent male insecurity. Though there is a passing mention of the Gulf with reference to the film market, it stops at that.

But what if we read these movies through the frame of Gulf migration? The 1980s in Malayalam cinema was a period of transition. The reign of the older stars, such as Madhu, Prem Nazeer, and Sathyan was over. Jayan, who was blazing his way forward in superstardom, met with an untimely death in 1980 when he was forty-one. There was a palpable need for new faces. A few new faces—Shankar, Nedumudi Venu, Ratheesh, Mohanlal, Mammootty—were expected to take over the reins of the third generation of Malayalam cinema. With more than a hundred movies each year, the film industry was going strong. At the beginning of the decade, the commercial cinema continued to produce spectacles with prominent action and dance sequences, the fantastic caves and undergrounds of precious stones and diamonds, the skyscrapers and thrilling encounters in imaginary locations, or the folkore with its mythical caves, martial arts, and persevering curses. There were also the social critiques by the likes of K. G. George and I. V. Sasi, both of whom began their careers in the early 1970s. The 'art' cinema, on the other hand, continued exploring the possibilities of a third aesthetic, one which would have a unique Keralan touch. As mentioned earlier, the mid-1980s saw the rise of what is called the 'middle-brow' cinema, most associated with the names of K. G. George, Bharathan, and Padmarajan. The middle brow was a compromise between the austere aesthetics of the art cinema, but plugged into some of the staples of the commercial cinema such as recognizable stars and the use of songs.

The 1980s was the time when Gulf money channelled its way into the Malayalam film industry, and the expatriates became a notable component of the audience.[56] The new money that was pouring into cinema from the migrants abroad and the plantation economy in Kerala made high-budget cinema possible. Some of these films, such as *Mandanmmar*

(Hyderabad: Orient Blackswan, 2010); Vipin Kumar, 'Politics of Laughter: An introduction to the 1990s' Malayalam popular comic film', *South Asian Popular Culture* 6, no. 1 (2008).

[56] Rajadhyaksha and Willemen, 'Mammootty', in *Encyclopaedia of Indian Cinema*, 143.

Londanil (*Stupids in London*) (Sathyan Anthikad, 1983), featuring London and *Iniyenkilum* (*At Least from Now*) (I. V. Sasi, 1985), partially shot in Tokyo, made use of these foreign locations as occasions to reflect back the living conditions in Kerala and to seep into the public imagination other possible ways of life. Paul Mathew notes that the influx of Gulf money and the establishment of the Gulf migrants as a prime audience for Malayalam cinema as factors that led to the change in the image regime of Malayalam cinema, from one that was literary and centred on the individual to that of a non-centred vision.[57]

It is in laughter films that this new image regime would manifest itself forcefully. The laughter films, which overlaps with the time of the middle brow, and is most associated with the names of Sathyan Anthikad, Priyadarshan, and Siddique-Lal, combined the austerity of the middle brow but substituted comedy for the brooding social commentary. The movies did have brief intervals of pathos, but comedy was the prominent element, and the comic scenes formed the spinal plot of the films, usually until the anticlimax of a mix of thrill and pathos, only to return to the world of laughter in the climax. A feature of the laughter film was the substitution of the single protagonist by a duo or a group of young men.[58]

Studies on laughter films have looked at them as a kind of resistance to the hegemonic bodies of Malayalam cinema. Vipin Kumar reads the comic films as resulting from the inability of the dominant bourgeois order to symbolize these youths who hail from the lower orders of the society. The laughter is, according to Kumar, a result of the failure of utopia that was promised to these youth as they left their belongings to find a place for themselves in the city. These films are therefore laughing at our own failures and are therefore acts of social criticism.[59] Jenny Rowena finds in the groups of young men who occupy the screen space of these movies, with their goof ups as well as their barely concealed lower social

---

[57] Paul Mathew, 'The Image-Regime of Cinema in Postmodern Malayalam Literary Fiction', *South Asian Review* 40, no. 4 (2019).

[58] While Mohanlal, who was a rising star at the time and had in his oeuvre films which belonged to a range of genres, played the lead in a good number of the laughter films, he was mostly paired with Sreenivasan. Jayaram, Mukesh, Jagadeesh, Siddique, Maniyanpilla Raju, among others, were the other staple faces of the laughter films, in various combinations. Innocent, Jagathy Sreekumar, and Mamukoya, actors who were not in lead positions and were known primarily for their comic prowess, comprised the formidable second row in these films.

[59] Kumar, 'Politics of Laughter'.

positions, as making fun of the reigning ideas of Malayalam cinema aesthetics. She reads these movies also as spaces that allowed for a pincer development in the following years, a development which can be, according to her, read from the subsequent careers of perhaps the most laughter-inducing and lovable duo of the laughter films—Mohanlal and Sreenivasan. While Mohanlal, the one who played the more prominent of the duo, went on to become one of the two reigning superstars of the Malayalam cinema (at least for two decades and running; the other being Mammootty, one who has had fewer appearance in laughter films) whose characters reeked of feudal entitlements, Sreenivasan went on to explore, in her words, 'the inner anxieties of the non-hegemonic masculine position'.[60]

I mostly agree with the basic detailing of the situation that is provided by Kumar and Rowena. The various shifts that characterize the moment are the rising mobility of the lower orders of society because of migration, the increasing visibility of women in public space coupled with the visibility and assertion of feminism, and the rising unemployment. The shortcomings of these assessments of the laughter films are that they are framed by the region and its domestic politics. That is, their reading of the laughter films confined itself to discussing these movies as being part of the narrowly circumscribed borders of the Kerala state. The diagnosis they arrive at, that the root cause of these forms being unemployment, increasing presence of women in the public sphere, the insecure masculinities, as well as the critique of the bourgeois utopia, all of these were diagnoses made in the precinct of the primacy and ultimacy of Kerala as a region defined in geographical terms. What they ignore is the fact that region is also a region in imagination. That is, in a polity like Kerala which is characterized by migration, and at a time when the migrant population came to fund cinema in a major way, Kerala as a region cannot be seen only from a position that is placed within, but also as a reflection from a place without. In other words, the region of Kerala is not what it is in itself but also one which we imagine it looks like when viewed from outside. And migration facilitates such an imagined vision from outside. It is also a matter of some consideration that in its own self-styling and in its statistic public-relations discourse, Kerala places itself along a global

---

[60] Rowena, 'Laughter-Film', 148.

narrative, be that of Communism or quality of living or progressive values, which makes a gaze from outside a constant presence.

A crucial symptom of the repressed Gulf in laughter films is their suggestion of a heterotopia. While there have been a few laughter films that do not leave the village in which they are set, the dominant trend is that the story usually unfolds in a strange place, or a strange place is visibly built into the narrative. Laughter films have been of plots involving wandering. In *Poochakkoru Mukkuthi* (*A Nose Ring for the Cat*) (Priyadarshan, 1984), the lead couple are both migrants to the city; a lot of the narrative happens in the streets, which doesn't belong to anyone. All of *Boeing Boeing* (Priyadarshan, 1985) happens in the city; there is no mention of a family background for the lead character (played by Mohanlal). In the CID trilogy of Mohanlal and Sreenivasan, the duo don't ever come back to the place where their journey began.[61] In the course of their journey they travel to Madras (now Chennai), New York, California, but don't ever feel the need to enquire about the people they once knew. This is because neither of them belonged to that place in the first place. Both were already people from outside in that village. Neither of them seems to have any relations worth remembering either. The plot of *Mazhapeyyunnu Maddalam Kottunnu* (*Drumming while Raining*) (Priyadarshan, 1986) unfolds in and around a house which doesn't belong to either the lead characters (played by Mohanlal and Sreenivasan) but is of the woman each of them wishes to marry. *Chithram* (*Picture*) (Priyadarshan, 1988), one of the biggest hits of Malayalam cinema, is similarly played out in a scenic verdant hill station in Tulunadu, home to neither of the leading couple (played by Mohanlal and Ranjini). So is the case with *Kilukkam* (*Jingle-Jangle*) (Priyadarshan, 1991), another grand success from the Priyadarshan–Mohanlal duo, with its setting in Ooty, where the male protagonist is a tourist guide, and the female protagonist a visitor. The whole of *Ramji Rao Speaking* (Siddique-Lal, 1989) takes place in a city where the young men at the centre of the narrative doesn't seem to have any familial bearings.[62] There are many more examples

---

[61] *Nadodikkattu* (*The Vagabond Wind*) (Sathyan Anthikad, 1987), *Pattanapravesham* (*Town Entry*) (Sathyan Anthikad, 1988), and *Akkare Akkare Akkare* (*Far Far Away*) (Priyadarshan, 1990) make the trilogy.

[62] I owe this point to a talk given by James Michael on comedy films in English and Foreign Languages University in c.2007. Michael's larger point was that the youngsters in these movies

of laughter films where unmoored male youngsters, devoid of a family and newcomers to the city, try to dodge the many hardships they face with much hilarity: *Odaruthammava Aalariyam* (*Don't Run Uncle, We Know You!*) (Priyadarshan, 1984), *Aram+Aram= Kinnaram* (*Sharpened to Sweetness*) (Priyadarshan, 1985), *Mukundetta Sumithra Vilikkunnu* (*Mukundetta, Sumithra Calling*) (Priyadarshan, 1988), *Nagarangalil Chenn Raparkam* (*Let's Stay in the Cities*) (Viji Thampi, 1990) to name but a few.[63] They lead very different lives in these other places, lives they would not dare to, had they stayed back in their villages. At home they are believed to be employed in white-collar professions, while in truth they are just eking out a living doing odd jobs or in modest conditions as waiters, barbers, or mechanics.

The double life that migration gives rise to finds its formal correspondence in the instability of the cinematic gaze. Laughter cinema is characterized by the deployment of two different modes of gaze, one, the shot–reverse–shot aesthetic that characterizes the family space (including intimate relations with opposite sex), and two, the tableau mode, which present the characters in the mode of theatre. The tableau mode takes over in moments of homosocial bonding or in times when the characters are trying to con their way out of the sticky situation. Roughly, though not always, these gazes also correspond to two different modes in which the characters are presented—one, as individuals with a pathetic back story, and two, as stick figures whose function is comedy.

To illustrate this point with reference to *Akkare Ninnoru Maaran*: the shot–reverse–shot aesthetic comes into play only in domestic scenes in the movie, and in the brief intimacy between the protagonist and his love

---

could afford to live without any hint of being employed because there was a source of hidden wealth, the Gulf.

[63] A minor tendency in the later years is to thematize the struggle to incorporate the outside world to the world of the family. In *Meleparambil Aanveedu* (*The Male House of Meleparamb*) (Rajasenan, 1993), the youngest of four male siblings seek and find a job elsewhere (in Tamil Nadu) while everyone else at family spends time in the household looking after family property and business. The young man (played by Jayaram) marries in secret the daughter of the local heavyweight and in the face of her murderous family when the truth gets out, runs back home with his wife. The problem is, however, in telling his family that he is married when none of his elder brothers are, and also to a non-Malayali (Tamil). The rest of the movie is about him trying to get his wife accepted by his family before he could tell them that she is his wife. *Mangalam Veettil Manaseshwari Gupta* (Suresh Vinu, 1995) is similarly about getting one's family back home to accept one's life choices made in the city and away from home.

interest. The character played by Sreenivasan is given a back story. As the owner of a lodge which is more of a liability, he is a young man who shares the frustrations and aspirations of the other youth in the film—a good job, money, and in his case, a career in acting. However, as the one in the disguise of an Arab later on in a village not his own, the realist space of cinema focuses the audience gaze on how well the disguise is able to fool the diegetic onlooker.[64] The turn from one organization of looks to another, from the shot–reverse–shot to tableau, is when these characters assume roles other than who they are, when they play along with the charade of financial success and conjuring a world of make-believe. The laughter is as much at the situation as it is at them.[65]

In their very function, the laughter films bring into being an ironic subject who cannot fully identify with the characters, and whose relation to the character is already built on a dramatic distance in which the character on screen and the audience have two different sensations of the same situation. The (social and geographical) location, performativity, and gaze overlap to produce two different registers of looking, one of which is the tableau. This is distant look. The look, as different from gaze, is one which makes available a different order of reality.[66] This distant look doesn't prevail throughout the film, but is one that intrudes upon the identifiable spaces of the Kerala imaginary, such as in *Akkare Ninnoru Maaran*, to stage heterotopias where the givenness of social location gives way to imposture.

How is one to understand the public involved in the look from afar? Prasad tells us in an aside how in moments in which some films induce an individual gaze approximating the bourgeois through a scene of physical intimacy between the lead couples, there will be someone in the

---

[64] One can observe this framing even in the films in which Sreenivasan plays the protagonist, such as *Vadakkunokkiyantram (Compass)* (Sreenivasan, 1989) or *Pavam Pavam Rajakumaran* (The Pauper Prince) (Kamal, 1990) in which the character is not available for identification but for observation.

[65] Tableau as an arrangement of look that invites the audience to deliberate upon a situation in a moment of national transition from one state to another has been elaborated upon by Ravi Vasudevan. See 'The Cultural Politics of Address in "Transitional" Cinema', in Ravi Vasudevan, *The Melodramatic Public: Film Form and Spectatorship in Indian Cinema* (Ranikhet: Permanent Black, 2010), 98–129.

[66] For a discussion on the concept of look, derived from Lacan, and its uses in film, see Colin MacCabe, 'Theory and Film: Principles of Realism and Pleasure', in *Film Theory and Criticism: Introductory Readings*, eds Gerald Mast, Marshall Cohen, and Leo Braudy (New Delhi: Oxford University Press, 1992).

hall who makes the calling sound of a night hawker, at which point the audience laughs, thus breaking the spell of the film and reconstituting the publicness of cinema.[67] In a similar vein, the laughter films induce laughter, a very communal, infectious mode of bringing into awareness that one is in a movie hall, or among people, or that one is actually laughing to oneself, all of which prevent the mode of bourgeois appreciation of films. Laughter foregrounds the communal nature of watching.[68] As a genre, laughter films acknowledge the public as laughter is a result of dramatic irony. It is the moment in which a public takes place facing the screen. The identification with the character is cut in favour of otherness. The identification of a public (as different from an individual) as the recipient of one's performance is at the heart of community formation.[69] The laughter films, in their very comicality perceived in tableau, brings into being this cinematic public.

Given the disjuncture in the organization of gaze in laughter films between identification and objectification of the *same* characters, [70] this is a text whose coherence is guaranteed by its public whose look provides the consistency of the film. The incredulous, almost ridiculous, thread which sustains the charade in laughter films makes it a visual contract emanating from a prior contract between the text and the viewer, one

---

[67] Prasad, *Ideology of the Hindi Film*, 104.

[68] 'When two or more people laugh, it establishes a common vantage point, a public space between them, an *entre nous*. It raises an awareness of something that the viewers are now, to a certain extent, aware of *together*.' See Julian Hanich, 'Laughter and collective awareness: The cinema auditorium as public space', *NECSUS: European Journal of Media Studies* 3, no. 2 (2014), 46.

In this vein, one could say the canned laughter that characterizes sitcoms is a compensation for the replacement of a viewing collective with the individual viewer at the laptop.

[69] A point argued by S. V. Srinivas with regard to NTR's success in Telugu cinema. See S. V. Srinivas, *Politics as Performance: A Social History of the Telugu Cinema* (Ranikhet: Permanent Black in association with The New India Foundation, 2013).

The distinction made here is with regard to the address of cinema—does the cinema address itself to a collective or an individual. As Julian Hanich points out, even quiet attentive viewing in a cinema hall has a collective dimension, such as in its intentionality, joint attention to the film, and joint action in terms of the reflectivity that the space of the auditorium offers for viewing itself as a jointly willed action. See Julian Hanich, *The Audience Effect: On the Collective Cinema Experience* (Edinburgh: Edinburgh University Press, 2018).

[70] A similar point can be made about horror films too, but with two major differences: one, the disjuncture involved in the gaze in horror films is between one in which the protagonist as a locus of identification offers us a view of the world while the other makes the protagonist an object of vision not that of the audience but of an assumed menacing diegetic character (and that of the audience only by relay); and two, the effect achieved thereby, fear, is aimed to be realized in an individualist mode—exactly why nervous laughter, which desperately recalls the public nature of the theatre, is often heard during horror sequences.

which is brought into being by its dependence on recognizable faces, the right resonance in titles, and the generic expectations arising therein. The public constituted thereby is an intimate public, one that is based upon prior truths of the genre rather than an evolving consensus based on interpretation and deliberation as the film is underway.[71] This intimate public is not based on identification with the characters in their vagabond heterotopia. The diegetic masquerade to enact a successful life elsewhere is always a matter of inspection and investigation by the public. The distant look turns the familiar into an object of enquiry. In the staging of the masquerade, laughter films manage to defamiliarize one's own home, bring out its pettiness, fit for a hearty laughter.

This look from afar, where cinema doesn't produce locus for identification, and thereby produce a distanced but not disinterested view is best thematized in *Sandesham* (Message) (Sathyan Anthikad, 1991), a movie for which Sreenivasan wrote the script. In this example, the look from afar is placed on the familiarity of home, for this is a movie which doesn't step outside the bounds of the native village of the protagonists. The film looks at the mutual animosity and its absurdities between the two electoral fronts in Kerala through the synecdoche of the rivalry between two siblings who work for these respective fronts.

At a particular juncture of the movie, a national leader of one of the two parties visits the village as part of his national campaign. What follows is one of the most memorable sequences in Malayalam cinema. There is a competition between the local workers of the party to serve the leader. That the house of the siblings has been selected as the place where the leader would stop to relax for a few hours before he moves along his campaign trail puts the house at the whim of the party and especially of the visiting leader. The film mocks the slavishness of the local leaders to the national leader while the latter can afford to be completely oblivious of his hosts. A request for *naariyal ka paani* from the leader leads to all round confusion as to what he could mean. The moment the lascivious sounding Hindi demand (*naari* means woman, as one among the crowd

---

[71] Lotte Hoek has shown, in the context of screening of pornography, that the public constituted by the film is not necessarily due to the coherence of the film, but could be an intimate public produced by the affordances of film to meet their collective demand, and inversely, by the recognition of the viewers that demands could be made. See Lotte Hoek, *Cut-pieces: Celluloid Obscenity and Popular Cinema in Bangladesh* (New York: Columbia University Press, 2013).

points out) is translated appropriately—'coconut water, he is asking for coconut water'—by a person whose face remains invisible and whose voice come from the very last of the file of the gathered leader-servers, the party men leave no coconut hanging in their bid to outdo each other for this moment in which the leader's eye might fall on them (and that will be their moment of escape from this swamp perhaps!). The visiting leader mocks the incomprehending villagers—'"*sampoorna saksharatha*" *bandar ke bacche!*' ('complete literacy', monkey offsprings!).

The sequence, in the mode of a tableau rather than one which follows the interplay of alternating point of view or eyeline matches, illustrates some of the elements of the imagined provinciality of Kerala. The comical servility before the (North Indian) outsider, the complete ignorance of the leader for his hosts in this village which stands for Kerala itself, the cluelessness before the 'national language', all of these instantiate the recurring theme of Delhi, where decisions are made, being far away. The choice of the actor to play the national leader—Innocent—a comedy actor whose repertoire has a rich collection of playing bungling ineptness, further hones the chagrin of the imagined servitude. A laughable people slaving for the attention of a laughable 'national' leader![72] Being at the margin of the nation with negligible presence in its daily life, a nation whose centre has been occupied by people one considers to be inept—uneducated, unruly, and arrogant—is at the heart of this imagined victimhood[73] Of what use is all our literacy if this servility is all we could aspire to?!

The irony and self-reflectivity of the laughter films makes it possible for a recuperative reading of the Gulf in the two decades it was completely absent as a location in Malayalam cinema. And this self-reflexivity mocks the mix of grandstanding and sense of inferiority. On the one hand there is the grandstanding about the advanced human development indices

---

[72] While this could be read as a criticism of the Congress Party alone, the film criticizes Communists for another kind of pettiness, for their high intellectualism devoid of any grounding in local realities, and mimicking political programmes from elsewhere that have no organic links to the situation at home.

[73] The importance of Delhi, the national capital, as the place where decisions are made, as well as the self-worth of individuals based on how near they are to this power centre is satirized in movies. The satire is partly effective because it is premised on Delhi being far away, a premise widely shared by the audience that can therefore provide for much surprise when upset in such a matter-of-fact way as in *Vellimoonga* (*Barn Owl*) (Jibu Jacob, 2014).

of Kerala, and as we like to put it, 'comparable to Western Europe'; on the other, there is also the bleak truth that one's dear ones at home can live with dignity only at the price of one's own migration.[74] There is the contradiction between seeing one's state as part of the world history because it traffics in discourse of international politics such as Communism and CIA, while also recognizing how far one's own world is from the marvels of the world, as seen in all those skyscrapers and technologies. It is these very ironic self-reflections on oneself that laughter films gave voice to.

It is perhaps also worth keeping in mind this dramatic irony which Vipin Kumar says that the comic films have incomplete symbolizations of the characters. For Kumar this is because the bourgeois language of hitherto Malayalam cinema is unable to capture the otherness of these characters.[75] Rather than celebrate this, one could see this as a mix of acknowledgement and wilful ignorance[76] which was crucial to migration in Kerala. The mobility of the family of the migrants, not just in terms of money but also along the social ladder, is compounded with the obfuscation of the nature of one's work abroad. On the one hand, migration is often a means to enhance one's social position, even if within limits.[77] But on the other hand, the migrants are often vagabonds in their countries of destination, eking their way out by hook or by crook.[78] The exact nature of the migrant's job needs to be wilfully ignored in public in order for migration to benefit not just the family but also the entire network through which his remittances, as well as his gifts, travel. The nature of the work also needs to be ignored for the fact that regardless of the nature, the remittances did make a difference. The possibilities of imposturing, and its real effects are crucial for migration to continue as an aspiration. The

---

[74] *Sandesham* has two migrant figures—the protagonist's father who used to work in Tamil Nadu, and the newly joined Agricultural Officer whose native place is elsewhere. Importantly, these two figures form the duo of hard-working dignified strugglers in contrast to the petty politics of the two brothers.

[75] Kumar, 'Politics of Laughter'.

[76] Rather than suggesting the absence of knowledge, recent studies have pointed out the strategic uses of not knowing for maintaining community cohesion and communal action. See Casey High, Ann H. Kelly, and Jonathan Mair (eds), *The Anthropology of Ignorance: An Ethnographic Approach* (New York: Palgrave Macmillan, 2012).

[77] Filippo Osella and Caroline Osella, *Social Mobility in Kerala: Modernity and Identity in Conflict* (London: Pluto Press, 2001).

[78] Hari Sreekumar and Rohit Varman, "Vagabonds at the Margins: Acculturation, Subalterns, and Competing Worth," *Journal of Micromarketing* 39, no. 1 (2019): 37–52.

laughter film is a staging of the failure of the Gulf as a public discourse in Kerala except as a public secret precisely because this epistemic failure is crucial in maintaining an economy that also produces cinema and allows people to have money to spend on making or watching movies. However, under the condition of circular migration to the Gulf that characterizes Kerala, there cannot be a total break between the migrant and the non-migrant. They keep changing places. The tableau cannot hold on its own. It must give way to identification every once in a while.

3

Translating the Gulf

Writing the Borderland I

In its broad sense, migration literature has had a small but critical presence in Malayalam. Dilip Menon has shown that migration was a key experience in the worlding of the early subaltern novels from Kerala.[1] These
novels questioned the easy correspondence between nation and novel,
assumed by the landmark study on nationalism by Benedict Anderson;[2]
they evoked in the public sphere an imagination that was oceanic rather than nation-centric. Another strand of migration literature in
Malayalam has been of the migration from the southern parts of Kerala
to its northern hinterlands. These migrants set out in search of economic
mobility and cultivable land, and in the process altered the landscape of
northern Kerala (popularly called Malabar). In the self-descriptions of
these migrants, they fixed themselves in the history of Malabar, seeing
themselves as the agents of an economic change which brought development to Malabar. The migrant community in these novels was mobilized
by evoking the binary of the migrant versus indigene, thereby erasing the
internal differentiations within the migrants.[3]

I invoke the term 'literatures of migration' to suggest a shift in the
conditions of transnational migration and the need for the study of migrant literature to change under these circumstances. Globalization has
destabilized early notions of fixed localities. With the accelerated flow

---

[1] Dilip M. Menon, 'A Place Elsewhere: The Nineteenth-Century Subaltern Novel in
Malayalam', *The Blindness of Insight: Essays on Caste in Modern India* (Chennai: Navayana,
2006), 73–109
[2] Benedict Anderson, *Imagined Communities: Reflections on the Origins and Spread of
Nationalism* (London and New York: Verso, 1991).
[3] V. J. Varghese, 'Migrant narratives: Reading literary representations of Christian migration
in Kerala, 1920–70', *The Indian Economic and Social History Review* 43, no. 2 (2006).

The Gulf Migrant Archives in Kerala. Mohamed Shafeeq Karinkurayil, Oxford University Press. © Mohamed Shafeeq
Karinkurayil 2024. DOI: 10.1093/9780198910619.003.0004

of images, ideas, people, and capital, we have formations (scapes) that are constantly in motion, defying fixed boundaries, including that of the nation state.[4] The vastly different means of communication and the greatly increased avenues of transportation, together with the prevalence of footloose labour and gig economy should make us reappraise the frame through which we have been reading migrant literatures. Carine M. Mardorossian had, in the early years of the 2000s, already suggested the move from a literature of exile to migrant literature. Mardorossian's departure is that the framework of exile impeded an ideological analysis of what made one exile, and foregrounded a binary between here and a lost homeland.

> The shift from exile to migrant challenges this binary logic by emphasizing movement, rootlessness, and the mixing of cultures, races, and languages … [The migrant] can no longer simply or nostalgically remember the past as a fixed and comforting anchor in her life, since its contours move with the present rather than in opposition to it. Her identity is no longer to do with being but with becoming.[5]

While Mardorossian insists on the migrant's 'ambivalence towards both her old and new existence',[6] it is precisely such a narrative of 'in-betweenness' that Leslie A. Adelson wants us to think against.[7] Taking Appadurai's theorization of the shifting scapes as her central plank, Adelson illustrates the continuities between home and 'here' in the (Turkish) migration literature (in German).[8] 'The imaginary bridge 'between two worlds' is designed to keep discrete worlds apart as much as it pretends to bring them together'.[9] Adelson argues for an evaluation of migrant literature whose site of transition and transformation is the here of the host culture and not a state of perpetual non-arrival.

---

[4] Arjun Appadurai, *Modernity at Large: Cultural Dimensions of Globalization* (Minneapolis, MN: University of Minnesota Press, 1996), 27–47.

[5] Carine M. Mardorossian, 'From Literature of Exile to Migrant Literature', *Modern Language Studies* 32, no. 2 (2002): 16.

[6] Mardorossian, 'From Literature of Exile to Migrant Literature', 16.

[7] Leslie A. Adelson, 'Against Between: A Manifesto', *New Perspectives on Turkey* 29 (2003), doi: 10.1017/S0896634600006099.

[8] Leslie A. Adelson, *The Turkish Turn in Contemporary German Literature: Towards a New Critical Grammar of Migration* (New York and Hampshire: Palgrave Macmillan, 2005).

[9] Adelson, 'Against Between', 22.

The conditions of migration that are the focus of this chapter are vastly different from the ones studied by those discussed so far. Unlike the conditions in Europe, or that of the migration from the south of Kerala to its north, the migration to the Gulf from Kerala is marked by the impossibility of integrating into the host country. The racial divide between the native and the migrant, and the forced temporary nature of migration is central to the nation-building process in the Gulf.[10] It is also in the interests of the ruling dispensation in the Gulf monarchies that the labour force is drawn from multiple nations and through a quota system. The various migrant communities live in ethnically segregated conditions; even in labour camps, the rooms are segregated ethnically, something that the migrants also prefer.[11] The migration to the Gulf also follows a networked pattern such that the home and away are welded as nodes of a continuity, thereby also requiring us to rethink our notions of migration as obsessively individualistic. It is therefore my contention that an age of increased connectivity, mobility, networked migration, and footloose labour is ill-served by a paradigm which deems migration as 'absolute discontinuity'[12] in which 'the past is a country from which we all have emigrated'.[13] While it is important both to remember the colonial-indentured phase of migrations and the immobility of the migrants even in the age of technological advancements and high speed travel, as Vijay Mishra reminds us,[14] we also need to take into account the specificity of the Gulf migration wherein, as we shall see, the recollected trauma of separation does not even have recourse to the imagination of a national collectivity.[15]

This chapter is interested in the translations of the Gulf space in Kerala and the redrawing of the boundaries of the Gulf in this process. Sandro

---

[10] See Introduction to this volume.

[11] William T Vollmann, 'I am here only for working: Conversations with the petroleum brotherhood in the UAE', *Harper's*, December 2017. https://harpers.org/archive/2017/12/i-am-here-only-for-working/ Last accessed on 11 May 2021.

[12] Ranajit Guha, *The Small Voice of History: Collected Essays* (Delhi: Permanent Black, 2002), 648.

[13] Salman Rushdie, 'Imaginary Homelands', *London Review of Books* 4, no. 18 (1982). https://www.lrb.co.uk/the-paper/v04/n18/salman-rushdie/imaginary-homelands. Last accessed: 11 April 2021.

[14] Vijay Mishra, *The Literature of the Indian Diaspora: Theorizing the Diasporic Imaginary* (New York: Routledge, 2007).

[15] The imaginary of nation as a collective formed in mourning of an original loss (lost in its very origin and therefore the embodiment of an absence), travel and translation, and a

Mezzadra and Brett Neilson[16] develop the concept of translation as the means to produce a common in a world crisscrossed by borders thanks to the new forms that global capital have taken, converting language, knowledge, and the whole of life into an arena of valorization of capital. The concept of translation, rather than referring to the transfer of codes from one established language to another, refers to the co-production of codes between foreigner and foreigner.[17] Such a concept of translation overcomes the unconscious centrality of state as the arena of social transformation that is present in formulations such as 'equivalence'[18] and 'disagreement',[19] and takes into account the multiple borders of politics, economics, and cognition that cut through people, nations, and territories.

In the context of Gulf Malayalam literature, Nadeen Dakkak[20] has argued that the distance from and therefore the opacity of Malayalam helps it to be the language of transnational solidarity. Dakkak demonstrates this with reference to Benyamin's twin novels *Jasmine Days* and *Al Arabian Novel Factory*, in which the plot revolves around a banned and now unavailable book, which however continues to live in its translation to Malayalam. While the novels point out the necessary risks involved even in this translation, with the entire state apparatus on the hunt for the translator, Dakkak's effort is to explore a language of transnational solidarity that literature can offer. Within the space of the aforesaid novels, it is about bridging the gap between the minorities within the fictional Arab state (which closely resembles Bahrain) and the migrant labourers, by showing them both as victims of the same system.

This chapter too uses the concept of translation as a creative bridging between incommensurables. Translation becomes the 'creation of a

---

recollected trauma is central to Mishra's theory of a diasporic imaginary. See Mishra, *The Literature of the Indian Diaspora*.

[16] Sandro Mezzadra and Brett Nielson, *Border as Method, or, Multiplication of Labor* (Durham, NC and London: Duke University Press, 2013).

[17] Mezzadra and Nielson, *Border as Method*, 275.

[18] Ernesto Laclau and Chantal Mouffe, *Hegemony and Socialist Strategy: Towards a Radical Democratic Politics* (New York: Verso, 1985).

[19] Jacques Rancière, *Dis-Agreement: Politics and Philosophy*, trans. J. Rose (Minneapolis, MN: University of Minnesota Press, 1998)

[20] Nadeen Dakkak, 'Malayalam literature as a transnational space of political change: Migration and Bahrain's 2011 uprising in Benyamin's *Jasmine Days* and *Al Arabian Novel Factory*', *Journal of Commonwealth Literature* 58, no. 1 (2023).

common', the 'forging of new idioms'. The creative labour here is to probe how Malayalam Gulf literature imagines common ground between migrants to the Gulf fraught by language, nationality, ethnicity, and status; between migrants and the natives in the Gulf; and between migrants and non-migrants in Kerala.

The chapter and the next, in differing ways and to different ends, pay attention to the formation of communities within the space of Gulf migration, and how this feeds on and departs from given communities and collectivities. The primary texts herein are read for their performance of bordering—that is, the process activating a space of epistemic clashes in which words, phrases, and idioms show signs of migrancy between registers and codes. Such instances become the sites in which existing boundaries are redrawn for different conceptions of togetherness. While, as mentioned, this chapter focuses on the bridging of the spaces of the Gulf and Kerala through textual strategies, the next chapter is on the breakdown of speech. In both breaking down as well as bridging together, the objective is to show the making of communities within the space and as an affordance of global capital.

Despite the longevity of Gulf migration, now five decades old and ongoing, the Gulf migration has been mostly mute. That is to say, the Malayali Gulf migrant has not produced a veritable oeuvre of literature. It is only towards the end of the 1990s, that is already three decades after the commencement of the large-scale circular migration, that we have some Gulf voices in the mainstream Malayalam literature. Much of the Malayali Gulf migrant literature is published in occasional souvenirs brought out by arts clubs in the Gulf or local chapters (i.e. a subset of people from one locality in Kerala) of bigger organizations such as the Kerala Muslim Cultural Centre (KMCC). The souvenirs are usually brought out annually sponsored by the advertisement fees collected from various commercial establishments. These establishments agree to placing advertisements in these souvenirs so as to be counted among the well-wishers of the migrant network. A typical souvenir carries a few articles by high standing members of the public sphere in Kerala and short felicitation notes by several others; profiles of a few outstanding Malayali migrants; essays, short stories, and poems by migrants; an annual report of the activities undertaken by the group in the past year; and a photo gallery. It has been an ongoing sentiment that these literary contributions are high on nostalgia about Kerala and do not seek to engage with the actual life in the Gulf, apart from the teary descriptions of the sweltering heat and boiling desert. There was, supposedly, an inability on the part of the Malayali writers in the Gulf to depict their daily lives. According to V. Musafer Ahammed, the Malayali writers in the Gulf find themselves waking up to a river back home rather than the desert right in front of them.[21]

The Gulf became a talking point as a personal experience in the public domain in the late 1990s, when Gulf in itself and in its resonance in Kerala was undergoing a shift, and Gulf narratives began appearing in mainstream outlets.

The Perils of Homophony: Sageer's *Gulfumpadi PO*

The first literary work focused on Gulf migration to break into the mainstream press was Babu Bharadwaj's *Pravasiyude Kurippukal* (*Notes of an Émigré*), published by Mathrubhumi Press, a prominent publishing house in Kerala, in the year 2000. Bharadwaj was an established face in the cultural scene in Malayalam and these memoirs of his life in the Gulf some twenty years before were therefore coming from a seasoned writer who already had a name in the mainstream press. Later, Bharadwaj published two more memoirs—*Pravasiyude Vazhiyambalangal* (*The Sojourns of an Emigrant*) came out in 2011, and *Pravasthinte Murivukal* (*The Wounds of Emigration*) in 2012.[22]

Another milestone in Malayalam Gulf literature from the period was Sageer's comic strip, titled *Gulfumpadi PO*, which started appearing in *Chandrika Weekly* from 2001. A compilation of this comic was published by the Kozhikode based Olive Books in 2005 and by Don Books in 2021.

---

[21] Musafer Ahammed, *Kudiyettakkarante Veedu* (Kottayam: DC Books, 2014), 111.

[22] Babu Bharadwaj, *Pravasiyude Vazhiyambalangal* (Kozhikode: Pratheeksha Books, 2011); Babu Bharadwaj, *Pravasathinte Murivukal* (Kozhikode: Mathrubhumi Books, 2012).

I have written on Bharadwaj's memoirs in a series of essays. See Mohamed Shafeeq Karinkurayil, 'The Arabian Gulf as Revelation in Malayalam Migrant Literary Narratives', in *Routledge Companion to Migration Literature*, eds Gigi Adair, Rebecca Fasselt, and Carl McLaughlin, forthcoming; Mohamed Shafeeq K., 'Can the Migrant Exist? Reading Gulf Migrant Memoirs in Malayalam', in *Reimagining Marginality: Exploitation, Experience, Expression*, eds Mohan Dharavath and Achuth A. (New Delhi: Authorspress, 2022).

The Malayalam litterateur N. S. Madhavan hailed *Gulfumpadi PO* as comparable to David Beauchard's *Epileptic*,[23] Art Spiegelman's *Maus*,[24] and Marjane Satrapi's *Persepolis*,[25] in that these graphic novels are all works which draw on personal experiences and reflect on the splintering of the family in the face of deep tragedies. Madhavan called *Gulfumpadi PO* the (then) only organic fiction that has come out in Malayalam of the Gulf migrant experience, highlighting their sacrifice and heroism, while mass culture derides and makes fun of the Gulf migrant like they do with the handicapped and cultural minorities of other countries. [26]

Arranged in two tiers of two panels each, *Gulfumpadi PO* is, as Sageer writes in the preface to the compilation, born out of his own migrant experience, and what he sees around him in Kerala. Sageer left for Saudi Arabia in 1984, when he was thirty-one years of age. He was then married for two years and father to a child of three months. He had gone there as a sign board artist, but found that the printing technology was already taking over. He was then employed in a photography studio, where his speciality would be to touch up enlarged photographs.[27] In the next ten years he would visit Kerala just thrice on short vacations. His long years of being away were, as he says in the preface to the compilation, caused by the avarice of his relatives and extended family. *Gulfumpadi PO* is his take on this parasitic lot who feed on the migrant toiling in the Gulf.

Back in Kerala in 1994, Sageer was employed by *Chandrika Weekly*. His main portfolio was to illustrate the last page, which, as a general convention in magazines, would carry cartoon strips. These strips, such as the Hoja jokes (aka Mulla jokes), Sardarji jokes, and a similar stock of humorous micro stories in Malayalam called *Mangattachanum Kunjayin Musliyarum*, were aimed at light-hearted humour. *Gulfumpadi PO* on the

---

[23] David Beauchard, *Epileptic* (Seattle, WA: Fantagraphics, 2002).

[24] Art Spiegelman, *Maus: A Survivor's Tale: 1. My Father Bleeds History* (New York: Pantheon, 1986); Art Spiegelman, *Maus: A Survivor's Tale: 2. And Here My Troubles Began* (New York: Pantheon, 1992).

[25] Marjane Satrapi, *Persepolis: The Story of a Childhood* (New York: Pantheon, 2003).

[26] The piece, originally written for the Onam special issue of the Pune-based *Pravasisabdam* magazine, is republished as the foreword to the compilation. N. S. Madhavan, 'Aamukham' ('Foreword') in *Gulfumpadi PO* (Kozhikode: Olive Books, 2005), 9–12 and reprinted in the Don Books edition: Sageer, *Gulfumpadi PO* (Kottayam: Don Books, 2021).

[27] Sageer, interviewed by the author, 17 January 2022.

other hand, had to work through the mesh of humour, dark humour, and satire that the readers at times complained were not that funny.[28]

The comic is populated mostly by a stock of characters, with occasional appearances by other characters, especially Gulf migrants on their short visits. At the centre of the comic is Abu, short for Abu Baker, who is never seen as he is already in the Gulf, his wife Sainu, who is forever praying for her husband's well-being and safe and speedy return. Also featured are: Abu's father Moidu, a glutton for chicken and fish, an indiscriminate freeloader who is forever complaining that Abu is not sending money home; Abu's mother who is forever glued to the television and has a weakness for cola; Abu's son Hameed who is of college-going age and is always whiling away his time on his mobile phone or on his motorbike; Abu's daughter Sofi who is now in her tenth standard, aka SSLC, considered the turning point for girls (at the time, in working-class homes) between marriage and higher studies; Abu's youngest son, the schoolboy Shareef; Bapu, the quintessential broker who is cutting deals all the time and is a middleman for everything from marriage proposals to real estate; and Master, who embodies wisdom and is a variant of R. K. Laxman's Common Man with uncommon perspicacity.[29]

Gulfumpadi is the fictional setting of the comic strip. The place name is made of two words, 'Gulf' and 'padi', and is a nod to the many places in Kerala which are named after foreign locations, and with a *padi* at the end, where *padi*, literally meaning a place to keep one's foot, in general means a small locality. One comes across a Vietnampadi or an Abudhabipadi along the bus routes in Kerala. The world history gets mapped as popular memory in these signboards of places. The *um* in Gulfumpadi links the two extremes into one entity. The locality is flushed with the Gulf—Gulf migrants, Gulf money, and Gulf news.

The Gulf and Gulfumpadi is in a translational relation that stretches the signifiers into distortion. An example is how the word 'cable' is brought in two different registers in the opening strip of the series. In this strip[30] we

---

[28] Sageer, 'Aamukham' ['Preface'], in *Gulfumpadi PO* (Kozhikode: Olive Books, 2005), np. The preface in the Don Books edition does not carry this suggestion.

[29] For a study of R. K. Laxman's cartoons, see Christel R. Devadawson, 'Uncommon Citizens: Laxman and the Common Man', in *Out of Line: Cartoons, Caricature and Contemporary India* (Hyderabad: Orient Blackswan, 2019), 78–119.

[30] Sageer, *Gulfumpadi*, 15.

learn that Abu is now admitted to a hospital in the Gulf because he was electrocuted by an electricity cable. But his father Moidu is more worried that he hasn't received any money from Abu for almost a month ('three days to a month') and that his cable television connection will be cut to the displeasure of his grandchildren. In the last panel, which has Moidu going away with his back faced to us and the Master facing frontwards, walking in the opposite direction from Moidu, exclaiming to himself 'cable tragedies', thus bringing the two contexts of cable, electric cable, and cable television, in short circuit. The tragedy of Abu and the farcicality of Moidu's tragedy offers at once a simultaneity and shuttle between the Gulf and Kerala, while also pointing towards its incommensurabilities.

Unlike the comic strips in newspapers, the comic strips in magazines are not bound by current affairs and are not expected to make a statement in their light. As mentioned earlier, *Gulfumpadi PO* appeared in a space which was earlier taken up by such timeless (evergreen!) jokes such as Hoja. Even so, the worldliness of *Gulfumpadi PO* cannot be missed. It is raining in Gulfumpadi when it is monsoon in Kerala, there is water scarcity in Gulfumpadi when it is summer in Kerala, the characters in Gulfumpadi too are fasting when it is the fasting month of Ramadan for the readers. The comic marks the time when electricity rates are hiked, when sand mining is banned, when it is illegal to level wetlands, when it is the time of the football World Cup or Euro Cup, the US war on Iraq, and the boycott of US products in Kerala. The interiors and exteriors in the comic strip change with the passing of time. The Malayalam signboard of the chicken shop changes to English, the television in the living room blurts out the latest songs, the changing vogue in gadgets pervade the private life and public transactions. As Sageer puts it, it is the record of a time when people who were fed on rice flakes and black tea shifted to cola.[31] Like in the comic strip *Cheriya Lokavum Valiya Manushyarum* by G. Aravindan, who Sageer mentions as his inspiration,[32] the characters in Gulfumpadi age.[33] There are continuities from one week to another. Indeed, there is the passing away of time and the intimation of mortality that seeps through these

---

[31] Sageer, interview.

[32] Sageer, interview.

[33] Cartoonist Gokul Gopalakrishnan notes that the ageing of characters was an innovation in cartooning brought in by G. Aravindan. See *The Comic Art Rambler* http://thecomicartrambler. blogspot.com/2008/09/g-aravindans-small-men-and-big-world-re.html Last Accessed on 25 January 2022.

strips, especially to underscore the wasted youth of the migrant toiling for an uncaring people. The comic can thus be seen in line with the post-millennial turn in graphic narratives, 'problematising erstwhile, safe, settled ideas and projections of Indian society ...' and opting instead for 'the narration of problematic, difficult and yet timely issues'.[34]

The central thrust of *Gulfumpadi PO* is to show that an entire world has been built back in Kerala on Gulf remittances, but this world has no place for the migrant. Indeed, the migrant feels lonely here. As one character says, he cannot find one friend in the whole of Gulfumpadi who will lend him some cash to get back to the Gulf sooner since life back in Gulfumpadi has become so unbearable.[35] The Gulf migrant is valued only as long as he is away and his money keeps coming in. In spite of the Gulf migrants stating how miserable their life is in the Gulf every once in a while, no one except Master seems to care. Master is the embodiment of History, that repository of justice and recorder of our deeds who alone seems capable of seeing what is hidden beyond the here-and-now and judging in the right measure of time. He has only contempt for the self-serving intellectualism of the rich Gulf migrant as he is all sympathy for the working-class migrant whose folks back home have forgotten their pasts. Moidu, the father of the absent migrant is a prime example—he used to be a cowherd but now there is no milk in his house if the shop has run out of packaged milk.

Consumerism is the prime evil that Sageer identifies with the post-Gulf Kerala. Here, no one is interested in working. Everyone seem to be wasted away by indulgences. The migrant's mother does not know what to do if the television is not working. The father Moidu is either buying meat, smoking foreign cigarettes, or at the local juice shop, and all the time leeching off someone else. The neighbourhood has become mediatized to the extent that people come to know of a death in the neighbourhood only if it is reported in the newspaper or on television.

A central theme in Sageer's visualization of Kerala is the stark difference that exists between the migrant and the non-migrant in almost everything, but especially in their relation to the land itself. In one strip (Fig. 3.1)[36] Sainu is reading a letter from Abu, sitting in the lobby of the

---

[34] E. Dawson Varughese, *Visuality and Identity in Post-millennial Indian Graphic Narratives* (London: Palgrave Macmillan, 2018), 16.

[35] Sageer, *Gulfumpadi*, 95.

[36] Sageer, *Gulfumpadi*, 52.

Fig. 3.1 From *Gulfumpadi PO*. Reproduced with permission from Sageer.

house locally called *kolaya* or sit-out. It is the threshold part of the house which receives visitors, is not covered by walls, and therefore visible to passers-by. The panel is framed as a view from the house with the exterior as the background, and we can see the long raindrops of monsoon in the backdrop, and the foregrounded heavy tears dropping from Sainu's eyes as she reads the letter. The content of the letter is presented as speech coming from the letter. In the letter, Abu says that (having lost his job) he is trying for a settlement through the labour courts, and that he would be back home once that is done. He also adds, and one does hear the tone of longing, that it would be raining so much back home while the desert is parched and so is his heart.

In the next panel, we see Moidu approaching the house from outside. He is in his regular dress of a plain white shirt and *mundu* (the white wraparound which covers the lower half of the body, not visible in this frame), and headwrap (suggestive of Muslim peasantry of south Malabar). He is holding his umbrella, while he has a black polythene bag in his other hand. In the frame we can see the side-view of both Moidu who is approaching the house from outside, and Sainu who is reading the letter facing the inside of the house. Abu (in the letter) recounts how he is sleepless in the nights, and then would fancy the hum of the AC to be the sound of the monsoon rains, and memories would come flooding in. The nostalgic tone of this letter in its soft pathos is brought into contrast with the harshness of Moidu who insultingly asks if the letter has anything to say other than Abu's complains of being jobless and penniless. The insult is as much directed at Sainu who is always accused of spending all her time reading and writing letters to Abu. What Moidu can see but doesn't care about are her tears.

In the first panel of the next grid the scene shifts to the interior of the house. The folded umbrella in Moidu's left hand with rain water still dripping from it and the black polythene bag in his right provides continuity with last panel. It's the drawing room. The panel, like the last one, gives a side view which brings into frame the non-mutuality of the characters as they don't face each other. Sofi seated on a fancy plastic chair and Shareef on her lap are watching television. The old song playing in the television invokes love and longing for the landscape of Kerala. The song, a very famous one—*Naalikerathinte naattilenikoru*—recounts a migrant singing about the woman who awaits him at his abode in the land of coconut (Kerala). Moidu asks her (one can hear him almost shouting) to switch off the television. Playing on the word for coconut in the song (*naalikeram*; the more common word is *thenga*), Moidu says that in this land of shamelessness (*naanakkaed*), he had to sell sixty coconuts to buy a kilogram of mutton.

In the next panel, presented as a side view, Moidu is handing over the polythene bag to Sainu who is now inside the house (on the way to the kitchen one presumes), her face looking down, the tears still rolling down on her face, Abu's mother is heading towards the TV, while Moidu is stationary with his eyes fixed on the polythene bag. Moidu tells Sainu the right way to prepare mutton, as it can be good for arthritis, while Abu's mother is miffed at whoever had the temerity to switch off the TV.

The imbalance between the migrant's life and of those at home is brought into stark relief here. The contrast extends to the climate, the lifestyle, and expectations from life. It is raining heavily in Kerala. For the migrant in the searing heat of the Gulf, there cannot be a more beautiful sight. The summer months in the Gulf roughly correspond with the first and the heaviest phase of monsoon in Kerala, when the verdant world blooms from the brown cracks of the dusty burnt-out summer. Looking from Kerala, while it is definitely a beautiful sight, it is also not very convenient for life to carry on as usual. One has to carry an umbrella, the water dripping from it wetting the floors inside. There are puddles on paths (the first panel features one) and one has to keep the *mundu* half folded up, as is Moidu's habit, to save it from getting muddy.

While the migrant is saving up the last penny to buy a ticket home, his father is buying mutton, the most expensive of all meat available in the market. And for this he has sold coconut, that fruit which stands for Kerala itself. Sixty coconuts is a good number of coconuts that would have been useful for the family for several months, and all of them sold for a mutton curry that would serve a day! The polythene bag, now as well as in the beginning of 2000s, stood in the public discourse for the bane of consumerism and lack of care for nature. The song on the television doubles up as the voice of the migrant. In the song, the migrant sings of the land of coconuts where he has a small patch of land, and in it a humble abode, and in there a woman like the stem of a banana tree who is waiting for him, fasting. While these are the ordained and celebrated desires of a migrant, the Gulf migrant is expected to build a concrete house (as opposed to a thatched hut or a house with tiled roofs), and Abu has already got one constructed for his family. The Gulf migrant is expected to accumulate land, and as we know, Abu has done that too, and that land is the source of the now sold sixty coconuts. But despite far exceeding the modest dreams of the poet, the Gulf migrant cannot come home. In fact, the home he sings about does not even exist. Gulfumpadi is a tough place to live, with its inflation, its occasional tremors and fungal rains, its wheeling and dealing. The rains may be the easiest to negotiate. The truth is that those at home know well that Abu's life is miserable. Yet they just do not see the merit in his coming home. The migrant finds himself incomprehensible to those back home, and those back home find the migrant unbelievable when the Gulf is spoken about as if it is a place affected by unemployment.

We have already discussed (Chapter 1) the centrality of the figure of the wife to imagining an unsympathetic household in the migrant imagination. The migrant is similarly depicted as an incongruence and unintelligibility in the public space of Gulfumpadi. In one strip we see a migrant who is back home for a holiday carrying a television on his shoulders.[37] When asked by Moidu who he sees on the way, as to why he is seen with a TV for the second time in a week ('is there an exchange-mela?'), the migrant replies, over the next two panels that the TV is so that he can watch the (football) World Cup, as the two other TVs in his house are not free. His wife is into bingeing on TV series while his children are into cricket on the other TV. In the last frame, the epistemic borders are drawn for us through Moidu who asks, 'but isn't it lowly (*chepratharam*—of a cheap nature) that you, a Gulf*karan* (a Gulf man) is lugging it by yourself?'. To this the migrant replies, 'but, this is exactly what I do in the Gulf, a porter's job'. Master responds with a question mark which might suggest incomprehensibility to the classist comment by Moidu, the incorrectness of which is accented by the fact that Moidu himself used to carry around cow dung before the Gulf changed him. The panel leaves the migrant with the last word, but there is no panel left to elicit any response from the character's interlocutors. The migrant has got the punchline. But who has to be punched to knowledge about the real conditions in the Gulf? The truth is, considering *Chandrika Weekly*'s readership is well ensconced

---

[37] Sageer, *Gulfumpadi*, 96.

in the heavily migrant-sending Muslim households in the Malabar region, essentially it is a missed punch. The incomprehensibility expressed by the Master could therefore be read in a different order. The dialogues in Sageer's comics do not follow a direction, and one has to assume who speaks first based on the content of the dialogue. The primacy is given to playing out the space between characters, with the angle of vision in the first panel taken to be the constant through the strip. Master's question mark of incomprehension could then very well be to the migrant's statement of being a porter in the Gulf: 'After all, who doesn't know you are a porter in the Gulf! What big secret do you think you are revealing?!'.

One should not assume that Sageer has drawn a thick line between the migrant and the non-migrant, or drawn a homogenous migrant lot. Peetambaran, for example, is a rich Gulf migrant who is now constructing a lavish house which has an attached swimming pool even as people find it difficult to pay electricity bills, and all this when he also covers the whole thing up in a discourse of love for nature wrought in an intellectual vocabulary. The Master has only disdain for Peetambaran.[38] Another Gulf migrant, who is back home after finding no work in the Gulf and witnessing the hardship there, is now scheming like anyone else to make a profit out of the Gulf migrant.[39] One does not know which is corrupting—the Gulf or Gulfumpadi, or is it the transaction between the two, always lost in translation?

Ultimately, the tragedy is that the corruption catches up with everyone. As Abu's remittance keeps getting delayed, the family has to sell off lands to keep up appearances. Moidu is at such desperation that he himself is thinking of going to the Gulf. It is an act of desperation precisely because, despite his constant advice to everyone else to go to the Gulf without wasting time in Gulfumpadi, he seems to be well aware that life in the Gulf is not easy. Towards the end of the comic strip one can see the world becoming more incomprehensible. Moidu seems to have developed a wisdom akin to the Master, while the Master seems to have slipped into an intellectual mode which he so derided once upon a time. In the end Abu does come home and in the last panel of the last strip, it's all darkness while speech bubbles suggest the ensuing love-making between Abu and

---

[38] Sageer, *Gulfumpadi*, 74.
[39] Sageer, *Gulfumpadi*, 38.

his wife. The spectacle that Gulf has lent itself to should now be shut out for a happy ending.

Race as Malleable: Reading *Barsa*

Khadeeja Mumthas's *Barsa* came out in 2007. 'Barsa' means defiance, as is explained in the novel, and refers to the argumentative stance adopted by its protagonist Sabitha, a Muslim convert, towards the injustice, mostly based on gender, that she finds around her. Sabitha is a gynaecologist working in Saudi Arabia, in the Muslim holy city of Makkah, where she comes face to face with the acute misogyny in dominant Islam. This includes the injunction to keep the woman's body, at times even the face, under wraps; the treatment of women as a sex tool; the permission for polygamy accorded to men; the (informal) treatment of housemaids as sex slaves and its justification as being part of the culture with slavery not categorically prohibited in Islam; and so on. Sabitha is vocal against these misogynies, but only when she is pushed to a corner. Even while she is critical of these practices, she also acknowledges other aspects where women and especially Saudi women, fare better in Saudi Arabia in comparison to their counterparts in Kerala. These include the dignified treatment women receive in hospitals (contrasting it to Kerala), the awareness that Saudi women have of their rights, and their bargaining power in the marriage market.

In the course of the plot, the novel often relapses into the early history of Islam, especially revolving around the transactions between Prophet Muhammad and his wives. Set in the holy city of Makkah, the place provides the necessary motivation for these explorations. The novel also has a magical realist element in the man who claims to be alive from the time of the Prophet and offers a counter narrative to some of the more established positions in Kerala Islam regarding Islamic history.

As is clear from the author's preface to the novel, the critical study which accompanies it, and the general response to the novel, the work is read as a feminist critique of Islam. The protagonist of the novel, Sabitha is a new convert to Islam (after falling in love with Rasheed, who is now her husband, has accompanied her to Saudi Arabia, and is working in a different hospital in Makkah as a physician) setting the stage for looking at Islam through the fresh eyes of someone who has just found it. The author's framing of the novel in the preface is completely from a woman's viewpoint of Islam. The preface tells us that though many of her well-wishers had warned her against publishing the novel, the work was received well, and she did not have to suffer the ill consequences of which she was warned.

However, what is lost in the din is the appraisal of this work as migrant writing. In the framing of the work, Saudi Islam was treated as universal Islam, and the occasional binary that the author posits between Islam as the protagonist experienced it in Kerala (as the sensorial pleasures in the get-togethers for Eid, the sweets, the neighbourly love) and its distance from what she knows about it in Saudi Arabia is completely erased, even by the author herself. Even as the author's preface towards its end, states that the novel is a product of the author's experiences in Saudi Arabia where she spent seven years as a medical practitioner, this fact has not had much bearing on the reception of the novel except as a setting to see the 'real' face of Islam. The author herself treats Saudi Arabia as the place that has (only) made 'more intense and clear' questions that she has had from her childhood.[40]

Precisely because *Barsa* offers valuable insights as a piece of migrant writing, it needs to be discussed as such.[41] The novel elaborates on the life of migrants in Saudi Arabia and offers an intimate view of the stark discrimination that female migrants suffer. The novel also gives detailed accounts of internal turbulences in Makkah, such as the siege of Makkah in 1979; and quotidian aspects of life in Makkah such as the constant construction and renovation of buildings and relocation of people. The novel features a wide range of institutional setting in the host country, such the hostel, hospital, police station, and so on.

Unlike the other Malayalam writings on the Gulf, the protagonist couple at the centre of *Barsa* have highly respected white-collar jobs. Both Rasheed

---

[40] Khadeeja Mumthas, Barsa (Kottayam: DC Books, 2021), 9.

[41] A recent and sole engagement with the work as a piece of diasporic literature is by Rajesh V. Nair who studies it along the template of alienation and displacement. While the novel indeed offers enough reasons to study it along those lines, my effort here, consistent with the rest of the chapter, is to see the host and home countries as connected.

See, Rajesh V. Nair, 'Remapping the Land: Displacement and Memory in Benyamin's *Aadujeevitham* and Khadeeja Mumtaz's *Barsa*', *Indian Literatures in Diaspora*, ed. Sireesha Telugu (Routledge, 2022).

and Sabitha are medical practitioners. Therefore, unlike in the other literary texts, the work-related issues in the novel are not of unemployment or concerning low wages. In the professional world of the couple, the jobs are not segregated based on race or gender. Nor are the men here 'bachelors' barred by law from bringing their spouses. It is a work space which has men and women working in close quarters, unlike the narrative of a menial labourer.

Sabitha's work space is teeming with many nationalities and languages. There are other (non-Malayali) Indians there, in addition to Egyptians, Filipinos, Pakistanis, Saudis, and Sudanese. The Saudis are paid four times that of the migrants.[42] The work place thus becomes a site in which racial and gender prejudices play out. Sabitha rues the advantage the Urdu-speaking Indians have over her because of the affinity of the Urdu script with Arabic. The entitlement of the Saudis, the partiality of the Egyptians, the cold professionalism of the Filipinos, are referred to in several instances. There is a constant undercurrent of patriarchy in Sabitha's workplace, which surfaces once in a while, and which is often at the receiving end of Sabitha's outspokenness. While the sartorial restrictions placed on women is on your face, the patriarchal undercurrent includes moral guardianship that some of the doctors display over the female migrant menial labourers who come to the hospital for various formalities connected to visa applications; discrimination in equal division of labour; and the hatred and fear around any instance of assertion by a female colleague. Rather than ignore them or read them as forms of Muslim patriarchy, as they have been framed in the vernacular scholarly literature, it is perhaps to be seen as the form taken by contestations around culture in a multicultural setting.[43] Thus, there are contestations around what constitutes Islamic practice among the characters even as they are all Muslim. An example is the criticism that female genital mutilation, acquiesced to by the Sudanese doctor, is a subject of criticism for the others. Importantly, these struggles point to a space of interaction among people belonging to various ethnicities, a zone which is denied

---

[42] Mumthas, *Barsa*, 118.

[43] An instance of the skewed reading of the novel can be seen in how the title itself is interpreted. The blurb of the novel says that 'Barsa' refers to a woman who does not cover her face, thus making it peculiar to a (sectarian) Islamic context, while in the novel the term is used to mean defiant women (86), an instance of which in the specific context is not covering the face.

to the existentially sedentary manual labourers we come across in Babu
Bharadwaj's memoirs.

Not only do we have in *Barsa* the workspace as a space of interracial
interaction, the novel also shows instances in which the seemingly im-
penetrable divide of racial and ethnic segregation is overcome. Unlike the
other Gulf migrant narratives in Malayalam, in *Barsa* we see and hear
of people who have acquired Saudi citizenship. Marriage becomes an instance in which the migrant subject can overcome one's locations at birth
and belong, in full respect, to the other. In *Barsa* we have Saudis engaging
in marital relations with the others, with the others enjoying the entitlement of the Saudis subsequently. The marriages happen both ways—that
is, Saudi men marrying migrant women as well as Saudi women marrying migrant men.

The racial nature of citizenship in the Gulf thus undergoes an interesting twist in Mumthas's writing. On the one hand, citizenship seems to
be not so exclusive after all. We come across people who have acquired
citizenship after long periods of stay in Saudi Arabia,[44] or through marriage. At the same time, the privilege of citizenship is so embodied that it
changes the bodily comportment of the new citizen. 'The Saudis cannot
work continuously. It is as if laziness is in their blood. Those other people
who acquire Saudi citizenship wear that laziness as if it is a right.'[45] The
cross-over from a migrant to the entitlement of a native is stark: they imitate the bodily comportment of entitlement in their newly beaming faces
and in their confidence. They can now be stern with their colleagues.

Ironically, it is not race but religion that stands in the way of integra-
tion. For Rasheed, the migrant life has been about going back to the roots
of Islam. He immerses himself in Islamic history, finds time to do Hajj
a few times even though imperfectly since medical practitioners are
not allowed to take leave during the peak season of the Hajj pilgrimage.
Rasheed then comes across an old man in a desolate street. The purpose
of the magic realist element in the novel, this old man who has been alive
since the time of the Prophet Muhammad and has experienced the history of Islam from its beginnings to the present, thus is able to give an

---

[44] Mumthas, *Barsa*, 44. Considering that *Barsa* recounts a time beginning in the late 1970s,
this aspect of citizenship suggests policies that were prevalent before the large-scale influx of migrant labourers.

[45] Mumthas, *Barsa*, 81. All translations from the book are mine unless specified otherwise.

intimate account of this history. This old man who has seen the Prophet's time, has been amputated by the Caliph Umar, one of the four righteous political successors of the Prophet, as a punishment for stealing. The old man has seen the corruption which set into the Islamic establishment after the reign of the first four Caliphs. His account is at odds with the version propagated by dominant Islam, to the point of denunciation of the dominant global Sunni Islam.

Ultimately, when they cannot resist the pull of their homeland, Sabitha has this to say to Rasheed: 'Rasheed, don't you have nostalgia? Was it me alone who decide to come back! I know you cannot be an Arabian Muslim. After seven years, it is not as if your roots have changed their soil.'[46] Rather than being the connector between the two lands, Islam becomes for the migrant, despite the fluidity of race and ethnicity, that the roots of which cannot be recovered in the present Arabia. It is precisely this nuanced reading of religion which the vernacular criticism, including that of the author herself, has overlooked in a unidimensional feminist framing of the novel.

The Oceanic Permanence in Krishnadas's Prose

Krishnadas occupies a very important position for the Gulf migrant publication in Malayalam. As the founder of the Thrissur-based Green Books, he is responsible for carving out a respectable position for writings on the Gulf in mainstream Malayalam literature. Established in 2003, the breakthrough for Green Books came in 2008 with the publication of Benyamin's debut novel *Aatujeevitham* which went on to become the most sold novel in Kerala's publishing history. The success of the novel announced the potential of Gulf narratives in terms of plots, themes, and marketability. In addition to adding fresh titles to their inventory, Green Books also republished some of the earlier Malayalam writings on the Gulf, such as Vijayan Puravur's *Salalah Salalah*.[47]

Krishnadas has also authored two books based on the Gulf: *Dubaipuzha*, which was initially published in 2001 and then republished by Green

---

[46] Mumthas, *Barsa*, 188.
[47] Vijayan Puravur, *Salalah Salalah* (Thrissur: Green Books, 2014).

Books in 2003[48], and *Katalirampangal*, published by Green Books in 2010. The time between the two books is marked by personal tragedies for the author, reflected in the melancholic tone of the latter when compared to the former. *Dubaipuzha*, a memoir which spans over three decades, begins with the migrant's landing in the Gulf as an undocumented migrant and the long walks through the barren lands that these migrants who reached the Gulf on a dhow had to undertake. While recollecting the Malayali migrant existence in the Gulf, the memoir gives glimpses of the political and cultural history of the Arabs beginning from the late 1960s. The memoir tells us of the time in which the British had their air regiment in Sharjah, of the coup in Sharjah, the formation of the Trucial States, and so on.

In Krishnadas the dominant mode of narrating the migrants is not as individuals but of their collective activities. The author recounts the functions of the arts club of the migrants, of the intense political debates, of the political naiveté and optimism of the left-leaning Malayali migrants in the waning years of the Cold War. One particular passage is worth recalling for what it says about the constantly changing world in the Gulf and the seeming nonchalance which age bestows on the disillusionments of one's youth. The passage is on Josephettan, a Communist sympathizer who used to argue (in the 1980s) that the absence of Russians and East Europeans in the Gulf points to the prosperity of the Eastern Bloc:

> Those were the eighties. Josephettan believed and made others believe in the infallibility and unassailability of the socialist block. Then, in the nineties Eastern Europe and Soviet Union disintegrated. For several of us it was a personal tragedy and we lost sleep for many days. I was sure Josephettan must have been shattered too. By that time he had returned to Kerala. And then, contrary to his belief, planeloads of Russians descended on Dubai, lured by the Arab riches.[49]

---

[48] The English translation of *Dubaipuzha* appeared under the same title in 2019. Krishnadas, *Dubai Puzha*, trans. Prabha R. Chatterji (Thrissur: Sand Dunes, 2019). The direct quotes are from this translation.

[49] Krishnadas, *Dubai Puzha*, 31.

In the collective acts of the Malayali literary club, the Gulf is thus turned into a space of existence.[50] In one poignant chapter he tells us of the destruction of the library, with all the books still in it, by the municipality authorities, as the migrants could not find another place to move the books. In Krishnadas's prose, narration turns the transience of the architecture of Dubai into the very means of constructing Dubai as a 'place of memory'.[51] Acts of memory become the sole means through which a historical continuity can be mapped in a world of constant change. With no 'museums, archives, cemeteries, festivals, anniversaries, treaties, depositions, monuments, sanctuaries, fraternal orders'[52] to commemorate them, words of remembrance become the act in which memory claims a place for itself.

One can already see on the part of Krishnadas a strategy of familiarizing the Gulf in the title, which literally translates as 'Dubai river'. What is referred to here is the Dubai creek, but the author translates a foreign geography into one which is more familiar to the Malayali audience. As the author notes:

Dubai puzha, Dubai river? There isn't anything like that—many summarily dismissed my imagery. A few others were little more accommodative: *Oh! You mean the creek?* Well, it is a matter of opinion, isn't it?. A narrow channel of seawater flowing inland—indeed it is a creek, the Dubai creek. But to my homesick mind it was a *river* and will ever remain so. *Dubai Puzha* brought back the riotous colors of my childhood and rejuvenated me.[53]

---

[50] 'Existence' in the sense in which Alain Badiou uses it; that is to suggest (borrowing from Heidegger) a worldliness and a stepping out, but with the focus away from the individual consciousness and insistence on multiplicity. See Alain Badiou, 'Towards a New Concept of Existence', *Lacanian Ink* 29 (2007). For Heidegger's concept of being, see Martin Heidegger, *Being and Time: A Translation of Sein und Zeit* (New York: State University of New York Press, 1996).

[51] On the transience of the urban space in Dubai, see Yasser Elsheshtawy, *Temporary Cities: Resisting Transience in Arabia* (London: Routledge, 2021). Pierre Nora identifies in 'places of memory' concretions which are required in a world in which the rituals of memory do not exist anymore. As can be seen, my use of him is contrarian, as that place which can only be through acts of memory, because all physical concreteness to them have been permanently lost. See, Pierre Nora, 'Between Memory and History: *Les Lieux de Mémoire*', *Representations* 26 (1989).

[52] Nora, 'Between Memory and History', 12.

[53] Krishnadas, *Dubai Puzha*, 19. Emphasis in the original.

On another occasion, the shore of Khor Fakkan is the scene of a ritual:

> Often my imagination takes wings and transports me to the shores of Khor Fakkan. There I stand clapping for the dear departed souls offering them a fistful of memories in homage ... Crows descend and crowd around me. Among them I search for Jawhar, Rajan, Babu ... and thousands more ... [54]

The shores of Khor Fakkan now substitutes for the shores in one's own land where the departed elders could be propitiated and their salvation sought. The familiar crows turn the foreign land into one's own. If the Gulf is temporary, it is in its temporariness, in the waves of the sea, and the flight of the crows, that one can relate back to familiar times.

Towards the end of the memoir, the author and his friends drive up the hills of Khor Fakkan and are greeted by the greenery there. Here, we come across this sentence, startling for its effect for its placement at the conclusion of a memoir that often referred to the land of the Gulf as alien:

> We drive through the mountain roads. Village farmers have set up roadside shops to sell their produce. In these fertile green valleys where tomato, tapioca, pomegranate, watermelon and cucumber flourish we wander with a sense of loss, not quite sure what exactly did we lose ... [55]

The sentence presents a searing sense of misplacement not only because of its placement at the end of the memoir, but also the setting of the action. Khor Fakkan is where the undocumented migrants disembarked after their adventurous journey on the dhow. It is that place where they first came face to face with the foreignness they were thrust into. 'Alien landscape, alien people, alien language, alien smells'[56] is how Khor Fakkan appears to the just arrived migrant. And yet, in three decades the alienation has transformed into an uncannily familiar sight, one which reminds of one's youth and of the land one left behind. Labour, of those in

---

[54] Krishnadas, *Dubai Puzha*, 186–187.
[55] Krishnadas, *Dubai Puzha*, 179.
[56] Krishnadas, *Dubai Puzha*, 42.

the cities and the countryside have created the familiar out of the strange. The labourer has created the world in his own image.

There are multiple levels of displacement here. One longs for home only to realize that one's surroundings have now transformed into what one was supposed to have left. In this process of destabilizing the otherness of the Other, the self is also destabilized. The self that longed for the effective geographies of home, when faced with the uncanny resemblance of the foreign to one's home, can only access the remembering self in a split subjectivity. One cannot but notice that even as the labourer recreates their environs in the harshness of the desert, his own world of ideation is now suffused with the foreign. Krishnadas's prose is especially remarkable for the evocation of Arabic literature, both from the pre-Islamic and Islamic eras to the time of Arab nationalism.[57] We come across lines from Amr bin Kulthoom, Badir Shakir al Sayyab, Imrul Qaiz, and so on. The self cannot speak without borrowing from the Other, thus suspending every community that finds its sustenance on presumptuous stable identities. Krishnadas's world is ever transforming and to belong to that world is to constantly move. Like with the spaces, the constant transformation is what provides Krishnadas's prose its locus of memory. In movement and change one grasps what one thought is lost.

As we move on to *Katalirampangal*, Krishnadas' second work on the Gulf—self-declaredly a novel but one that reads as if a continuation to the first memoir—the mood is dark and melancholic. The title refers to the roar of the seas. Deeply personal, the novel is a departure from the predominantly optimistic mood in *Dubaipuzha*. The migrants still exist

---

[57] Gulf is heavily mediated by figures of World literature in Bharadwaj's and Krishnadas's prose. The use of motifs and quotations from these writers are a way of mediating the strangeness of the Gulf at a time when the representation of the Gulf has to convey the strangeness of the place in the wake of the oil boom and the collective memory of Arabia as a place one is familiar with, against the erasure affected by the fast transformations in the Gulf as well as in the migrant practices in Kerala.

However, one could see more to the use of the world literature icons. Pascale Casanova alerts us to the field of struggle that literary production is and the role that it plays in this as authorities of consecration and as resource of accumulation. See Pascale Casanova, 'Consecration and Accumulation of Literary Capital: Translation as Unequal Exchange', trans. Siobhan Brownlie, in *Critical Readings in Translation Studies*, ed. Mona Baker (London and New York: Routledge, 2010).Though not strictly in the sense employed by Casanova, the invocation of the world literary figures is aimed at bolstering the intellectual credentials of the Gulf writer. For a discussion, see Mohamed Shafeeq Karinkurayil, 'Indian Gulf Writing', in *Oxford Handbook of Modern Indian Literatures*, eds Ulka Anjaria and Anjali Nerlekar (Oxford University Press, 2023 [published online ahead of print]), doi: 10.1093/oxfordhb/9780197647912.013.38.

in their collective bodies and engage in collective and creative acts, but death, as the final word on all association, haunts these pages. The death of the author's mother casts heavy shadows on the narrative, and one after the other, it is a saga of losses—the loss of one's youth, of intimate relations, of the capacity to connect with others. Even as the collective life moves forward, there is always the pulling back to the personal, as if a look of mortality now defines every scene. Take this example from the time in which the author's comrades are imprisoned in the UAE for staging a play deemed to be blasphemous:

> Then I meet T. K. Ramakrishnan,[58] the minister for cultural affairs [of Kerala—*auth.*]. He began shouting like he has lost all sense of the setting, 'It seems Bhuvanachandran's complaints won't end. (He says) That we haven't done anything to rescue him and his friends in jail. This is not right!' T.K. began explaining his position. He is trying to speak like an energetic youth. I paid attention. But in the flow of time he has become old. His voice fails, there is confusion in it.[59]

One cannot miss the allusion to life being a poor player strutting and fretting its way to death. The revolutionary zeal gives way, as if in a reflection of the shift in global politics, to a tone of helplessness. Just like the poor player who is observed, the self finds itself unable to be completely in the scene. The intimations of death offer a new look at the scene, a vision that refuses to be subsumed in it and exists as an excess to it. It is as if everyone finds themselves out of place and memory is the only place where one could properly belong.[60]

---

[58] T. K. Ramakrishnan (1921–2006) was a Communist leader and served several terms as an elected representative in the Kerala Legislative Assembly.

[59] Krishnadas, *Katalirampangal* (Thrissur: Green Books, 2010), 178. Translation mine.

[60] In these memoirs, what is remembered is the time in the Gulf, where the migrants have migrated to. When memory is studied with relation to migration, it often gets associated with 'home'. See Sabine Marschall, 'Memory, migration and travel: introduction', in *Memory, Migration and Travel*, ed. Sabine Marschall (London and New York: Routledge, 2018).

While this is true for much of Gulf literatures of migration, this relation is also inverted once the memoir looks back on the Gulf. Here then, it is the Gulf that is remembered, from the vantage of home and the years that has passed between one's years of migration and the present. Bharadwaj's memoirs takes shape after he is back in Kerala and so is the case with Krishnadas. This inverted relation should draw our attention to how circular migration, such as the one from Kerala to the countries of the Gulf, in which the migrants are not offered the possibility of settling down in the receiving countries, is mostly invisible in diaspora studies.

Creatures of a Different World

Sonia Rafeek's *Herbarium* (2017) narrates the transformation of a boy, Tipu, from an online game junkie to one who is deeply sensitive about nature around him. Tipu, his father Asif, and mother Fathima were residents of Dubai, and after his mother disappears by a lake in the UAE, Tipu is sent to Kerala by his father. In Kerala Tipu discovers, much like his mother in her childhood, the distinctive multi-sensorial dimensions of the day and night, the various forms of life around him, and the enchantments of the serpent grove in the neighbourhood. These are under attack, however, from a motley group of antagonists who include the indifferent landowner of the grove, the property developer who is concerned only about money, and the cunning wildlife enthusiasts whose eyes are set on the profits of trafficking wildlife. The events that follow in the novel pitch Tipu and his friends and their parents against these villainous forces. Just as Tipu discovers nature around him, Asif gets to know more about his wife through her short notes he finds in various nooks and corners of their house in Dubai and in Kerala, and the two individual trajectories of discovery converge in the need to protect the serpent grove from the marauders.

The novel's narration switches between various registers. The ongoing present is interwoven in narration with dreams, memories, the augmented reality of the video games, lessons in natural history, and a brief interlude with a tortoise in the first person. The novel brings to its narrative agency the simultaneity of the various modes we inhabit, that of the disenchanted development, the fantasy spaces of computer games, the altered realities of the dreams, and of the life around us. The novel pleads with us to see about us more clearly and do something about the destruction of the wildlife around us. The figure of the boy from elsewhere provides the locus through which our surroundings can now be freshly apprehended. In this scheme of things, Dubai and Kerala are the two sides of the binary, in which the former stands for unbridled capitalist expansion and an artificial form of life, and the other for a life in which one is conversant with nature around it. However, the two spaces are in relay, and there are occult portals that connect them. These connections offer us a new idiom to think about migration, one that is based on a language of care rather than of right.

The novel begins with Asif's recollection of Fathima's efforts to grow the curry tree in the balcony of their Dubai apartment. The curry leaf is known to be sturdy and resilient, and yet it cannot stand the burning summer of Dubai. Fathima's characterization of the fate of the curry tree is in a self-reflexive vein, that she, too, however resilient and open to change, finds herself challenged to the core in Dubai. Her husband Asif, however, is at home in Dubai, precisely because he has no home. In a different episode, Fathima compares Asif to the migratory birds, who 'will never be migrants wherever they are'.[61] To migrate is also to belong elsewhere.

As a novel that shows the embeddedness of human life in the elements around it, Rafeek's novel exhibits a migrant consciousness which brings the migrant and the creatures that inhabit it but is invisibilized in human culture into a single register. Here is her description when a housefly enters their apartment in Dubai:

A housefly has entered through the gap on opening the balcony. Now Asif will have to show it the way out. Or else it will wander in this flat, not knowing if it is a guest or an invader. 'The unwise move of the one coming in without an idea of the way out', thought Asif, and decided to let it suffer for it.[62]

The confusion of one's own status between being a guest or an invader alludes to the status of migrant workers in the Gulf as 'guest workers' while the uneven structures that order their stay, work, and life in the Gulf treat them belligerently, as if they were an invader. The worker who enters the Gulf 'temporarily' however finds themselves unable to get out due to the indebtedness that define their stay. This indebtedness takes the discourse of being hosted by a foreign country and its benevolent rulers, being indebted to the establishment one is working for, being indebted to the host of people who facilitated the migrant's stay including those who lent them money at home, and the middlemen who arranged their employment visa. The cosmopolitan view of life, in which one's agency

---

[61] Sonia Rafeek, *Herbarium* (Kottayam: DC Books, 2018), 25. All translations from the book are mine.

[62] Rafeek, *Herbarium*, 11.

to negotiate borders is paramount, represented here by Asif, scoffs at the situation as the sufferer's *choice*.

In another context, the migrant workers are compared to the microbes that are all around, but unknown, to us:

> What would these people's lives be like! No visa, no passport, just living somehow, eight-ten people in a matchbox, like boxed sardines; these were Fathima's words on the Bangaldeshi who comes to clean the apartment. An alter life form who descends from another world to ours to mop and wash dishes and sweep away cobwebs. The way they send their roots down the earth and absorb energy is different [from ours]. Fathima had written in her notes too that only the sun, moon and wind stay the same between them and us. The Bangladeshi and friends have a different world, like bacteria in a petri dish; a world which goes unnoticed even though it doesn't require a microscope [to see it].[63]

The life of the precarious migrant labour is compared to the world of the microbes and that of the critters below the leaf litter of the grove. The brief paragraph also brings to the fore the class and ethnicity differences between the migrants, and how often class and ethnicity go together in migrant conditions, thanks to the networked nature of migrations where 'networks migrate, categories stay put'.[64] The impossibility of a migrant solidarity overlooking the many differences that mark the migrants is transposed as the invisibility of the worlds the precarious migrant subjects inhabit.

The precarity of the low-class migrant labour is matched by the precarity of the life forms we don't care to see. Among these life forms is the serpent grove in Kerala which is now threatened by the local rich man who made his riches in the Gulf by buttering up his Arab *arbab*. While the Gulf extends its arms to Kerala, the serpent grove and its elemental forces find their portals in the Gulf. The Tilapia Lake in Al Ain, that eerie oasis teeming with the flesh-eating tilapia in the middle of the desert is the portal in the Gulf that propels the plot forward in the novel. Fathima

---

[63] Rafeek, *Herbarium*, 102.

[64] Charles Tilly, 'Transplanted Networks', in *Collective Violence, Contentious Politics, and Social Change*, eds Ernesto Castaneda and Cathy Lisa Schneider (New York: Routledge, 2017), 312.

finds her final resting place devoured by the elements in the tilapia lake. Her demise finally makes her vicariously alive through her letters, and through Tipu discovering the world around him, the world which was Fathima's as she was growing up, the one she had to leave behind in leaving for Dubai as Asif's wife. By ordering the life of her loved ones from an invisible place, Fathima achieves an analogical parity with the labouring migrant class, relayed among others through the figure of fish, among whom she now resides.

In a world marred by class differences and indifference to nature, to properly belong is to be with the elements around us, in a relocation of one's ontic moorings against egocentric epistemology. Fathima's consummation in a lake in the middle of the desert that is reminiscent of the grove in the neighbourhood of her home in Kerala allows the time in the novel to return to a past, as a way of recounting the similarities between her and her son, and as the voice in the letters that frames and drives the lives of those she left behind. The world of the invisible, which marks the precarious migrant labour and of the life around us, is the final destination of freedom and self-determination. In the depths of the lake and the impenetrability of the forests, Rafeek's characters find the vitality to move the world. It is by displacing the life force of the central characters from one of human volition to one which requires jettisoning any episteme of seeing human as distinct from nature that this novel seeks to reorient the world. Taking the analogy further, the novel is an indictment of any schema which presupposes an original. The community, whether that of nation, of native, or of migrants, is made in depths opening itself to other worlds. The creation is *ex nihilo*, out-of-nothing where 'nothing' is 'the interstice of the intimacy of the world: the *among-being* […] of all beings'.[65]

Even though ghettoized in the Gulf, the migrant writing gives us several instances in which the migrants make possible a world of translation, transaction, and traversal of identities. Some of these movements fail, such as in Sageer's *Gulfumpadi*, some others try to build links anew. While the space of the memoir becomes the only one in which the Gulf migrants can be brought together to form a community in Bharadwaj's work, as has

---

[65] Jean-Luc Nancy, *Being Singular Plural*, trans. Robert D. Richardson and Anne E. O'Byrne (Stanford, CA: Stanford University Press, 2000), 16.

been noted elsewhere, in Krishnadas, the work of translation transposes identities such that Dubai becomes Kerala and vice versa. The stark cuts and blurs that Krishnadas deploys in his text through these transpositions which effects time–space alterations ultimately puts to question the very truth of migration. Rather than comforting, Krishnadas' transversal of the spaces is confusing and disturbing. If Khor Fakkan has become Kerala, then has one migrated after all? Interestingly it also therefore implies a different question—that of the native who can now only live his present in a similar disjuncture because the memory of the place appears as if it belongs to an other. It is in these disjunctures, in the story of loss, that Krishnadas can imagine a community.

While the effort in this chapter has been to look at the connections sought through Malayalam across spacetimes, in an act of minor cosmopolitanism, in the next chapter the focus is on the carving out of exclusive and intimate zones of belonging within the speech community. The motive and rationale for such a community is found in the condition of imposed silence. Speech and silence intersect in these ciphers.

4

The Dead Ends and Alleyways

Writing the Borderland II

The Gulf migration can be a zone of the breakdown of speech and the zone of silence. It can be distancing for those who have not experienced it. As we have seen in the last chapter, it would take a final outpouring of speech to make the experience (partly) relatable.[1] This chapter, however, is interested in its obverse: is it possible for us to imagine a community with the breakdown of speech as its condition of possibility? What would be the structural conditions of this breakdown? What form will such a community take? What will keep it together, and what will drive it in directions? These are the concerns of this chapter. If the overarching unity of the novel might be consummated only in the figure of the reading subject through 'the process of anticipation and retrospection, the consequent unfolding of the text as a living event, and the resultant impression of life-likeness',[2] this chapter will show the frustration of this overarching unity in the texts under study. The chapter will illustrate that such dead ends of language make these texts instances of performances that cleave a zone of alternate public.[3] Caused by the logic of global capital as it operates in the specific migratory relation between Kerala and the Gulf, such an alternate

---

[1] For an exploration on this, see also Gayathri Prabhu, 'A gulf of secrets: Priya Kuriyan's graphic memoir "Ebony and Ivory"', *Journal of Commonwealth Literature* 58, no. 1 (2023).

[2] Wolfgang Iser, 'The Reading Process: A Phenomenological Approach', *New Literary History* 3, no. 2 (1972), 296.

[3] The 'public' is a discursive performance. Texts and genres are integral to the constitution of a public sphere. As Michael Warner puts it, 'The making of a public requires conditions that range from the very general—such as the organization of media, ideologies of reading, institutions of circulation, text genres—to the particular rhetorics of texts.' See Michael Warner, *Publics and Counterpublics* (New York: Zone Books, 2002), 14.

The Gulf Migrant Archives in Kerala. Mohamed Shafeeq Karinkurayil, Oxford University Press. © Mohamed Shafeeq Karinkurayil 2024. DOI: 10.1093/9780198910619.003.0005

public points to the limits of migrant assertions while also telling us of the efficacy of communities formed under the sign of globalization.

The logic of migration to the Gulf depends, on the one hand, on the network of the migrant labourers and its tenacity, but also on the other, the possibility of betrayal lurking within this very network as an agent who is out to make money selling one's trust and goodwill. The logic of migrant flows organized in the *kafala* system is dependent on a host of middlemen. These middlemen are often other migrants. In most Malayalam migrant literary works, the Arabs are mostly absent except as lessors, while much of the exploitation (which benefits the Arabs too) is undertaken by migrants themselves.[4] This logic suspends any already available migrant community as the starting point of analysis, and requires us to investigate the construction of a community as a tentative act. The community of the migrant literature to the Gulf therefore has to be seen as transient in themselves, and enacted through translations. In this chapter we look at untranslatability as the means of producing an affective community. The focus is here on communities formed through exclusions and through a breakdown rather than the bridging capacity of speech.

This chapter looks at two novels of Gulf migration for their enactment of borders which temporarily activate a community in the face of the structural impossibility of community formation. These novels are Benyamin's *Aatujeevitham/Goat Days* and Deepak Unnikrishnan's *Temporary People*. The novels are read as instances of 'borderland writing', generating a conceptual field where "word and act, varying idioms, intellectual legacies, and cultural memories are engaged in confrontation, negotiation, and conversation".[5] My method in what follows is to look at the epistemic discontinuities and incongruences in these two novels

[4] Mohamed Shafeeq Karinkurayil, 'Indian Gulf Writing', in *Oxford Handbook of Modern Indian Literatures*, eds Ulka Anjaria and Anjali Nerlekar (Oxford University Press, 2023 [published online ahead of print]), doi: 10.1093/oxfordhb/9780197647912.013.38.

[5] Azade Seyhan, *Writing Outside the Nation* (Princeton, NJ and Oxford: Princeton University Press, 2001), 103. This is in contrast to the more dominant approach to the relation between novels and nations. In his landmark study on nationalism, Benedict Anderson shows the form of the novel to be that which made possible the imagination of a homogenous empty time. Novels have been credited with the arrival of a new subjectivity which can place itself in the world along a horizontal organization and have a totalizing vision of the world. In that respect it has been studied as the cognitive infrastructure for the birth of bourgeoisie. See Benedict Anderson, *Imagined Communities: Reflections on the Origins and Spread of Nationalism*

and read them as the tentative erection of a border in which the pleasurable intimacies of an affective community find temporary refuge. In referring to the affective nature of this community, I am also moving away from the notion of a public sphere as formed through debate and dialogue.[6] It has been shown that when identities cannot be acknowledged in the public sphere, they often take the form of affective communities converging around icons.[7] Affect sustains the public when dialogue and debate fail.[8] In turning to affective communities, I am looking at the ways in which community formation happens among the migrants to the Gulf in the face of the active denial of a public sphere through the segregatory practices and surveillance, a condition which affects not just the Gulf but increasingly even the so-called liberal democracies. In the absence of a common public sphere, the communities have to be formed in silences and ciphers, and participated in, in a mode of belonging rather than of deliberation. At the same time, the belonging as attachment to fetishes and symbols and ciphers is also to be seen as part of the effecting a particular type of public sphere, one which can as well be a part of dominant design as it can be a site of resistance.

The Secret Pleasures of Transliteration: *Goat Days*

In the preface to his spectacularly successful novel *Aatujeevitham*, the novelist Benyamin terms his work to be the final fulfilment of that

---

(London and New York: Verso, 1991); Nancy Armstrong, *How Novels Think: The Limits of British Individualism from 1719–1900* (New York: Columbia University Press, 2006).

[6] This conceptualization of public sphere is the legacy of Jurgen Habermas, *The Structural Transformation of the Public Sphere: An Inquiry into a Category of Bourgeois Society* (Cambridge, MA: MIT Press, 1989). Such a notion of public sphere might be more fanciful than reality, as pointed out by Nancy Fraser with relation to gender. Oskar Negt and Alexander Kluge have questioned the seeming openness of the public sphere, arguing it to be rather multiply localized. See Nancy Fraser, 'Rethinking the public sphere: A contribution to the critique of actually existing democracy', *Social Text*, nos 25/26 (1990); Oskar Negt and Alexander Kluge, *Public Sphere and Experience: Analysis of the Bourgeois and Proletarian Public Sphere* (London and New York: Verso, 2016).
[7] Thomas Blom Hansen, *Wages of Violence: Naming and Identity in Postcolonial Bombay* (Princeton, NJ: Princeton University Press, 2002); M. Madhava Prasad, *Cine-Politics: Film Stars and Political Existence in South India* (Hyderabad: Orient Blackswan, 2014).
[8] William Mazzarella, 'Affect: What is it Good for?', in *Enchantments of Modernity: Empire, Nation, Globalization*, ed. Saurabh Dube (London, New York, and New Delhi: Routledge, 2009).

age-old wish that the Gulf (migrant) may produce literature on the real conditions of living in the Gulf. Benyamin was a migrant labourer in the Gulf state of Bahrain for more than two decades. *Aatujeevitham* was his debut novel, originally published in Malayalam in 2008 and translated into English in 2012 by Joseph Koyippally as *Goat Days*.[9] The novel won several awards including the Abu Dhabi Shakti Award and the Kerala Sahitya Akademi Award. It is also among the most sold novel in the history of Malayalam literature. Benyamin, who is now a prolific novelist and a mainstay of Malayalam literary culture, would write two more novels—*Mullappooniramulla Pakalukal* (2014, trans. Shahnaz Habib, 2018[10]—winner of JCB Prize for Literature 2018) and *Al Arabian Novel Factory* (2014, trans. Shahnaz Habib, 2019)[11], centred on life in the Gulf. The unexpected and unprecedented success of *Goat Days* has made the appearance of Gulf migrant literature more feasible than it was previously in the mainstream press in Kerala. While Green Books, the publisher of *Aatujeevitham*, has expanded its catalogue of Gulf migrant writing, the dominant players in the field—Kottayam-based DC Books and Kozhikode-based Mathrubhumi books—now feature many Gulf-migrant writings in their offering.

Goat Days, written in the first person, is the story of Najeeb, a migrant labourer from Kerala, who finds himself in the deserts of Saudi Arabia, having to tend the goats of his Arab master, in conditions approximating slavery if not slavery itself, with no human company except for his *arbab*, or the Master, with minimal food and water and no shelter, under constant threat of physical violence and even extermination—'an alien planet inhabited by some goats, my *arbab* and me'.[12] The novel narrates Najeeb's extraordinary life in the desert and his eventual escape. The 'Author's Note' which appears at the end of *Goat Days* attributes the novel to the conversations that the novelist had with (the real life) Najeeb, the (referential) protagonist of the novel.

---

[9] Benyamin, *Goat Days*, trans. Joseph Koyippally (Gurgaon: Penguin Books India, 2012).
[10] Benyamin, *Mullappooniramulla Pakalukal* (Kottayam: DC Books, 2014); Benyamin, *Jasmine Days*, trans. Shahnaz Habib (New Delhi: Juggernaut Books, 2018).
[11] Benyamin, *Al Arabian Novel Factory* (Kottayam: DC Books, 2014); Benyamin, *Al Arabian Novel Factory*, trans. Shahnaz Habib (New Delhi: Juggernaut Books, 2019).
[12] Benyamin, *Goat Days*, 125.

When I went to meet Najeeb for the first time, I had no intention of creating a novel out of his story. I was curious only to know a man who had been through so much in life. But as I learned more about his experience, I couldn't fight the urge to write about it. How many millions of Malayalis live in the Gulf? How many millions have lived and returned to the homeland! But how many of them have really experienced the severity of the desert? I didn't sugarcoat Najeeb's story or fluff it up to please the reader. Even without that, Najeeb's story deserves to be read.[13]

The novelist discounts his own creativity and wants to place himself as a mere scribe. This assertion of relayed authorship, even as a literary device, merits attention. By turning himself into a scribe, the novelist points towards real life experiences that one wouldn't believe had one not learned it from the experienced themselves. These two aspects, one, a story which is too strange to be believed, and two, the need to believe it nevertheless because it is coming straight out of a person's experience sans any creativity involved in transit, thereby implies the mode of revelation. In the appendix to the Malayalam novel, Benyamin calls *Aatujeevitham* a story for which the Gulf literary mind has been thirsting, and himself as the one who was destined to say it.[14] This characterization of the novel as the story which narrates the hitherto untold story of the Gulf experience and the novelist himself as the scribe, is therefore the novel's own plea to be taken as representative of a population.

Benyamin, in the appendix to the Malayalam novel (not available in the English translation), tells us that for many years now every litterateur from Kerala who has visited the Gulf has been urging the writers there (from among the Malayali community) 'to tell the world a story from among you. That the world of readers is awaiting it'.[15] As the first novel which set out to open up this world to the literary public of Malayalam, it is therefore instructive to look at how this unique experience is translated into the language which forms the literary public at home. The example cannot be more literal (and allegorical) than this:

[13] Benyamin, *Goat Days*, 255.
[14] Benyamin, *Aatujeevitham* (Thrissur: Green Books, 2008), 212.
[15] Benyamin, *Aatujeevitham*, 212. Translation mine.

Lying on my sheet, I tried to remember the Arabic words I learned that day and their meanings. It had only been two days. But I felt that I had learned more words than necessary.

arbab	saviour
masara	house of the goats
khubus	the only food that I might get here
mayin	a very rare liquid to be carefully used (Please do not trivialize it as mere 'water.' What the *arbab* feels about *mayin* is not comparable to our attitude towards water).
ganam	goat
haleeb	milk
thibin	grass
barsi	hay
jamal	camel
la	no
ji haam	yes, *arbab*
yaallah	get lost[16]

Instead of giving us a straightforward glossary, the Arabic words that Najeeb learned in the first couple of days comes to us wrapped in his own life. Perhaps the name of the oppressive Master translating itself as 'saviour' is a cruel irony. But as we move on, we aren't sure if the meanings are thus neutral. *Khubus* is the only food he might get there. But what food is that? An elementary familiarity with fast food shops in Kerala will let us know that it is the Arabic bread. Like *roti*. The meaning provided for *khubus* indicates that this glossary is not to be treated as a dispassionate truth. We move on to *mayin* to figure out that it is both water and not water. The account for what *mayin* is is both sober and playful at the same time. It is sober for it is linked to how miserable Najeeb's life is. It is at the same time playful, because in the very warning to not trivialize, there is the account of the absurdity of the situation in which Najeeb finds himself. The impossibility of translating *mayin* is not because it doesn't have a linguistic equivalent, but because the translator finds himself unable to bridge between the feelings of the language user with the substitute word

---

[16] Benyamin, *Goat Days*, 96.

that he is familiar with. Language finds itself in an uncanny relation with itself, when faced with these foreign feelings. The playfulness is having to call water a very rare liquid, while at the same time being aware that it is water, what defines life on earth itself. One would recall here that before migrating to the Gulf, Najeeb was a sandminer who had to spend long hours in the riverbed and had developed a persistent cough and cold because of this continuous exposure to a body of water.

Having encountered such interested and congealing prose, words cannot be taken at face value anymore. We reach *ji haam* and it punctures a hole in the narrator's credibility. Isn't that Hindustani? Can the author even identify languages before he gives us his dictionary? Or does it mean that even in that alien space of words and things, that primordial desert when the story of humankind is staged in the purest of class struggle, a foreign language is reserved to register servility? *Ji haam* brings in a defamiliarizing effect on the boundedness of our imagined origins. For an *arbab* who is said to understand no language other than Arabic, *ji haam* becomes the foreign expression that guarantees the stability of his universe. Having destabilized the host language through a teasing take on *khubus* and *mayin*, the dictionary now seeks to unsettle the assumed stability of the foreign Master by inserting a somewhat familiar (for the reader, but not for Najeeb, however) migrant word among the unfamiliar ones of the Master's tongue. At the same time, one cannot but see that this in itself is provided as a cipher. Either you are familiar with it or you are not, either you get it or you don't, suggesting the many possibilities at play in language.

My next example is when Najeeb is tasked by his *arbab* and the latter's friend (another *arbab*) to catch some goats, to be taken to the market:

> They would point to the masara and say, 'Aadi abiyad.' I wouldn't understand which one. Thinking that it was the goat next to me, I would try to catch it. 'Himar, maafi aswad, abiyad, abiyad,' the arbabs would holler. Realizing that it was not that one, I would try to catch a bigger one. 'Himar, much maafi inti, aadi abiyad,' the arbab would hit my head. Only after many mistakes did I finally realize that the arbab was asking me to catch the white he-goat.[17]

---

[17] Benyamin, *Goat Days*, 102–103.

What exactly do those italicized words mean? '*Himar, maafi aswad, abiyad, abiyad*', '*himar, much maafi inti, aadi abiyad*'—all those words just to indicate the colour of the goat to be caught? That cannot be. But we are not told what they mean. This is arguably so that we experience what Najeeb goes through—that these are just sounds shrouded in mystery.

Aatujeevitham/Goat Days is internally focalised and written from the first-person perspective. What we have in the novel is the desert as a dystopian space. Playing out for much of the narrative between the protagonist and his Arab master, it is as if the novel dramatizes the primal struggle between the migrant and the native. Najeeb doesn't understand the Master's language, and vice versa, making this a confrontation with the absolute Other, the one who, ironically in this instance, guarantees the openness of this world.[18] Given that this paragraph is from the first-person perspective and that that first person is uncomprehending of the strange word sounds that light up the paragraph, it surely doesn't matter if the reader too doesn't understand these words. By the logic of the paragraph, to identify with the protagonist would be to not get these words. The schema of the paragraph is attained in its last sentence. Najeeb did realize that the *arbab* was asking him to catch a particular goat, which he does. We also realize that Najeeb doesn't understand the language.

The foreignness of the world and the language in which that world is worlded has already been communicated. Clearly one can move on. But, anyone with a rudimentary knowledge of Arabic, that is, among others, anyone with a minimal experience of migration to the Gulf, may be expected to recognize these words. Recognition, more visceral than cognition, flashes through in these 'foreign' words. These words are not the guttural nonsense that parodies the Arab in stand-up comedies. These are words that are now part of the migrant's bodily archive. And they are available for the flash of recognition despite what the paragraph tells us and implies in function: that these are unintelligible words, that Najeeb doesn't understand them, and that since we are let into this world only through Najeeb's perspective, its function is to stay unintelligible.

---

[18] The absolute Other is Emmanuel Levinas' figure to think beyond all cloistering thought systems. See Emmanuel Levinas, *Totality and Infinity* (Pittsburg, PA: Duquesne University Press, 1969).

These words usher the flash of recognition because the author has transcribed actually existing words into Malayalam (Malayalam does not have markers for several sounds in Arabic). The migrant recognizes in them not their meanings, but also the force with which these words unleash themselves and lodge themselves in the jitteriness of one's hand, in the sudden vacuity in the midriff. '*Himar*', the word rings in him, twice in the paragraph, perhaps many times over. The issue is not of puns, or polysemy, but multiple pathways of selective admission to recognition that are open behind the screen, leaving minimal clues to the public who enter the lobby of this fiction.

The assumed primal struggle between the native and the migrant appears more complicated now. Clearly the text speaks in ciphers. The words '*aadi abiyad, himar maafi aswad*, etc. operates as border checks. The supposed homogeneity that make up the speech community is divided at the border. Some can pass through while some cannot. The border is of course not set in stone. They move. These words can be translated by someone in the know. You would have then crossed the border. Everyone may forget these words some day. The border would have moved again. Even more interestingly, the border does not even present itself as a border. It operates as the zone of recirculation where those who are turned back may not even recognize there being a border precisely because the paragraph orders the word as ultimately inconsequential, serving its diegetic purpose in its unintelligibility. In Azade Seyhan's words, 'borderlands accommodates many variants of unofficial, hybrid, and carnivalesque speech forms, languages for which there are no official dictionaries'.[19] And yet these words do have meaning, and more importantly, these words affect.

What these words have done is to carve an exclusive zone of enjoyment. An intimate public with a specious oneness with the linguistic community but which has now been ordered and bordered by the experience of migration. Some are in the know. Words become the site of secret pleasures. They congeal with affects in their meanings, in the superfluity of their meanings. The words erect a cult of experience. It is because these words can hide in their foreignness that these words can become the site

---

[19] Seyhan, *Writing Outside the Nation*, 116.

of secret recognitions. The hollowness of the words in the paragraph hide the immense pleasure that fill these words at the moment of the particular readings of it. In effect, while playing out the existential duel between the Master and the Slave, the migrant narrative effected another less noticed border, between the migrant and the non-migrant within the sending community. The migrant jealously guarded a zone of exclusive enjoyment over the non-migrant; a fragile one at the same time. In doing this, the Arab figure is turned into the empty image of the primitive slave owner for some, but detailed with Arab masters of one's life for the others. The secret pleasure thus also becomes the zone of incommunicability of the migrant experience.

The instability of a boundary between the Arab and his migrant slave, as witnessed in the seepage of words from one universe into the other on both sides of the divide, of *ji haam* from here to there, of *abyad*, *aswad*, and others from there to here, also signals the insecurity of this world. This is a world of *kafala*, variously identified by scholars as a type of bonded labour or even slavery. In this system, the migrant labourer is bound to his sponsor, known as the *kafeel* and usually a native, without whose permission he is not allowed to switch jobs or even return home.

However, what is also corrosive about the system is how it is a system which benefits not just the state and the native sponsor but also a host of middlemen which include even people from amongst the migrants. It is therefore a system which breaches the barricades of the migrant community, thus problematizing any migrant solidarity that is taken for granted. Such a system is bound to generate a pervasive sense of mutual suspicion and of being exposed. In the world in which *kafala* operates in pervasive tentacles of self-interest and betrayal, where the middlemen blur the possibilities of migrant solidarity, the pleasures of the cipher is a desperate attempt to imagine a community despite the hopelessness. After all that transpired in Najeeb's life, the excruciating life of the slave, the dehumanization involved, and the eventual escape from the dystopic desert, a question lingers in his mind, one that he wants to get over, not because it is unimportant but because it is overwhelming:

Karuvatta's brother-in-law later swore that he had not arranged for a shepherd's visa for me. It was the visa of a helper in a construction company. Lord only knew who spoke the truth. I am not going to lose my

sleep thinking about it. It was my destiny to walk into that life. I over-
came it. I am not going to think any deeper about it. If I did, I would
surely become crazy.[20]

While the novel highlights the role of the migrant Malayali community in the Gulf in helping Najeeb through various stages after his escape
from the desert, and despite the security he feels around them, this is ultimately a question that remains in Najeeb. This impossibility to be sure
of the affinities of one's extended social network upsets the earlier neat
contrast between the oppressor and the oppressed. On whose side is the
friend's brother-in-law? This question, the indulgence of which the narrator is afraid will lead him to losing his sanity, is so overwhelming because it denies the migrant a safe zone of belonging. 'Lord only knew who
spoke the truth.' It points out that a community of migrants is of porous
borders and it is not possible anymore to have a neat division between the
oppressor and the oppressed.

To go back then, to the question of the foreign words—*masara, mayin,
khubus, himar, abyad, aswad*—what are all these foreign tongues doing
in a Malayalam novel? What do they intend to convey? What foreignness
flashes through in a novel that should have been an act of confiding?

The borderland is characterised by a multitude of languages and epis-
temologies. The borderland does not allow a walling in of the community
from what is outside. The borders are porous. The community is therefore
always tentative, and beset by risks of infiltration. Words are burdened
with extra tasks here—to be a cipher even as it dissimulates universal intelligibility. The paradigm of border allows us to study the gulf within the
homogenous speech community that hides behind obscurities and enacts its intimacies away from the public gaze.

Here, a community is performed without addressing them, in the guise
of neglecting their existence, in the order of an intimacy expressible only
in sweet and terrible nothings. Aided by a network, 'every migrant makes
their journey through unformed signifiers and sounds that do not mean
anything but play in the background of his sleep with their curious twists,
suspenseful pauses, unforeseen elongations, startling comebacks and

---

[20] Benyamin. *Goat Days*, 251.

happy conjoinings'.[21] Someday these words would be familiar, someday the migrant would be different. And that day he/she would know how to be familiar with those who are different, in a desperate act to keep faith.

Benyamin's *Goat Days* is perceived to be that novel which finally dynamited the dream that was the Gulf by exposing the harsh conditions of labour that existed for most migrant labourers.[22] The novel aims to 'expose the alienation, deception and exploitation to which low-class migrant workers in the Gulf are vulnerable because of policies such as *kafāla*'.[23] While the Gulf migrants have steadily been writing for their longing to return, the fact that they do not return has often cast their nostalgia as of purely poetic value and devoid of any real intent. The migrant on the other hand does not make public the actual conditions of his labour, because employed in a multitude of jobs that are considered lowly—such as that of cleaner, cook, gardener, farm labourer, domestic labourer, sex worker, etc.—in the home culture which had a history of caste-assigned jobs (which in some ways still persists), the ignorance about their actual living conditions benefitted both the status of the migrant and of his/her folks back home. While the migrants have been producing literature, often in publications brought out by migrants themselves, such as the annual souvenirs of their cultural organization, the fact that Benyamin's *Goat Days* came as a revelation is not to be attributed to the migrants' low skills as writers, but to the inability of the harsh conditions of the Gulf being said out in a genre of public speech for it would destroy not just the migrants' own value but also call out the pleasures of those at home. What Benyamin did was to expose the silence while also sustaining the pleasures of an inside knowledge.

As illustrated earlier, my argument is that *Aatujeevitham/Goat Days*, despite being the eye-opener it is supposed to be, found for the migrant enclaves of belonging away from the prying eyes of the non-migrants at

---

[21] Mohamed Shafeeq Karinkurayil, 'Have we forgotten what Migration means?', *Ala: A Kerala Studies Blog*, no. 8, 30 April 2019. https://alablog.in/issues/issue-8/what-migration-means. Last accessed on 24 November 2022.

[22] For an example, see Maya Vinai and M. G. Prasuna, 'Re-mapping the Anxieties of the Gulf Diaspora: A Study of Benyamin's *Goat Days*', *South Asian Review* 36, no. 2 (2015), doi: 10.1080/02759527.2015.11933021.

[23] Nadeen Dakkak, 'Migrant Labour, Immobility and Invisibility in Literature on the Arab Gulf States', in *Mobilities, Literature, Culture*, eds Marian Aguiar, Charlotte Mathieson, and Lynne Pearce (New York: Palgrave Macmillan, 2019), 206.

home. While Benyamin subsequently authored novels which were not concerned with Gulf migration and secured his place among the mainstream of Malayalam writers (and not remain a *pravasi*/migrant writer), in 2014 he brought out a twin novel which aimed to lay bare the political turbulence in the Gulf for the Malayali public sphere, pulling away the veil of willed ignorance in which the migrants seemed to have found refuge.

The continued crisis of Palestine, the imperial designs of the US in Iraq from the early 2000s, the after-effects of which are still ongoing, the Arab Spring of 2011 and its repercussions in the Gulf—all of these brought to the fore the question of political existence of the Gulf migrants from Kerala. While the general mood in Kerala was against the US action in Iraq,[24] and is sympathetic to the causes of Palestine and the Arab Spring, the fact that the state also derives much of its fiscal energy from those countries which did not seem to share their enthusiasm, and the contradictions this caused on the public life of Kerala was not lost on some. As Babu Bharadwaj wrote in 2012, in his memoir *Pravasathinte Murival* (*The Wounds of Emigration*):

The ideology of imperialism has started enslaving the human minds and tastes, like the Cola. And in the midst of this, it feels like the Malayali migrant is looking for an ever narrower strip of survival [s/he can carve out] of these developments. It feels like they are trying to distance themselves from a big political theme. A British woman I met recently criticized the British Prime Minister vehemently and told me in no ambiguous terms that the British people were not with their Prime Minister's imperial efforts. Are the Malayali migrants able to take a stand similarly? Aren't they still on the side of the hunters?

The Malayali migrant is beginning to be disturbed by the anguish and disappointment of being expelled from a paradise. He is disturbed by [the resistance in] Iraq and Palestine and Lebanon. He is deeply convinced by [the term] 'terrorism.' His desperation is not that of Arab

---

[24] There was a widespread boycott of American consumer goods at the onset of the war, spearheaded by various groups. The Communist Party of India (Marxist), the most prominent party in Kerala in terms of its organizational efficacy, carried out spontaneous demonstrations all across Kerala on the day Saddam Hussein was executed.

nationalism. His is a frustration over being outcast. He is angry towards resistance. He is willing to happily submit to imperialism. I hope my observations are not true. This is the cause of my wounds.[25]

While Babu Bharadwaj's concern is with the Arab states' role in international politics and the Malayali migrants' (non-existent) political position on this, Benyamin turned attention to the internal repression in the Gulf countries. In *Jasmine Days*, we are made privy to the first-person narrative of a young woman, a second-generation migrant from Pakistan whose family members are employed in higher echelons of the host administration. The novel is about the discrimination faced by the Shiite population in an unnamed Gulf country which closely resembles Bahrain. Set in the days that led to the failed 'Jasmine revolution', the novel narrates the travails of the structurally minor but numerically greater Shia population through Ali, the narrator's friend and romantic interest. The novel dramatizes the enabling role played by migrants in the continuing discrimination of the minority population within the host countries, thereby seeking from its readers a vote of conscience. As Nadeen Dakkak points out, the novel's mission is to demonstrate both the migrants and the minorities in the Gulf to be victims of the same system, and to imagine solidarities across the native/migrant binary.[26]

The epigraph to *Jasmine Days* quotes a verse from the Qur'an which says 'Allah will not change the condition of a people till they change their own condition', and a line from Thomas Mann's *Magic Mountain*, 'We must wash our eyes with darkness to see what we want to see', signalling the themes that dominate the novel, those of political existence and the need to wake up to social reality around us. Benyamin quit his two-decade-long migrant life in Bahrain with the writing of the twin novels, speaking against the political oppression in the Gulf, bolstering his image as a leftist writer in Kerala's public sphere.

Jasmine Days is framed as the translated version of a (fictional) novel *A Spring without Fragrance*, a novel banned by the unnamed Gulf kingdom, one extant copy of which has fallen into the present (fictional) author's

[25] Bharadwaj, *Pravasathinte Murivukal* (Kozhikode: Mathrubhumi Books, 2013), viii–ix.
[26] Nadeen Dakkak, 'Malayalam literature as a transnational space of political change: Migration and Bahrain's 2011 uprising in Benyamin's *Jasmine Days* and *Al Arabian Novel Factory*', *Journal of Commonwealth Literature* 58, no. 1 (2023): 36–51, doi: 10.1177/00219894221145452.

hands. The fictional novel has been written by Sameera Parvin, a young Pakistani woman who has now settled in Pakistan. Could there be anything to the frame other than its novelty? One notices that the first-person narrative of the young Pakistani woman who has spent time in Pakistan is not always believable. For example, in her early days of acquaintance with Ali she writes, 'I had no idea who Shias were and what they believed in'.[27] Coming from someone (Sameera Parvin) who seems inclined to understand society around her, and who has grown up in Pakistan where conflict between the Shias and Sunnis are not unheard of, such a confession is hardly credible. Even if one is to admit that through peculiar circumstances our novelist–protagonist was unaware of such happenings, it is easier to see that such ignorance is easier in the Kerala context where the terms of religious debate and sectarian violence are vastly different. But even in that context this ignorance is not very credible. One might then have to assume that the naivety of the novelist–protagonist is a necessary step back from an already formed language to articulate a novelty. The choice of a non-Malayali as the protagonist of *Jasmine Days* could be read as a bid to see the Gulf through fresh eyes, away from the discourse that has shaped it in Kerala for decades before it.

The twin novel of *Jasmine Days*, *Al Arabian Novel Factory* is similarly captured in a frame narrative which posits the novel as ghost-written by the (fictional) novelist for Prathapan, the protagonist of the latter novel, in exchange for the sole existing copy of *A Spring without Fragrance*. These two novels present the Gulf beyond the image of skyscrapers, holiday destinations, and the rich Arab and the toiling-migrant-who-gets-rich-fantastically that is prevalent in the Malayali imagination of the Gulf. One of the costs of racial segregation in the Gulf has been that the Arabs of the Gulf host societies have been given a uniform appearance in the Kerala imagination. This uniformity is often expressed in the white long cloth called *kandoura* and the guttural sounds, which are often evoked for comedic effect. The host communities of the Gulf countries have been unavailable to the Kerala public sphere except as grotesque caricatures. One could see in hindsight that the attention paid by Benyamin to the transcription of Arabic in *Goat Days* is thus also a cleaving of those for whom Arabic is a real language with visceral recall, from those for whom

---

[27] Benyamin, *Jasmine Days*, 63.

it is only a caricature. The news that Benyamin wants to introduce to the Malayali audience is the heterogeneity of the host communities in the Gulf, thus directly confronting the migrant/native binary.

An Outlaw at the Border: *Temporary People*

In Deepak Unnikrishnan's *Temporary People* (2017), a son who now lives in the US but was raised in Abu Dhabi, UAE, wants to spend time by his dying father in a hospital in Abu Dhabi. He is anguished that despite having lived all his childhood in the UAE, the state would not allow him enough time there even as his father lay dying, because as far as the state is concerned, he is an alien. His plan is to get arrested at the Abu Dhabi airport under circumstances in which his wish to be near his father in the latter's final hours will be granted. His plan goes awry thanks to a series of unforeseen twists, and he now stands before the airport control authority at the Abu Dhabi airport. He has a dead man's parts in his body, and is asked to explain:

> "My name is ദീപക് ഉണ്ണികൃഷ്ണൻ," I begin, "I used to live here."
> Popeye [Immigration Officer—*auth.*] leans against the table, stroking his chin.
> "Go on," he prompts, "about the man you killed—"
> "My sister's name is ▇ ▇▇▇. She was born here."[28]

There are two kinds of screenings here. The first one is an opacity that is caused by the foreign letters. I will come back to this in a while. The second one, the black blocks, could be seen to perform a range of functions. The black boxes are, by this point in Unnikrishnan's book, a familiar device. What it most approximates is the state's censorship of information. The Gulf states are infamous for a strict regime of surveillance, and the black boxes signify their success in not letting any light

---

[28] Deepak Unnikrishnan, *Temporary People* (Brooklyn, NY: Restless Books, 2017), 248.
    This example is a confirmation of Fredric Jameson's argument that in postmodern fiction, the word itself is turned to an image: 'Postmodernism … only knows too well that the contents are just more images'. See Fredric Jameson, *Postmodernism, or, The Cultural Logic of Late Capitalism* (Durham, NC: Duke University Press, 1991), ix.

out on sensitive information. However, the black box could also be a conformity to the ethics of privacy upheld by the progressive tenets of society. It could be a gesture of respecting the privacy of one's sister who does not have to be dragged into one's own muddles. As such, it can thereby be the antonym of a surveillance regime; insisting on the ethic of privacy, the black box could be on the side of freedom, this time for a woman who can have an existence independent of this man's perversity. Either way, it is the space and moment in which the text has been purportedly intruded upon by the outside world. This is a moment in which writing bares its performative nature, as an originary inscription brought to the fore by the all obfuscating reinscription. This performative fusing of the world of the text and the world outside it is, as I shall now proceed to show, the very site in which literature produces a fractal inside and outside within it, such that it can now stage the eruption of characters within, without. What one can see here is the attempt of aesthetic representation to recapture itself as political representation—a bid to speak for by speaking as.[29]

Deepak Unnikrishnan, the author of *Temporary People*, is a second-generation Gulf migrant. In his work, variously described as a novel or a collection of short stories, Malayalam and Arabic acquires the solidity of iconic representation while English remains the meta-language. The pervasive presence of Malayalam words and the connection to Malayalam and Kerala asserted in the novel, justifies the inclusion of the piece in this book.

Unnikrishnan describes Abu Dhabi, the city he grew up in, as 'the city where citizenship is not an option'.[30] The law which states that the male children of immigrant parents had to leave the country when they are past minority, and could come back only for work meant that the children of migrant parents could only belong to their home as if an outsider. The migrant parents themselves have to leave the place when they retire from their jobs, no matter how long they have been there. The temporariness

---

[29] For a discussion on the two kinds of representation, see Gayatri Chakravorty Spivak, 'Can the Subaltern Speak', in *Colonial Discourse and Postcolonial Theory: A Reader*, eds Patrick Williams and Laura Chrisman (New York: Columbia University Press, 1998).

[30] Deepak Unnikrishnan, 'Abu Dhabi: The city where citizenship is not an option', *Guardian* (13 December 2017). https://www.theguardian.com/cities/2017/dec/13/abu-dhabi-citizenship-uae-foreigner-visa-india Last accessed on 24 November 2022.

of the only place one could call home bears heavy on the space and time. Temporariness becomes the state of being which lends the labouring life in the Gulf a ghostly nature. It is from the vantage point of this transience that Unnikrishnan approaches the question of migrant labour in the Gulf:

> Once the last brick is laid, the glass spotless, the elevators functional, the plumbing operational, the laborers, every single one of them, begin to fade, before disappearing completely. Some believe the men become ghosts, haunting the facades they helped build.[31]

The inevitability of exit and the ghostly presence it creates forms the essence of migration, or *pravasam*, for Unnikrishnan. This allows the novel to be read from the vantage point of the absent–present, in an explanatory framework drawn from the figure of haunting.[32]

To be temporary is in fact to be devoid of that space which can record one's growth, that permanence against which the vagaries of time can be indexed as such. In the age of double revolution, when Europe plunged into modernity, nation was that space in which the ever-growing promise of the youth that is modernity could be delimited, such that novels could be brought to an end. It was in the consummation of a nation as the endpoint of individual development that these novels could finally resolve themselves.[33] What is denied to the Gulf migrants is exactly this anchor. As Nadeen Dakkak illustrates, *Temporary People* is a work of diasporic fiction in that it is also an assertion in the face of the state policies and everyday practices of exclusion and discrimination that the Gulf is an ineradicable part of the second-generation migrants.[34] In the rest of this chapter, I read Unnikrishnan's *Temporary People* as elucidating the

---

[31] Unnikrishnan, *Temporary People*, 3.

[32] See Priya Menon, '"*Pravasi* Really Means Absence": Gulf-*Pravasis* as Spectral Figures in Deepak Unnikrishnan's *Temporary People*', *South Asia: Journal of South Asian Studies* 43, no. 2 (2020), doi: 10.1080/00856401.2020.1719628.

[33] Tobias Boes, *Formative Fictions: Nationalism, Cosmopolitanism, and the Bildungsroman* (New York: Cornell University Press and Cornell University Library, 2012). Also see Franco Moretti, *The Way of the World: The Bildungsroman in European Culture* (London and New York: Verso, 2000).

[34] Nadeen Dakkak, 'The Gulf as an Unhomely Home: Reconfiguring Citizenship and Belonging in Diasporic Narratives on Second-Generation Migrants', in *Migration in the Making of the Gulf Space: Social, Political, and Cultural Dimensions*, eds Antia Mato Bouzas and Lorenzo Casini (New York and Oxford: Berghahn Books, 2022).

conditions under which, in the face of official denial of citizenship and the reality of the *kafala* system which corrupts the migrant community from inside through the middlemen, a community is nevertheless produced. I read in the novel the enactment of borders which temporarily provide the effect of boundedness.

Temporary People is what would be generally referred to as postmodern fiction. Devoid of an overarching narrative or a consistent voice or uniform focalizing techniques, the 'novel' is fragmented—a collection of disparate narratives some of which have loose connections between them. The novel is playful, it riffs on words, deploys strange spellings for known words, and inserts strange words. The chapters are arranged in books, but there are portions which are within books but are not chapters. At times words give way to pictures, and given the strangeness of some of the words, one could say that at times words give way to sounds. The fragmented narratives take place in various locations, in Abu Dhabi, in an apartment that could be anywhere, in Kerala, in an unnamed tiny desert kingdom where men are grown in farms, and on the pages of a foreign book.

Brian McHale[35] characterizes a postmodern novel to be a reordering of the elements of the modernist novel such that while the elements remain the same, a trait which was marginal earlier now acquires prominence, while the previously prime characteristic now exits the centre stage. The prominent element or characteristic is what he calls 'the dominant'. McHale identifies the dominant in the postmodern to be ontological, while it was epistemological in the modernist novel. That is, while the modernist novels staged the relation to world as a question of knowledge, probing on what is possibly known, the postmodernist novel poses the question fundamentally as a question of being itself. That is, 'what world is this?', rather than 'how do I know this world?'. *Temporary People* performs the suspension of ontological certainty in many of its chapters, and the postmodernism of the novel becomes the mode in which a community can be imagined. The ontological question becomes the staging for the construction of a domain of mutuality which is performed in the mode of adhering to epistemological certainties, as I shall illustrate. Paying attention to the construction of this community even as the

---

[35] Brian McHale, *Postmodernist Fiction* (London and New York: Routledge, 2004).

contours of the world seem out of grasp helps us in decoding the pleasures and precarity of belonging in a migrant world.

Fredric Jameson identifies the condition of possibility of postmodernism with the new multinational economy where production and consumption have lost their visible links to each other. It is the disconnect in this ordering of economy which makes possible an imagination which is devoid of the arch of grand narratives. This disconnect brings into being an order of randomness in spatial and temporal imaginations. The architecture does not converge on a centre, the painting folds into itself, and history is propped with anachronism. Postmodernism for Jameson is the culture transforming into 'a field of force in which the dynamics of sign systems of several different modes of production can be registered and apprehended'.[36] While at any point of time there exists different modes of production which shows itself in the narrative form, what is specific about the postmodern condition is the global division of labour. Like McHale, Jameson also sees in postmodernism not a break with but a reconstitution of what existed earlier. Postmodernism is the cultural logic of a multinational capitalism which is nothing but the latest stage of capitalism.[37]

An example of the multiple modes of production available at a moment can be seen in the Malaysian factories studied by Aihwa Ong.[38] There, the influx of multinational capital plugs into the sexual division of labour. Women gets selected for their nimble hands and keen eyes, thus disassembling their body in the corporate imagination and substituting them for machines in a Fordist assembly line. At the same time, the multinational capital in Malaysia also banks on the prevailing morality of self-control, of not speaking back in the face of elders, etc., to produce a docile workforce. Ong shows that in such a curious mix, the resistance to such strategies of disciplining too is formed along 'non-capitalist' registers. Women tend to get possessed by spirits in ways that affect the smooth functioning of work space and even causing shut downs.

---

[36] Fredric Jameson, *The Political Unconscious: Narrative as a Socially Symbolic Act* (London and New York: Routledge, 1983), 84.

[37] Jameson, *Postmodernism*.

[38] Aihwa Ong, *Spirits of Resistance and Capitalist Discipline: Factory Women in Malaysia* (Albany, NY: State University of New York Press, 1987). See also Aihwa Ong, 'The Gender and Labor Politics of Postmodernity', *Annual Review of Anthropology* 20 (1991).

The multiple modes of production that condition the Gulf combines the petro-economy, on which the world runs, and a labour force whose terms of contract runs counter to the received ideas of capitalism. To explicate the enactment of borders which give rise to the community under the sign of global capital that is the petro-economy, I employ the trope of the outlaw. The outlaw is the one who defies the law and is a law unto itself. At the same time, being an outlaw also conveys the simultaneous existence of another law according to which one is deemed an outlaw. Derrida famously referred to Literature as an outlaw. While on the one hand literature is subject to laws—laws pertaining to authorship, copyright, defamation, etc.—within the precincts of the work literature executes its own law. Derrida makes this observation with reference to Kafka's parable 'Before the Law'.[39] Pointing to how the parable ends with a declaration of its ending ('I will shut it now'), Derrida reads it as an instance of Literature becoming a law unto itself. It says what it performs, thus bringing forth the sovereignty of the text, emanating, as sovereignty does, from a place beyond law itself,[40] or as Derrida would point out, the empty place (like the inside of a tabernacle) of the law that is nevertheless guarded. In a more general sense, Literature is an outlaw because its very task is to push the boundaries of the ordered and to enact a world which cannot be reduced to a set of laws.[41]

To deploy the trope of the outlaw then is to point out the performance of a sovereignty within a text while also illustrating the law according to which one is an outlaw. The outlaw brings forth the border as well as the modality of the border. The foregrounding of performance is also to suggest that my interest here is to point out the ways in which the text affords an alternative space of sovereignty.

The trope of the outlaw nudges us to read the text as a law which is concretized in its reading, breaking the boundaries between the fictional universe and a referential world. When the guard in Kafka's 'Before the Law' shuts the door within the fictional universe, he also brings our reading to a close. The text becomes that space bound by the law within the universe

---

[39] Jacques Derrida, 'Before the Law', in *Jacques Derrida: Acts of Literature*, ed. Derek Attridge (New York: Routledge, 1992).

[40] 'That constitutive, specific element of a decision is, from the perspective of the content of the underlying norm, new and alien. Looked at normatively, the decision emanates from nothingness', Carl Schmitt, *Political Theology: Four Chapters on the Concept of Sovereignty* (Chicago, IL and London: The University of Chicago Press, 1985), 31–32.

[41] Derrida, 'Before the Law'.

of which the law is nevertheless suspended so that a new one can be executed as a unique instance. In other words, the text is where the law is a decision (as opposed to the banality of execution), performed in the there-and-then and not available for replication.

I now return to the figure of the outlaw, the eldest son of a dying parent who is now detained at the airport. A dead body has been detected inside him. He is now asked to explain the dead body in him. It is one of those instances where, to evoke McHale's categories, the primary question is of ontology. For a chapter which begins in a realist mode, it soon slips into the surreal. To put it very briefly, we have a situation in which a police officer frisking our protagonist in Frankfurt airport has lodged himself within the protagonist. The officer had gone there, all the way up inside, when he had subjected the protagonist, whom we shall leave nameless (for reasons we will soon come to), to a rectal search. Once inside the protagonist, the officer refuses to come out, and his colleagues treat the matter as if routine and go about their duties elsewhere. The protagonist has now reached Abu Dhabi airport, and to silence the many German puzzles that are coming from inside him, he requests the passport control at the airport to give him some TNT that he can swallow. Soon he has a dead man inside him.

The protagonist is asked to explain the dead man inside him, to which he answers with the paragraph reproduced earlier in this section. As mentioned earlier, we have two kinds of obfuscations in the protagonist's answer to the passport authority when he is asked to explain the dead man in him. These two kinds of opacity are very different from each other. The second one of these, the black boxes, is an act of superimposition. Whether it is the state censorship or the respect towards the privacy of another person, it is an authority which has imposed itself on the speech from outside. The opacity is between the reader and the text. For in the fictional universe, one can assume that the sister's name was pronounced. The intrusion of the black boxes, their powerful muteness, brings to the fore the act of reading. A fictional universe, and the narrative authority which guarantees it, is maintained by the suspension of disbelief as well as belief. On the one hand one should be willing to believe the fiction, on the other hand, one should not take it to be real either.[42] The black boxes

---

[42] Ronald Sukenick, *In Form: Digressions on the Act of Fiction* (Carbondale and Edwardsville, IL: South Illinois University Press, 1985), 99.

become a space where the fictional world meets reality, fractally. That is, it reproduces the distinction between the fiction and reality within itself. The black boxes become the strategy through which an outside agency can be performed inside. That is, it becomes the site of an exercise of the law of the land, staged so that the outlaw can be brought to relief.

If the second instance of opacity is a straightforward act of silencing, whether voluntary or not, the first instance, that of the foreign letters, is speaking as if in silence. It is the speech of the ghosts, the absent–present who haunt the Gulf space. It is both speech and its refusal, both silence and its annulment. The foreign letters pronounced by the outlaw, erect the zone of a private pleasure as it erects a border among the readers. Some readers are able to read these strange letters. The others fail, or have to figure it out through other means, perhaps over the internet. Again, for both kinds of readers, the act of reading is foregrounded. The foreign script becomes the nodal point through which the bonds of an intimate community emanates from the fictional universe to the referential one. The outlaw enacts his own law, one that is illegible because it belongs to another episteme. One may just skip over these foreign alphabets, for it seems to have already served its purpose in being illegible. In a way, the black boxes and the foreign alphabets cease to be language, and announce the limits of language, where the signifier and the signified are arrested in their sliding and have now fused into each other. At this point all communication has broken down, or so it would seem.

However, for some others privy to another episteme, the irrealist nature of the chapter allows for communal recognition to flash through in an instant of danger (of having to account for a dead body while it was not one's fault that the body chose to be there). To reiterate, my argument regarding *Temporary People* is that the dominant ontological question provides the ground on which epistemology can order people. Some know, others don't.

Temporary People is presumably a book targeted at the global audience. In its many transcriptions and symbolisms, the book is meant to convey the alterity of the Gulf experience. The Arabic version of the Arabic numerals used extensively in the book, while existing as an image for one reader, exists as a grapheme for the other. For one, the number suggests alterity, for the other the alterity has a substance and a meaning to it. The symbol brings alive the sense of distinction. In such a book, the presence of those occult alphabets carves out an even more exclusive enclave. In case you have not figured it out yet—those foreign letters are Malayalam alphabets. What is written in those Malayalam alphabets, if it were to be transcribed to English, would read 'Deepak Unnikrishnan'. The sentence therefore says, 'My name is Deepak Unnikrishnan'. The homonym of the author's name emerges as a cipher in a story that is surreal. It emerges as if from another layer, erupting from below to what is above reality (*sur-real*) like an alien, a migrant. This migrant brings with him, in this narrative that is irrealist, the homonym from a real world.

The presence of the occult tongue brings to the fore the alienness of a migrant in a world which will only host him as an alien and only with the guarantee that he will never be one's own. In a world which is racially de-marcated, the racial difference and alienation are the very conditions of belonging. The foreignness of the foreign body allows it to continue on this foreign soil. In a racially segregated world where English and what it connotes is held in a higher esteem than an Indian language, this erup-tion of the tongue of a migrant makes us think of the many possibilities of the performance of difference. This is the opposite of mimicry. Homi Bhabha's exposition of mimicry[43] is based, like in our own case, on the need for the Master to defend their racial difference, for this was the basis of the colonial governance. At the same time, the colonial Master also kept alive the spectre of the civilizational process, the premise of which was an ultimate equality of all humankind, given the necessary training and disciplining. It is the disjuncture between the two principles of co-lonialism that is brought to the fore when the native speaks and acts like their colonial master. While it would appear that the colonized (a part of them) have now been civilized, this forces the unconscious of coloni-alism to come to the fore, this unconscious being white racism according to which the native can never be an equal to the white. In this world, the 'civilized' native can only exist in a state of mimicry, their acts will only be an imitation and never the thing itself. And it is precisely here that the hollowness of the civilizing mission is visible for all to see. The for-eign alphabets and the wayward tongue of *Temporary People* is, on the other hand, an act of coming out. It is when the object language arrogates

---

[43] Homi Bhabha, 'Of Mimicry and Men: The Ambivalence of Colonial Discourse', *October*, 28 (1984).

to itself the function of meta-language—the language which is the governing logic of the narrative.[44] The deciphering of the foreign alphabet to be the homonym of the author's name, as a name that can pass itself off as the author's name itself, as the underground act of collapsing the border between the fictional and referential world accents the performativity. It is the one act in which the potential of a parody is undone in an act of bravado. By proclaiming one's own strangeness, the act allows for an imagined stability of the world which rests on racial difference. In other words, the foreign alphabets give the world the relief of borders still in place. It reassures that the identities have not been blended beyond redemption; that one's essence still belches out in unanticipated moments.

While the foreign alphabets stand for difference in general, it also offers the joy of recognition for the reader who is privy to these alphabets. Allowing for the moment of filiality,[45] the presence of the foreign tongue becomes the site in which the aesthetic representation fuses into a political representation. Again, this is performed at two distinct levels. On the one hand, the presence of the Malayalam alphabets for the Malayali reader short circuits the fictional text with the reality of his being. While English can pass off as neutral by posing to be the meta-language of the text so far, and thereby become transparent, the presence of the Malayalam scripts performs an opacity while at the same time being intelligible. However, to be intelligible is not to be transparent. The word becomes the site where the text clings to a recognition of a community which is not based on a discursive public sphere but an affective attachment to symbols. The alphabets themselves are symbols of affective attachment. A zone of intimate belonging is activated, and the condition to belong to this community is extra-diegetic. The alphabets transcribe the name of the author (while it may also be a fictional character). This

---

[44] Meta-language and object language are terms used by Colin MacCabe to distinguish between the (authorial) voice that is representing the world (meta-language) and the voice that is represented within it, by using inverted commas, for example. See Colin MacCabe, *James Joyce and the Revolution of the World* (London and Basingstoke: Macmillan, 1979), 13–38. Postmodern fiction by questioning the nature of representation, does not allow for the free rein of meta-language. However, looking at a moment in which the meta-language is in the process of suspension, I am also drawing attention to the fact of its existence before the breakdown.

[45] For Edward Said, exile becomes the condition in which communities of affiliation can replace an earlier one of filiation; see Edward W. Said, *The World, the Text, and the Critic* (Cambridge, MA: Harvard University Press, 1983), 16–24. The migrant conditions of late capital, as explicated in the Introduction to this book, is perhaps making this less possible.

act becomes the declaration on the part of the author to belong to that intimate community as well. The book thus not only represents the Malayali migrant; it also installs the author as the speaking tongue of this community. The one who acts as, now also speaks for.

The pleasure of the surreal text is now eclipsed by the irruption of the real in the surreal. Rather than be the invisible hand of this fictional world, the author makes a dramatic appearance. By placing itself towards the very end of the book, this performance of speaking out one's own name in an exclusive code also allows the book to be a talking out of a migrant; a speech act rather than representation. It foregrounds the act of representing and thus allows the migrant the speaking voice rather than one which is heard. Very much under the gaze of the law, it performs a private language, and therefore a law for oneself.

This chapter has been interested in the formation of communities at the limits of language. If argumentative communities—a characteristic essential to democratic public sphere according to Habermas—is formed primarily through the function of discourse, these communities that this chapter illustrates are formed where the discourse meets the signifier with no significance in the public domain, and can be accessed only as private archive. The community is an autonomous domain insofar as the language of the public sphere is unable to comprehend this language of the community. Rather than opposing capital, however, these communities are formed in conditions dictated by extractive capitalism. The chapter reads in these strange signifiers the affective resource that affords a community of experience. These signifiers signal a border. These are exceptional signifiers. If empty signifiers pronounce the paradigm that defines the borders of a language from a place within, the exceptional signifier pronounces it from a place without. The exceptional signifier reorders the object language as that place of exception from which one can have a view of the meta-language. Rather than therefore subjecting the object language to the meta-language, the exceptional signifier offers a place from where the meta-language is provincialized.

The private nature of the exceptional signifier arrests it from overarching into the hegemonic. What is at stake here is the pleasure such a privacy offers. It is the pleasure of a private recognition that reading offers that makes it amenable to the consolidation of a community of affect. We have seen the structural conditions that require the migrant to speak about migration as if it is a private affair, even though migration might have become fairly routine over generations for communities. Even as we recognize that a migrant imagination of language (as opposed to the dominant territorial based imagination of linguistic communities) has a formidable task to naturalize itself, we should also recognize that domination need not be the imagined destination, and that the occult can have its special appeal. The fascination around migration need not be for its explicit purposes, but the secret pleasures on the side. The exceptional signifier enthrals, with the aura of refusing what it could not be.

Conclusion

It is common sense that what drives Gulf migration is the combination of lack of jobs or poverty at home with the relatively higher wages for jobs in the Gulf and the higher exchange rates of the Gulf currencies in relation to the rupee. The stories of dire poverty of the 1960s and 1970s, of the time when there was famine and one had to depend on tapioca because rice was unavailable is part of the lore of the first phase of migration to the Gulf in the 1960s. The Gulf migration has been a great leveller in the economic situation in Kerala, and held the promise of breaking the social hierarchies in the 1980s. However, this scholastic economic determinant common sense leaves many aspects out. Any study of migration necessarily needs to incorporate the crucial cultural work for and against it in order to understand it in its multi dimensions. The desirability of mobility, the legitimacy of money towards acquiring it, the relationship vis-à-vis the state that may or may not facilitate this mobility, the means of expression of mobility, are all questions that demand a closer look at the culture of migration. This study of cultural work should include not only the discourse and its resonance, but also of the unspoken traces that have left their impressions on one's sensations.

In the process of illustrating the alleyways of pleasure and the contours of belonging in Kerala's Gulf migrant archives, this book places migrant expressivity in a historical cultural context while also paying attention to the partial objects, such as isolated sounds, gestures, and words, that stick out of the context and engender exclusive pathways of understanding and being. What this book has attempted to do is to show the making of communities and collectivities in conditions imposed by global capital. Moreover, these communities are not read as always opposed to capital. The Gulf migrant is rather an agent of community endeavours and changes back home. Theirs is a counter story to the one in which they cut the sorry figure of the wannabe-upper class. It is from the Gulf that they

The Gulf Migrant Archives in Kerala. Mohamed Shafeeq Karinkurayil, Oxford University Press. © Mohamed Shafeeq Karinkurayil 2024. DOI: 10.1093/9780198910619.003.0006

draw the cultural resources for what the future could look like. Kerala's modernity is built on the aspirations of a life elsewhere. It is in the Gulf that Kerala experienced *uber*-modernity as a world made completely strange.

Remittance and Ignorance

The lure of the Gulf in Kerala, its attractiveness as a labour destination, and the very social conditions that deem it to be successful (or not) is noted by Robin Jeffrey:

> people will do overseas, where the neighbours cannot see them, what they would not do at home. Just as the early migrants to Ceylon some-times worked as menials, today examples are deplored—or celebrated—of 'the graduate of the Kerala university [who] works in Saudi Arabia as a headload worker in a construction firm'. What is important is that 'he sends home a handsome amount'.[1]

What is striking about this paragraph is that the real nature of the migrant's job, even if the neighbours cannot see them, is after all not un-known. Jeffrey knows. Nor are the others ignorant. The public deplores or celebrates. So, even though the migrant may be out of one's sight, that is hardly an iron curtain of ignorance. The reality of the Gulf migrant is not lost on anyone. But, as we have seen, there is a discourse around the Gulf as if what happens in the Gulf is a secret. This discourse occasions the migrant literature and the films. This book has illustrated that the dis-course of ignorance is a rhetorical consensus which allows the Gulf to figure in Kerala in all its contradictions. These are contradictions of the aspiration for the Gulf vis-à-vis the nostalgia about Kerala, the complains of harsh labour vis-à-vis the lure of a life of adventure, the discursive tem-porariness of Gulf migration vis-à-vis its inter-generational continuity. The knowledge–ignorance allows for selective owning and disowning of the Gulf, a result of which has been that the Gulf mostly figures only as a source of remittance. That the Gulf is also a cultural force is ignored.

---

[1] Robin Jeffrey, *Politics, Women and Well-Being* (London: Palgrave Macmillan, 1992), 152.

The point of the book is not that the Gulf experience is shrouded in silence, but that the mode of secretiveness is the mode in which the Gulf has been spoken about. It can only be acknowledged *as if* in a rumour. The real versus fantastic Gulf is the proto-narrative form through which this disavowal is resolved in Malayalam. This ideologeme of real versus fanstastic Gulf has its most concrete formal intervention in 'revelatory narratives', that is, those narratives which seek to explain the 'real' Gulf.

Chapter 1 offers a contrapuntal reading of the Gulf, as seen through the migrant photographs. The chapter showed that in migrants' self-representation of themselves in photographs, the Gulf exists more than as a space of labour and toil. These photographs construct the Gulf as a space of adventure and thrills, as a space where a new community can be forged into being, as the background for one's own aspirations (artistic and otherwise), and as the phantom space where discourses in Kerala can be transformed and returned back to it. Though the photograph discussed in the chapter is fairly representative of migrant photographs in their general tone, the attempt has been to read them symptomatically, that is, as a particular instantiation that can tell us of the collective unconscious.

While the chapter celebrates the insurgent modernity in the migrant photographs, this is only half the story. The other half is that of the push back by the hegemonic forces in Kerala which forged a discourse of austerity in which austerity was upheld as the national culture on the one hand, and as sign of rationality and therefore modernity on the other. As opposed to this, the insurgent migrant modernity was just the bumbles of the nouveau riche whose garrulous nature was the sign of their distaste, irrationality, and the general corruption they bring in. The Gulf labour could not register itself as a political identity either, given that the political identity was already fashioned along the lines of governmental identity, among which the Gulf did not figure.

Chapter 2, focusing on cinema, traced the figuration of the Gulf in Malayalam films from 1980 to the present. After its appearance in 1980, the Gulf began to reappear in Malayalam cinema only in the late 1990s. But the Gulf kept appearing in films in refracted forms during this time. The wonder that is the Gulf as well as the disdain towards the Gulf migrants are both more or less the legacies of Malayalam cinema until the 2000s. Chapter 2 also looks at the countercultural cinema, Home Cinema, of Salam Kodiyathur, as a practice that is moulded by particularistic ideas of private and public, of the seen and unseen, the collective experience of migration, and the attendant negotiations of visibility. The chapter reads in Home Cinema a negotiation of the same insecurities that ail other migrant expressions—that in the face of an infiltrating logic of the border generated by the *kafala* system, the binaries of migrants/citizens, guests/hosts do not provide adequate platforms to generate community. The recent films from the main-stream film industry features the Gulf and the Gulf migrants in greater numbers. However, the ideologeme of knowledge–ignorance is hard to shake off in the discourses on the Gulf, often serving itself as the frame of the movies on the Gulf migrants.

In Chapter 3, I have pointed out the rhetorical strategies through which this the singular migrant experience is translated onto the language of the sending culture, thus redrawing of the boundaries of Gulf and Kerala under the experience of migration. With reference to the comics *Gulfumpadi PO*, the study highlights the staging of the epistemic borders and the impossibility of an understanding of the migrant in the Keralan public sphere. In this comic as well as the novels and memoirs, we have various translations and transactions that redraw the Gulf–Kerala in unexpected ways, upsetting the common sense about these spaces and migration as a process itself. Deviating sharply from other migrant narratives, we saw how even race as an embodied fact is malleable in Khadeeja Mumthas's *Barsa*. Krishnadas's writings similarly deconstruct the migrant–native binary, while Sonia Rafeek stages migration to question the human–non-human binary.

While in Chapter 3 the focus was on the translation of the Gulf in Kerala, across the languages, registers and genres, in Chapter 4 the focus is on the breakdown of public speech around exceptional signifiers in language. These signifiers do not easily translate to signifieds except through a cleaving of the reading community. These signifiers provide a space of exception to look back at the meta-language, and in the process form a meta-language of the experience of reading. The chapter illustrates the process of community building around affect at a time when the speech seems to have been emptied of its capacity to be a platform of dialogue, and has crystallized into icons of belief.

To conclude, a book is a record of its time. In the immediate aftermath of the fall of the Berlin Wall, there was a sense of a time gone forever, and a general optimism of a more connected world, one which under-stood each other better, the critical theory shared that optimism mostly. The concepts of hybridity, of dynamic scapes, of the capacities of migrant archives in the era of greater movements and newer technologies, all partook of the optimism, even as there were also some premonitions of the fork in history that we had come to—as the time to choose between routes and roots.[2] While at one time the migrant might have always been a resistor of all fundamentalisms, the experience of the last four decades had been less than ideal. Migrants have been found to be neither particu-larly averse to hierarchies or exclusions. Rather than melting down, the borderization as a process has become ever more present in our lives even if far from any international border. In a state like Kerala, which is also a prime target for inward migration from various parts of India, one often sees signboards put up by local authorities instructing that the land/flat owners should collect the identity cards of migrant labourers. Some of the modalities of the Gulf migration replicate itself in the internal migra-tion from other states of India to Kerala, such as networks of migration, ghettoization of migrant labourers along professions as well as places of residence.[3] The migrant labour to Kerala is subjected to prejudice, often amplified through social media.

In hindsight, one can only remember with disbelief the glee at the prospect of a borderless world that was promised in the last decade of the last century. The end of Cold War, rather than being the promised end of History, was a redrawing of boundaries. At a time when borders abound and public life has increasingly become an exercise in echo chamber, the conditions and avenues of intimacy that this book analyzes and illustrates is not limited to the migrants alone. The epistemological breakdown that this book takes as its focal point is the characteristic of our present world

---

[2] Stuart Hall, 'Cultural Identity and Diaspora', in *Identity: Community, Culture, Difference*, ed. Jonathan Rutherford (London: Lawrence and Wishart, 1990), 222–237.

[3] A few studies on internal migration to Kerala are: Sumeetha M., 'Exploring the Capital-Labour Dynamics: Migrants in the Gold Jewellery-making Industry in Kerala', in S. Irudayarajan (ed.), *India Migration Report 2017* (New Delhi: Routledge, 2018); Md Selim Raja and Bhaswati Das, 'Labour Migrations Within India: Motivations and Networks', *South Asia Research* 39, no. 2 (2019), 125–142, doi: 10.1177/0262728019842018; Jajati K. Parida, Merry Elizabeth John, and Justin Sunny, 'Construction Labour Migrants and Wage Inequality in Kerala', *Journal of Social and Economic Development* 22 (2020), doi: 10.1007_s40847-020-00104-2; Jayaseelan Raj, 'Categorical Oppression: Performance of identity in South India', *The Australian Journal of Anthropology* 31, no. 3 (2020), doi: 10.1111/taja.12375.

increasingly conditioned by algorithms that tend to augment the world according to our preferences or others' designs, declared or otherwise. While this book does not offer modes of resistance or hold out figures as guarantors of a better world, and even as it takes the bleak state of affairs as its starting point, there are moments when the possibilities instil confidence.

Postscript: Rearticulating the Migrant

The Gulf might not be the Eldorado it was once supposed to be,[4] but it continues to attract migrants, but not just as the place of the Arab gold, but as the street of the world, as the theme song of the first Dubai Shopping Festival characterizes the eponymous city. The visa regime and the labour laws in the Gulf are undergoing fast and welcome transformation. The *kafala* system seems to be seeing its last days for some professions at least in some of the Gulf countries. The Gulf countries' rebranding as tourist hotspots, and the diversification of the economy seem to make the visa regime more flexible.

The dependency of Kerala's economy on the remittances from the Gulf has in recent years led to anxieties about the possible end of the era of migration to the Gulf and concerns about rehabilitating the permanently returning migrants from the Gulf. The Covid-19 pandemic and the large-scale immobility it forced upon the world, made the emergency even more acute.[5]

This book has also been an effort to salvage the migrant archive in Kerala. Commenting on the paucity of Keralan Gulf migrant cultural production, Babu Bharadwaj has likened it to the echoless desert. The fact remains that our insistence on the written word has cost us from studying

---

[4] For a conversation on this see Lorenzo Casini and Deepak Unnikrishnan, 'Conclusion: The Gulf Space in Words: In Conversation with Author Deepak Unnikrishnan', in *Migration in the Making of the Gulf Space: Social, Political, and Cultural Dimensions*, eds Antia Mato Bouzas and Lorenzo Casini (Oxford and New York: Berghahn Books, 2022).

[5] Devaki Vadakepat Menon and Vanaja Menon Vadakepat, 'Migration and reverse migration: Gulf Malayalees' perceptions during the Covid-19 pandemic', *South Asian Diaspora* 13, no. 2 (2021), doi: 10.1080/19438192.2020.1820668; Mufsin Puthan Purayil and Muhsin Puthan Purayil, 'Return migration amidst a Pandemic: Reflections on Kerala's Gulf Migration', *Journal of Migration Affairs* 3, no. 1 (2020), doi: 10.36931/jma.2020.3.1.99-107.

many other forms of migrant expressions. Even within written word, we are yet to harness the resource of the personal letter. In *Pravasiyude Kurippukal*, Bharadwaj puts forward this important observation that the Gulf migrant personal letters would give us insight into the formation of the Kerala mind.[6] The emotional history of Kerala cannot ignore the Gulf, just as its economic or social or political history cannot either. The Gulf memoirs by Babu Bharadwaj, Krishnadas, Musafar Ahammed, et al., provide us glimpses of the migrant subjectivity. These are resources for a scholar to look at the affective resonances of Kerala's Gulf migration.

The urgent task now is to take cue from Bharadwaj's statement and see how a history of Kerala can be written giving Gulf migration its due. The task is not just to look at migrant creativity, to recreate their life in the foreign land, or to look at the history and society from their perspective. What we have to do is to speak about migration as it is part of this soil and our bodies and the trajectory of our collective existence. And for this we need to develop a language that is as yet in its elementary stage.

Our perceptions of home and homeland has been predominantly terrestrial under the weight of a landed ideology. The sea is understood to be in this imagination the border of a geographical unit. In this terrestrial imagination, the ocean becomes a hindrance to travel. But recent scholarship has debunked this idea. Kerala has a host of origin stories for different communities, many of which suggest travelling to Kerala from other lands. Gulf migration was hardly the first migration of labour from Kerala. Though not as large-scale as the Gulf migration, Kerala has a history of migration to the South-east Asian region and to the other regions within South Asia. Far from being an isolated region, Kerala has been connected to the wider Indian Ocean region through movement of goods, people, and ideas.[7] However, when it comes to our national imagination of Kerala, we tend to follow a terrestrial model, forgetting that we as a people have a history which is beyond the strictly administrative

---

[6] Babu Bharadwaj, *Pravasiyude Kurippukal* (Kozhikode: Mathrubhumi Books, 2013), 146.

[7] Amitav Ghosh's book on his fieldwork in Egypt, *In an Antique Land*, which came out in 1992 in the immediate aftermath of the first Gulf War, brought into popular imagination the historical interconnections between Egypt, the Arabian Peninsula, and India based on oceanic travel. The book connects and contrasts the connectedness of the present and that of the medieval times. See Amitav Ghosh, *In an Antique Land* (Delhi: Ravi Dayal Publishers, 1992). In recent years, the Indian Ocean as a region of connectedness across distant lands has acquired much salience. A few examples of recent scholarship are: Fahad Ahmad Bishara, *A Sea of Debt: Law and Economic Life in the Western Indian Ocean, 1780–1950* (Cambridge: Cambridge

boundaries of the state of Kerala. We will have to invent a language to speak about our interconnectedness in history.

The task before us is to imagine Gulf migration as part of Kerala's narrative as the journey towards progress. Our story of Gulf migration as it exists now is that of migrants who had to leave their beloved families and the homeland for a life of toil in the harsh desert because of the privation at home. If we look closely, we will find that this story is connected to many other ideas that are prevalent in the dominant imagination—that the migrants are, to begin with, coming from low stations of life, that their money is new money and therefore not worthy of respect. While this is a feudal imagination, it is actually more powerful than the whimper of a dying feudal culture. This dominant imagination of the Gulf migrant is in fact aided by what passes for progressivism, and that is the anti-capitalist bend which is ingrained in Kerala's collective consciousness. In this narrative, the Gulf migrant often becomes the one who injects vast amounts of money to the village, upsets the balance, brings in consumerism. This common sense is so dominant that an entire generation of Gulf migrants have been made to relate to Gulf migration as a necessary evil rather than for all the great things it has done for those around them. Why is it that all the Gulf memoirs sound like personal tragedies?

The other story is of those people who had adventurous hearts, who dared to jump off ships, who made the cities in the Gulf, who made new friendships, who could imagine their lives beyond their village, who had the acumen to invest collectively in educational institutions and small-scale businesses, who were generous with what they earned with those around them, and who brought a lot of smiles to people around them. This migrant's story is also the story of the people around him or her and of the land he or she managed to rescue from the brink of poverty. We know this story. But the moment we start speaking about it, it starts slipping back either to the victim who lived his or her life under order from others, or the villain who forgot his or her roots.

University Press, 2017); Engseng Ho, *The Graves of Tarim:Genealogy and Mobility Across the Indian Ocean* (Berkeley, CA: University of Caifornia Press, 2006); Wilson Chacko Jacob, *For God or Empire: Sayyid Fadl and the Indian Ocean World* (Stanford, CA: Stanford University Press, 2019); Mahmood Kooria, *Islamic Law in Circulation: Shafi'i Texts across the Indian Ocean and the Meditteranean* (Cambridge: Cambridge University Press, 2022); Sebastian R. Prange, *Monsoon Islam: Trade and Faith on the Medieval Malabar Coast* (New Delhi: Cambridge University Press, 2018).

This book has also been about recognizing the ideological blind spots of the individual-centric discourse around the Gulf migration and about the need to build upon the translation of the Gulf into an experience of Kerala. The hospitals we go to, the buses that ply the interiors of our village, the colleges we went to, are products of Gulf money. All around us what we see is an increasing dependence on Gulf money for almost everything, then it is time to assert that Kerala is made by the foreign money and the spirit of community that was prevalent among the migrants for the improvement of those around them.

However, and precisely for the money the migrant brings in, the Gulf migrant has been turned into just an economic agent. And because what s/he brings in is money which our collective consciousness abhors, even if he is a hero, he has to be a tragic hero. What we need urgently is a reconfiguration of this figure. We have to see migration for its role in ushering in a world of progressivism, where more people can dream of going to schools, getting into higher education, working in respectable professions, and standing up to the world.[8] If the Kerala myth is built around the idea of a progressive people, and if Kerala's history is the history of freeing oneself from the shackles of old habits, then migration has to figure in this story as that which makes it possible every day, as Kerala's most consistent tryst with the world.

Thirdly, we need to think of migration of sending in not only money which can buy things, but also as an intimate act which changes us as sensory human beings. Once we go beyond the remittance discourse, we can see how modern Kerala is made by the Gulf migrants at the most minute levels. It was the Gulf migrants from India who first brought in the audio cassette players. India soon became the second biggest producer of cassettes in the world. The cassette technology changed not only Indian market equations, but also changed the demography of cassetted songs.

---

[8] J. Devika, in her article 'Migration, Transnationalism and Modernity' makes a case for looking at the celebrated Kerala Renaissance as a product of Malayali migration to many parts of the world. She is, however, sceptical of the impact of Gulf migration. See J. Devika, 'Migration, transnationalism, and modernity: Thinking of Kerala's many cosmopolitanisms', *Cultural Dynamics* 24, nos 2–3 (2012). In general Gulf migration is associated with strengthening patriarchy and the resurgence of religion and rituals. But these are at the same time tied to notions of social mobility, as shown by Filippo Osella and Caroline Osella, *Social Mobility in Kerala: Modernity and Identity in Conflict* (London: Pluto Press, 2001). So, it demands that we also see the self-respect and confidence that was brought in by the Gulf money.

The Gulf migrants and their families back home used these cassettes to send letters. Far from being a capitalist mass production, the cassettes turned into a technology of personal use, and a testament to the creativity of the migrant. The Gulf was also the source of cheap cameras in the 1980s, and the major funding resource for Malayalam film industry. The audio and video cassettes, the camera, and the cinema, are not just new technologies. These are technologies which change the way in which our senses and our desires are conditioned. The Gulf has intimately changed the way we hear, speak, and see. And yet, we are yet to pay adequate attention to the ways in which the Gulf migration remade Kerala in these intimate and affective dimensions. In other words, we are yet to pay adequate attention to how the Gulf migration in Kerala made the contemporary sensorium of a Keralan.

Thanks to the important studies conducted by the Centre for Development Studies (CDS) and others, we have data on the socio-economic impact of Gulf migration on Kerala. However, we have lost invaluable data on the cultural aspects of migration. Much of the literature produced by Gulf migrants was published in low-key supplements by cultural organizations in the Gulf. This literature was often derided by the literati for their 'nostalgia' for Kerala and their inability to speak about their real lives in the Gulf. The derision from the established culture has meant that, having been deemed as not worthy of literary merit, we have lost these. What is available and accessible now are those works which are published by the established publishing houses like DC Books and Mathrubhumi. What we have lost is a host of literature by labourers in the Gulf. While it is important to represent the migrants, the representations *by* migrants can have a very different moral and creative thrust. What we lose by losing this 'poor' literature is an account of how the migrants would have represented their own lives, even if it is through 'nostalgia' or '*painkili*' (inadequately translatable as 'sensationalism').

Similarly, the photographs of Gulf migrants are rotting away. Not only are these photographs records of how the Gulf looked at one point of time, or the changing fashions or aesthetic sense, these photographs are records of a counter history by the Gulf migrants. While almost all mainstream literature on the Gulf migrants presents their lives as tragic, the photographs tell us a different story. In the photographs not only do we see migrant creativity in terms of angles and framing, we also see how the migrants would make sense of their lives. And these are often narratives of freedom, thrills, adventure, comradeship, and joint missions. What we see in the migrant photographs are migrants fashioning themselves in new ways, like people who are explorers or are in the midst of modernity and feeling and seeing themselves as new human beings, unmoored from their villages, rather than caught in the rainclouds of nostalgia. The Gulf photographs can help us narrate an alternative history of Gulf migration, about a people who crossed the seas to found a utopia of freedom from the debilitating moorings of their own villages, who explored the unknown to invent the magic of modernity that will deliver a people from humiliation.

The cassette letters sent between the Gulf and Kerala are not only an oral record of a period, but it are also a record of the changing geography of intimacy in Kerala. Without a sustained effort to retrieve these cassettes, an important facet of Kerala's contemporary period will be forever lost to us. A similar case can be made for the personal letters too. We know that the telephone conversations in the 1970s to 1990s between the Gulf migrant and their family back home were either non-existent or too brief and almost always public rather than private. This is because the rare phone sets were always thronged on holidays by the household members and neighbours, all of who were expecting calls. The personal letters were the more detailed form of communication. Usually, an envelope would contain more than one letter, and each letter had different purposes. Some were to be read aloud while some were confidential notes for the eyes of select people only. Letters were not only avenues of expressing emotions, they were also detailed documents on household expenses, debts, and other transactions. These letters would therefore give us not only facets of transnational emotional ties, but also glimpses of the ways in which the kinship bonds were realized through monetary transactions. These letters would help us get a unique and priceless picture of the informal economy.

It should be a matter of priority that we build an archive of the cultural products of Gulf migration. Such an initiative can go a long way in giving the migrants their due as the makers of contemporary Kerala's everyday life. A lot can be done if we realize the potential this project has for re-narrating Kerala and decide to pursue it.

Filmography

Akkare. Dir. K. N. Sasidharan. 1984. Malayalam.

Akkare Akkare Akkare. Dir. Priyadarshan. 1990. Malayalam.

Akkare Ninnoru Maaran. Dir. Girish. 1985. Malayalam.

Aliyanoru Free Visa. Dir. Salam Kodiyathur. 2007. Malayalam.

America America. Dir. I. V. Sasi. 1983. Malayalam.

Arabikkatha. Dir. Lal Jose. 2007. Malayalam.

Aram+Aram=Kinnaram. Dir. Priyadarshan. 1985. Malayalam.

Ayal Kadha Ezhuthukayanu. Dir. Kamal. 1998. Malayalam.

Boeing Boeing. Dir. Priyadarshan. 1985. Malayalam.

C U Soon. Dir. Mahesh Narayanan. 2020. Malayalam.

Chithram. Dir. Priyadarshan. 1988. Malayalam

Devasuram. Dir. I. V. Sasi. 1993. Malayalam.

Diamond Necklace. Dir. Lal Jose. 2012. Malayalam.

Dubai. Dir. Joshiy. 2001. Malayalam.

Ezham Kadalinakkare. Dir. I. V. Sasi. 1979. Malayalam.

Garshom. Dir. P. T. Kunju Muhammed. 1999. Malayalam.

Ghazal. Dir. Kamal. 1993. Malayalam.

Iniyenkilum. Dir. I. V. Sasi. 1985. Malayalam.

Kallu Kondoru Pennu. Dir. Shyamaprasad. 1998. Malayalam.

Khaddama. Dir. Kamal. 2011. Malayalam.

Kilukkam. Dir. Priyadarshan. 1991. Malayalam.

Kuttikkuppayam. Dir. M. Krishnan Nair. 1964. Malayalam.

Love in Kerala. Dir. Sasikumar. 1968. Malayalam.

Love in Singapore. Dir. Baby. 1980. Malayalam.

Mampazhakkalam. Dir. T. A. Shahid. 2004. Malayalam.

Mandanmmar Londanil. Dir. Sathyan Anthikad. 1983. Malayalam.

Mangalam Veettil Manaseshwari Gupta. Dir. Suresh Vinu. 1995. Malayalam.

Manithali. Dir. M. Krishnan Nair. 1984. Malayalam.

Maniyara. Dir. M. Krishnan Nair. 1983. Malayalam.

Mazhapeyyunnu Maddalam Kottunnu. Dir. Priyadarshan. 1986. Malayalam.

Meleparambil Aanveedu. Dir. Rajasenan. 1993. Malayalam.

Meow. Dir. Lal Jose. 2021. Malayalam.

Momo in Dubai. Dir. Ameen Aslam. 2023. Malayalam.

Mukundetta Sumithra Vilikkunnu. Dir. Priyadarshan. 1988. Malayalam.

Nadodikkattu. Dir. Sathyan Anthikad. 1987. Malayalam.

Nagarangalil Chenn Raparkam. Dir. Viji Thampi. 1990. Malayalam.

Neeyum Njanum. Dir. A. K. Sajan. 2019. Malayalam.

Ningalenne Branthanakki. Dir. Salam Kodiyathur. 2000. Malayalam.

Odaruthammava Aalariyam. Dir. Priyadarshan. 1984. Malayalam.

Oru Marubhoomikkadha. Dir. Priyadarshan. 2011. Malayalam.

Paadam Onnu: Oru Vilapam. Dir. T. V. Chandran. 2003. Malayalam.

Parethan Thirichu Varunnu. Dir. Salam Kodiyathur. 2004. Malayalam.

Passport. Dir. Manoj Mohan Mynagappally. 2015. Malayalam.

Pathemari. Dir. Salim Ahamed. 2015. Malayalam.

Pattanapravesham. Dir. Sathyan Anthikad. 1988. Malayalam.

Pavam Pavam Rajakumaran. Dir. Kamal. 1990. Malayalam.

Poochakkoru Mukkuthi. Dir. Priyadarshan. 1984. Malayalam.

Ramji Rao Speaking. Dir. Siddique-Lal. 1989. Malayalam.

Samantharangal. Dir. Balachandra Menon. 1998. Malayalam.

Sandesham. Dir. Sathyan Anthikad. 1991. Malayalam.

Sharja to Sharja. Dir. Venugopan. 2001. Malayalam.

Shawarma. Dir. Jimmy Joseph. 2018. Malayalam.

Shutter. Dir. Joy Mathew. 2012. Malayalam.

Vadakkunokkiyantram. Dir. Sreenivasan. 1989. Malayalam.

Vellimoonga. Dir. Jibu Jacob. 2014. Malayalam.

Vilkkanundu Swapnangal. Dir. Azad. 1980. Malayalam.

Visa. Dir. Balu Kiriyath. 1983. Malayalam.

Visit Visa. Dir. Shafi Orange. 2014. Malayalam.

Bibliography

Adelson, Leslie A. 'Against Between: A Manifesto'. *New Perspectives on Turkey* 29 (2003): 19–36, doi: 10.1017/S0896634600006099.

Adelson, Leslie A. *The Turkish Turn in Contemporary German Literature: Towards a New Critical Grammar of Migration*. New York and Hampshire: Palgrave Macmillan, 2005.

Ahammed, Musafar. *Kudiyettakkkarante Veedu*. Kottayam: DC Books, 2014.

Ahmad Moulavi, C. N. and K. K. Mohammad Abdul Kareem. *Mahattaya Mappila Sahitya Paramparyam*. Kozhikode: Azad Book Stall, 1978.

Akkach, Samer. 'Nazar: The Seen, the Unseen, and the Unseeable'. In *Nazar: Vision, Belief, and Perception in Islamic Cultures*, edited by Samer Akkach, 12–32. Leiden and Boston, MA: Brill, 2022.

Alavi, Seema. *Muslim Cosmopolitanism in the Age of Empire*. Cambridge, MA and London: Harvard University Press, 2015.

Alpagu, Faime. '<<I am DOIng well in Austria>> Biography, photography and migration memories of a 1970s *guest worker*'. *Rassegna Itaiana di Sociologia* 1 (2019): 47–74, doi: 10.1423/93559.

Anderson, Benedict. *Imagined Communities: Reflections on the Origins and Spread of Nationalism*. London and New York: Verso, 1991.

Anil, Anagha. 'Portrait Populism: On Communist Iconography of Kerala'. In *Populist Mediations- Aesthetics and the Politics of Affect in (Digital) Media*, edited by Catherine Bublatzky and Simone Pfeifer (forthcoming). AllegraLab.

Ansari, M. T. 'Within/Without the Naalukettu: More on the Muslim in Malayalam Literature'. *Humanities Circle* 2, no. 1 (2014): 71–88.

Appadurai, Arjun. *Modernity at Large: Cultural Dimensions of Globalization*. Minneapolis, MN: University of Minnesota Press, 1996.

Appadurai, Arjun. 'Archive and Aspiration'. In *Information is Alive: Art and Theory on Archiving and Retrieving Data*, edited by Arjen Mulder and Joke Brouwer, 14–25. Rotterdam: NAI Publishers, 2003.

Arafath, P. K. Yasser. 'Muslim Ulema in the Shafiite Cosmopolis: Fitna, Piety and Resistance in the Age of Fasad'. *The Medieval History Journal* 21, no.1 (2018): 25–68, doi: 10.1177/0971945817750506.

Arafath, P. K. Yasser. 'Cassetted emotions: intimate songs and marital conflicts in the age of *pravasi* (1970–1990)'. In *Cultural Histories of India: Subaltern Spaces, Peripheral Genres, and Alternate Historiography*, edited by Rita Banerjee, 135–148. New York: Routledge, 2020.

Armstrong, Nancy. *How Novels Think: The Limits of British Individualism from 1719–1900*. New York: Columbia University Press, 2006.

Arunima, G. 'Imagining communities—differently: Print, language and the (public sphere) in colonial Kerala'. *Indian Economic Social History Review* 43, no. 1 (2006): 63–76, doi: 10.1177/001946460504300103.

Arunima, G. *There Comes Papa: Colonialism and the Transformation of Matriliny in Kerala, Malabar, c.1850–1940.* Hyderabad: Orient Blackswan, 2008.

Assaf, Laure. '"Abu Dhabi is my sweet home": Arab youth, interstitial spaces, and the building of a cosmopolitan locality'. *City* 24, nos 5–6 (2020): 830–841, doi: 10.1080/13604813.2020.1837562.

Babar, Zahra. 'Migration Policy and Governance in the GCC: A Regional Perspective'. In *Labor Mobility: An Enabler for Sustainable Development,* edited by Ali Rashid Al-Noaimi and Irena Omelaniuk, 121–142. Abu Dhabi and Cambridge: The Emirates Centre for Strategic Studies and Research and Cambridge University Press, 2013.

Badiou, Alain. 'Towards a New Concept of Existence'. *Lacanian Ink* 29 (2007): 63–72.

Banks, Marcus and Howard Morphy (eds). *Rethinking Visual Anthropology.* New Haven, CT and London: Yale University Press, 1997.

Barthes, Roland. *Image, Music, Text.* Translated by Stephen Heath. London: Fontana Press, 1977.

Basheer, Vaikom Muhammad. *'Me Grandad 'ad an Elephant!': Three Stories of Muslim Lives in South India.* Translated by R. E. Asher and Achamma Coilparambil Chandrasekharan. Edinburgh: Edinburgh University Press, 1980.

Basheer, Vaikom Muhammad. *Ntuppuppakkoranandarnnu,* 21st edn. Kottayam: DC Books, 2008.

Beauchard, David. *Epileptic.* Seattle, WA: Fantagraphics, 2002.

Benhabib, Seyla. *Another Cosmopolitanism.* Oxford: Oxford University Press, 2006.

Benjamin, Walter. *Illuminations.* Translated by Harry Zohn. New York: Schocken Books, 1968.

Benjamin, Walter. 'Small History of Photography (1931)'. In *On Photography: Walter Benjamin,* edited and translated by Esther Leslie, 59–105. London: Reaktion Books, 2015.

Benyamin. *Aatujeevitham.* Thrissur: Green Books, 2008.

Benyamin. *Goat Days.* Translated by Joseph Koyippally. Gurgaon: Penguin Books India, 2012.

Benyamin. *Al Arabian Novel Factory.* Kottayam: DC Books, 2014.

Benyamin. *Mullappooniramulla Pakalukal.* Kottayam: DC Books, 2014.

Benyamin. *Jasmine Days.* Translated by Shahnaz Habib. New Delhi: Juggernaut Books, 2018.

Benyamin. *Al Arabian Novel Factory.* Translated by Shahnaz Habib. New Delhi: Juggernaut Books, 2019.

Bhabha, Homi. 'Of Mimicry and Men: The Ambivalence of Colonial Discourse'. *October* 28 (1984): 125–133.

Bharadwaj, Babu. *Pravasiyude Vazhiyambalangal.* Kozhikode: Pratheeksha Books, 2011.

Bharadwaj, Babu. *Pravasathinte Murivukal.* Kozhikode: Mathrubhumi Books, 2012.

Bharadwaj, Babu. *Pravasiyude Kurippukal,* 3rd edn. Kozhikode: Mathrubhumi Books, 2013.

Bishara, Fahad Ahmad. *A Sea of Debt: Law and Economic Life in the Western Indian Ocean, 1780–1950.* Cambridge: Cambridge University Press, 2017.

Boes, Tobias. *Formative Fictions: Nationalism, Cosmopolitanism, and the Bildungsroman*. New York: Cornell University Press and Cornell University Library, 2012.

Bruslé, Tristan. 'What Kind of place is this? Daily Life, Privacy and Inmate Metaphor in a Nepalese Workers' Labour Camp (Qatar)'. *South Asia Multidisciplinary Academic Journal* 6 (2012), np, doi: 10.4000/samaj.3446.

Carling, Jørgen and Francis Collins. 'Aspiration, desire and drivers of migration'. *Journal of Ethnic and Migration Studies* 44, no. 6 (2018): 909–926, doi: 10.1080/1369183X.2017.1384134.

Casanova, Pascale. 'Consecration and Accumulation of Literary Capital: Translation as Unequal Exchange'. In *Critical Readings in Translation Studies*, edited by Mona Baker, translated by Siobhan Brownlie, 287–303. London and New York: Routledge, 2010.

Casini, Lorenzo and Deepak Unnikrishnan. 'Conclusion: The Gulf Space in Words: In Conversation with Author Deepak Unnikrishnan'. In *Migration in the Making of the Gulf Space: Social, Political, and Cultural Dimensions*, edited by Antia Mato Bouzas and Lorenzo Casini, 135–153. Oxford and New York: Berghahn Books, 2022.

Centre for Development Studies. *Poverty, Unemployment and Development Policy: A Case Study of Selected Issues with Reference to Kerala* (Bombay: Orient Longman, 1977).

Chambers, Thomas. 'Continuity in Mind: Imagination and Migration in India and the Gulf'. *Modern Asian Studies* 52, no. 4 (2018): 1420–1456, doi: 10.1017/S0026749X1700049X.

Chatterjee, Partha. *Nationalist Thought and the Colonial World: A Derivative Discourse*. London: Zed Books, 1986.

Chouliaraki, Lilie. 'Cosmopolitanism as Irony: A Critique of Post-Humanitarianism'. In *After Cosmopolitanism*, edited by Rosi Braidotti, Patrick Hanafin, and Bolette Blaagaard, 77–96. New York: Routledge, 2013.

Cohn, Bernard S. *Colonialism and Its Forms of Knowledge: British in India*. Princeton, NJ: Princeton University Press, 1996.

Creet, Julia. 'Introduction: The Migration of Memory and Memories of Migration'. In *Memory and Migration: Multidisciplinary Approaches to Memory Studies*, edited by Julia Creet and Andreas Kitzmann, 3–26. Toronto, Buffalo, NY, and London: University of Toronto Press, 2011.

Dakkak, Nadeen. 'Migrant Labour, Immobility and Invisibility in Literature on the Arab Gulf States'. In *Mobilities, Literature, Culture*, edited by Marian Aguiar, Charlotte Mathieson, and Lynne Pearce, 189–210. London: Palgrave Macmillan, 2019.

Dakkak, Nadeen. 'The Gulf as an Unhomely Home: Reconfiguring Citizenship and Belonging in Diasporic Narratives on Second-Generation Migrants'. In *Migration in the Making of the Gulf Space: Social, Political, and Cultural Dimensions*, edited by Antia Mato Bouzas and Lorenzo Casini, 54–89. New York and Oxford: Berghahn Books, 2022.

Dakkak, Nadeen. 'Malayalam literature as a transnational space of political change: Migration and Bahrain's 2011 uprising in Benyamin's *Jasmine Days* and *Al Arabian Novel Factory*', *Journal of Commonwealth Literature* 58, no. 1 (2023): 36–51, doi: 10.1177/00219894221211452.

Dale, Stephen Frederic. *Islamic Society on the South Asian Frontier: The Mappilas of Malabar, 1498–1922*. Oxford: Clarendon Press, 1980.

Das, Veena. *Life and Words: Violence and the Descent into the Ordinary*. Berkeley and Los Angeles, CA a nd London: University of California Press, 2006.

Derrida, Jacques. 'Before the Law'. In *Jacques Derrida: Acts of Literature*, edited by Derek Attridge, 181–220. New York: Routledge, 1992.

Desai, Manali. 'Indirect British Rule, State Formation, and Welfarism in Kerala, India, 1860–1957'. *Social Science History* 29, no. 3 (2005): 457–488, doi: 10.1017/S0145553200013018.

Devadawson, Christel R. *Out of Line: Cartoons, Caricature and Contemporary India*. Hyderabad: Orient Blackswan, 2019.

Devika, J. 'Egalitarian Developmentalism, Communist Mobilization, and the Question of Caste in Kerala State, India'. *The Journal of Asian Studies* 69, no. 3 (2010): 799–820, doi: 10.1017/S0021911810001506.

Devika, J. 'Migration, transnationalism, and modernity: Thinking of Kerala's many cosmopolitanisms'. *Cultural Dynamics* 24, nos 2–3 (2012): 127–142, doi: 10.1177/0921374013482359.

Devika, J. 'Cochin Creoles and the Perils of Casteist Cosmpolitanism: Reading *Requiem for the Living*'. *The Journal of Commonwealth Literature* 51, no. 1 (2016): 127–144, doi: 10.1177/0021989414563150.

Dhareshwar, Vivek and Tejaswini Niranjana. '*Kaadalan* and the Politics of Resignification'. In *Making Meaning in Indian Cinema*, edited by Ravi Vasudevan, 191–214. New Delhi: Oxford University Press, 2000.

Elizabeth Edwards. 'Beyond the Boundary: a consideration of the expressive in photography and anthropology'. In *Rethinking Visual Anthropology*, edited by Marcus Banks and Howard Morphy, 53–80. New Haven, CT and London: Yale University Press, 1997.

Elsheshtawy, Yasser. *Temporary Cities: Resisting Transience in Arabia*. London: Routledge, 2021.

Fargues, Philippe. 'Immigration without Inclusion: Non-Nationals in Nation-Building in the Gulf States'. *Asia and Pacific Migration Journal* 20, nos 3–4 (2011): 273–292, doi: 10.1177/011719681102000302.

Fernandez, Bina. 'Racialised institutional humiliation through the Kafala'. *Journal of Ethnic and Migration Studies* 47, no. 19 (2021): 4344–4361, doi: 10.1080/1369183X.2021.1876555.

Fraser, Nancy. 'Rethinking the public sphere: A contribution to the critique of actually existing democracy'. *Social Text*, nos 25/26 (1990): 56–80.

Gardner, Andrew M. *City of Strangers: Gulf Migration and the Indian Community in Bahrain*. Ithaca, NY and London: Cornell University Press, 2010.

Ghosh, Ghosh. *In an Antique Land*. Delhi: Ravi Dayal Publishers, 1992.

Ghosh, Amitav. *The Imam and the Indian: Prose Pieces*. Delhi: Ravi Dayal Publisher and Permanent Black, 2002.

Guha, Ranajit. *The Small Voice of History: Collected Essays*. Delhi: Permanent Black, 2002.

Gulati, Leela. *In the Absence of their Men: The Impact of Male Migration on Women*. New Delhi: Sage Publications, 1993.

Habermas, Jurgen. *The Structural Transformation of the Public Sphere: An Inquiry into a Category of Bourgeois Society*. Cambridge, MA: MIT Press, 1989.

Hall, Stuart. 'Cultural Identity and Diaspora'. In *Identity: Community, Culture, Difference*, edited by Jonathan Rutherford, 222–237. London: Lawrence and Wishart, 1990.

Hall, Stuart. 'Reconstruction Work: Images of Post-war Black Settlement'. In *Writings on Media: History of the Present*, edited by Charlotte Brunsdon, 78–94. New York: Duke University Press, 2021.

Hanafin, Patrick. 'A Cosmopolitics of Singularities: Rights and the Thinking of Other Worlds'. In *After Cosmopolitanism*, edited by Rosi Braidotti, Patrick Hanafin, and Bolette Blaagaard, 40–56. New York: Routledge, 2013.

Hanich, Julian. 'Laughter and collective awareness: The cinema auditorium as public space', *NECSUS: European Journal of Media Studies* 3, no. 2 (2014): 43–62.

Hanich, Julian. *The Audience Effect: On the Collective Cinema Experience*. Edinburgh: Edinburgh University Press, 2018.

Hansen, Thomas Blom. *Wages of Violence: Naming and Identity in Postcolonial Bombay*. Princeton, NJ: Princeton University Press, 2002.

Heidegger, Martin. *Being and Time: A Translation of Sein und Zeit*. New York: State University of New York Press, 1996.

Heller, Patrick. *The Labor of Development: Workers and the Transformation of Capitalism in Kerala, India*. Ithaca, NY and London: Cornell University Press, 2000.

High, Casey, Ann H. Kelly, and Jonathan Mair (eds). *The Anthropology of Ignorance: An Ethnographic Approach*. New York: Palgrave Macmillan, 2012.

Ho, Engseng. *The Graves of Tarim: Genealogy and Mobility Across the Indian Ocean*. Berkeley, CA: University of Caifornia Press, 2006.

Ho, Engseng. 'Custom and Conversion in Malabar: Zayn Al-Din Al-Malibari's Gift of the Mujahidin'. In *Islam in South Asia in Practice*, edited by Barbara Daly Metcalf, 403–408. Princeton, NJ: Princeton University Press, 2009.

Hoek, Lotte. *Cut-pieces: Celluloid Obscenity and Popular Cinema in Bangladesh*. New York: Columbia University Press, 2013.

Honig, Bonnie. 'Another Cosmopolitanism? Law and Politics in the New Europe'. In *Another Cosmopolitanism*, edited by Seyla Benhabib, 102–127. Oxford: Oxford University Press, 2006.

Howes, David and Constance Classen. *Ways of Sensing: Understanding the Senses in Society*. Oxford and New York: Routledge, 2014.

Ilias, M. H. 'Malayalee Migrants and Translocal Kerala Politics in the Gulf: Reconceptualising the 'Political'. In *Diasporas of the Modern Middle East: Contextualising Community*, edited by Anthony Gorman and Sossie Kasbarian, 303–337. Edinburgh: Edinburgh University Press, 2015.

Ilias, M. H. 'South Asian Labour Unrests and Non-Citizenry Aspects of Popular Politics in the Gulf'. In *Asianization of Migrant Workers in the Gulf Countries*, edited by S. Irudaya Rajan and Ginu Zacharia Oommen, 55–67. Singapore: Springer, 2020.

Ilias, M. H. and Shamshad Hussain. 'Literate Illiterates'. In *Cosmopolitan Cultures and Oceanic Thought*, edited by Dilip M. Menon and Nishat Zaidi, 181–196. Oxford and New York: Routledge, 2023.

Iqbal, Sabin. *Shamal Days*. Noida: Harper Collins, 2021.

Iser, Wolfgang. 'The Reading Process: A Phenomenological Approach'. *New Literary History* 3 no. 2 (1972): 279–299.

Jacob, Wilson Chacko. *For God or Empire: Sayyid Fadl and the Indian Ocean World.* Stanford, CA: Stanford University Press, 2019.

Jahan, Nusarath. 'Transnational relationships and virtual technology: an ethnographic study of the left-behind wives in Kerala'. *Gender, Technology and Development* 25, no. 2 (2021): 146–162, doi: 10.1080/09718524.2021.1928875.

Jain, Kajri. *Gods in the Bazaar: The Economies of Indian Calendar Art.* Durham, NC and London: Duke University Press, 2007.

Jameson, Fredric. *The Political Unconscious: Narrative as a Socially Symbolic Aact.* London and New York: Routledge, 1983.

Jameson, Fredric. *Postmodernism, or, The Cultural Logic of Late Capitalism.* Durham, NC: Duke University Press, 1991.

Jeffrey, Robin. *Politics, Women and Well-Being.* London: Palgrave Macmillan, 1992.

Jureidani, Ray and Said Fares Hassan. *Migration and Islamic Ethics: Issues of Residence, Naturalisation and Citizenship.* Leiden and Boston, MA: Brill, 2019.

Kadavath, Vipin K. *Historicising Kshemam: A Study of Vernacular Political Discourse.* Unpublished PhD Diss., English and Foreign Languages University, 2015.

Kakande, Yasin. *Slave States: The Practice of Kafala in the Gulf Arab Region.* Winchester: Zero Books, 2015.

Kant, Immanuel. *Kant: Political Writings*, edited by H. S. Reiss, translated by H. B. Nisbet. Cambridge: Cambridge University Press, 1991.

Kapur, Geeta. 'Mythic Material in Indian Cinema', *Journal of Arts and Ideas*, nos 4–15 (1987): 79–108.

Karassery, Dr M. N. *Pulikkottil Krithikal.* Thrissur: Kerala Sahitya Akademi, 1979.

Karinkurayil, Mohamed Shafeeq. 'Have we forgotten what Migration means?'. *Ala: A Kerala Studies Blog*, no. 8 (30 April 2019).

Karinkurayil, Mohamed Shafeeq. 'The Islamic Subject of Home Cinema of Kerala'. *BioScope: South Asian Screen Studies* 10, no. 1 (2019): 30–51, doi: 10.1177/0974927619855451.

Karinkurayil, Mohamed Shafeeq. 'Reading Aspiration in Kerala's Migrant Photography'. *South Asia: Journal of South Asian Studies* 43, no. 4 (2020): 598–612, doi: 10.1080/00856401.2020.1759000.

Karinkurayil, Mohamed Shafeeq. 'The days of plenty: images of first generation Malayali migrants in the Arabian Gulf', *South Asian Diaspora* 13, no. 1 (2021): 51–64, doi: 10.1080/19438192.2020.1767895.

Karinkurayil, Mohamed Shafeeq. 'On Stale Images: A Photo Essay'. *Dastavezi: The Audio-Visual South Asia* 3 (2021): 68–81, doi: 10.11588/dasta.2021.1.15080.

Karinkurayil, Mohamed Shafeeq. 'The Political Language of Minority Islam in the Indian State of Kerala: The Works of C. H. Mohammed Koya'. *Journal of Muslim Minority Affairs* 41, no. 4 (2021): 658–668, doi: 10.1080/13602004.2022.2028461.

Karinkurayil, Mohamed Shafeeq. 'A Strangeness One Can Occupy: Clothes and Their Codes in the Photographs of Gulf Migrants from Kerala'. In *Migration in the Making of the Gulf Space: Social, Political, and Cultural Dimensions*, edited by Antia Mato Bouzas and Lorenzo Casini, 115–134. New York and Oxford: Berghahn Books, 2022, doi: 10.1515/9781800733510-008.

Karinkurayil, Mohamed Shafeeq. '"Dubai" as a Place of Memory in Malayalam Cinema'. *International Journal of Politics, Culture, and Society* 36 (2023): 459–474, doi: 10.1007/s10767-022-09422-1.

Karinkurayil, Mohamed Shafeeq. 'Indian Gulf Writing'. In *Oxford Handbook of Modern Indian Literatures*, edited by Ulka Anjaria and Anjali Nerlekar, np. Oxford University Press, 2023 (published online ahead of print), doi: 10.1093/oxfordhb/9780197647912.013.38.

Karinkurayil, Mohamed Shafeeq. 'The Arabian Gulf as Revelation in Malayalam Migrant Literary Narratives'. In *Routledge Companion to Migration Literature*, edited by Gigi Adair, Rebecca Fasselt, and Carl McLaughlin, Routledge, forthcoming.

Kathiravelu, Laavanya. *Migrant Dubai: Low Wage Workers and the Construction of a Global City*. New York: Palgrave Macmillan, 2016.

Kavil, Sadiq. *Outpass*. Kottayam: DC Books, 2014.

Kaviraj, Sudipta. *The Imaginary Institution of India: Politics and Ideas*. New York: Columbia University Press, 2010.

Kendall, David. 'Always let the road decide: South Asian labourers along the highways of Dubai, UAE: a photographic essay'. *South Asian Diaspora* 4, no. 1 (2012): 45–55, doi: 10.1080/19438192.2012.634561.

Kodiyathur, Salam. 'Puzhuvarikkatha Drshyamadhyamangal'. *Prabodhanam* (25 August 2007): 17–19.

Kooria, Mahmood. 'Pothumandalam, Drishyadhyamangal, Matham: Oramukham'. In *Matham Drisyabhashayil: Keraliya Pothumandalathil Islam Thedunna Puthuvazhikal*, edited by Mahmood Kooria, 23–66. Kozhikode: Islamic Sahitya Academy, 2011.

Kooria, Mahmood. 'An Abode of Islam under a Hindu King: Circuitous Imagination of Kingdoms among Muslims of Sixteenth-Century Malabar'. *Journal of Indian Ocean World Studies* 1, no. 1 (2017): 89–109, doi: 10.26443/jiows.v1i1.21.

Kooria, Mahmood. *Islamic Law in Circulation: Shafi'i Texts across the Indian Ocean and the Meditteranean*. Cambridge: Cambridge University Press, 2022.

Krishnadas. *Katalirampangal*. Thrissur: Green Books, 2010.

Krishnadas. *Dubaipuzha* (20th edn). Kozhikode: Green Books, 2019.

Krishnadas. *Dubai Puzha*. Translated by Prabha R. Chatterji. Thrissur: SandDunes, 2019.

Kumar, Udaya. 'Shaping a Literary Space: Early Literary Histories in Malayalam and Normative Uses of the Past'. In *Literature and Nationalist Ideology*, edited by Hans Harder, 19–50. New Delhi: Social Science Press, 2010.

Kumar, Udaya. 'Ambivalences of Publicity: Transparency and Exposure in K. Ramakrishna Pillai's Thought'. In *The Public Sphere From Outside the West*, edited by Divya Dwivedi and Sanil V., 79–96. New Delhi: Bloomsbury, 2015.

Kumar, Udaya. *Writing the First Person: Literature, History, and Autobiography in Modern Kerala*. Ranikhet: Permanent Black in association with Indian Institute of Advances Study and Ashoka University, 2016.

Kumar, Vipin. 'Politics of Laughter: An introduction to the 1990s' Malayalam popular comic film'. *South Asian Popular Culture* 6, no. 1 (2008): 13–28, doi: 10.1080/14746680701878513.

Kunhi, P. K. Muhammad. *Muslimkalum Kerala Samskaravum*. Thrissur: Kerala Sahithya Akademi, 1980.

Kurien, Prema Ann. 'Non-Economic Bases of Economic Behaviour: The Consumption, Investment and Exchange Patterns of Three Emigrant Communities in Kerala, India'. *Development and Change* 25 (1994): 757–783, doi: 10.1111/j.1467-7660.1994.tb00535.x.

Kuttappan, Rejimon. '"He Held a Gun to My Neck": Modern Slavery and Forced Labour in the GCC'. In *Uncertain Journeys: Labour Migration South Asia*, edited by A. S. Pannerselvan, 23–38. New Delhi: Speaking Tiger, 2018.

Kutty, V. M. *Mappilappattinte Charitrasancharangal*. Kozhikode: Lipi Publications, 2007.

Laclau, Ernesto and Chantal Mouffe. *Hegemony and Socialist Strategy: Towards a Radical Democratic Politics*. London and New York: Verso, 1985.

Levinas, Emmanuel. *Totality and Infinity*. Pittsburg, PA: Duquesne University Press, 1969.

Lindberg, Anna. *Experience and Identity: A Historical Account of Class, Caste and Gender among Cashew Workers of Kerala, 1930–2000*. Lund: Department of History, University of Lund, 2001.

Lukose, Ritty A. *Liberalization's Children: Gender, Youth and Consumer Citizenship in Globalizing India*. Durham, NC: Duke University Press, 2009.

MacCabe, Colin. *James Joyce and the Revolution of the World*. London and Basingstoke: Macmillan, 1979.

MacCabe, Colin. 'Theory and Film: Principles of Realism and Pleasure'. In *Film Theory and Criticism: Introductory Readings*, edited by Gerald Mast, Marshall Cohen, and Leo Braudy, 79–92. New Delhi: Oxford University Press, 1992.

Madhavan, N. S. 'Aamukham'. In *Gulfumpadi PO*, 9–12. Kozhikode: Olive Books, 2005.

Mannathukkaren, Nissim. *Communism, Subaltern Studies and Postcolonial Theory: The Left in South India*. London and New York: Routledge, 2022.

Manuel, Peter. *Cassette Culture: Popular Music and Technology in North India*. Chicago, IL and London: University of Chicago Press, 1993.

Mardorossian, Carine M. 'From Literature of Exile to Migrant Literature'. *Modern Language Studies* 32, no. 2 (2002): 15–33.

Marschall, Sabine. 'Memory, migration and travel: introduction'. In *Memory, Migration and Travel*, edited by Sabine Marschall, 1–23. London and New York: Routledge, 2018.

Mathew, Nisha. 'Layered Cities, Shared Histories: Gold, Mobility and Urbanity between Dubai and Malabar'. In *Routledge Handbook of Indian Transnationalism*, edited by Ajaya Sahoo and Bandana Purkayastha, 253–265. London: Routledge, 2019.

Mathew, Paul. 'The Image-Regime of Cinema in Postmodern Malayalam Literary Fiction'. *South Asian Review* 40, no. 4 (2019): 319–336, doi: 10.1080/02759527.2019.1624124.

Mazzarella, William. *Shoveling Smoke: Advertising and Globalization in Contemporary India*. Delhi: Oxford University Press, 2003.

Mazzarella, William. 'Affect: What is it Good for?'. In *Enchantments of Modernity: Empire, Nation, Globalization*, edited by Saurabh Dube, 291–309. London, New York, and New Delhi: Routledge, 2009.

Mazzarella, William. *Censorium: Cinema and the Open Edge of Mass Publicity*. Durham, NC and London: Duke University Press, 2013.

Mazzarella, William. *The Mana of Mass Society*. Chicago, IL and London: The University of Chicago Press, 2017.

McHale, Brian. *Postmodernist Fiction*. London and New York: Routledge, 2004.

McKay, Deirdre. 'Ghosts of Futures Present: Photographs in the Filipino Migrant Archive'. *Visual Anthropology: Published in cooperation with the Commission on Visual Anthropology* 21, no. 4 (2008): 381–392, doi: 10.1080/08949460802156466.Menon, Bindu. 'Malayalam Middle Cinema and the Category of Woman'. In *Women in Malayalam Cinema: Naturalising Gender Heirarchies*, edited by Meena T. Pillai, 105–121. Hyderabad: Orient Blackswan, 2010.

Menon, Bindu and T. T. Sreekumar, ' "One More Dirham": Migration, Emotional Politics and Religion in the Home Films of Kerala'. *Migration, Mobility, & Displacement* 2, no. 2 (2016): 4–23, doi: 10.18357/mmd22201615029.

Menon, Dilip M. 'Lost Visions? Imagining a National Culture in the 1950s'. In *Land, Labour & Rights: Daniel Thorner Memorial Lectures*, edited by Alice Thorner, 250–268. New Delhi: Tulika Books, 2001.

Menon, Dilip M. 'Things Fall Apart: The Cinematic Rendition of Agrarian Landscape in South India'. *The Journal of Peasant Studies* 32, no. 2 (2005): 304–334, doi: 10.1080/03066150500094519.

Menon, Dilip M. *The Blindness of Insight: Essays on Caste in Modern India*. Chennai: Navayana, 2006.

Menon, Dilip M. 'A Local Cosmopolitan: Kesari Balakrishna Pillai and the Invention of Europe for a Modern Kerala'. *Tapasam* 2, nos 3–4 (January and April 2007): 383–412.

Menon, Dilip M. 'Becoming "Hindu" and "Muslim": Identity and Conflict in Malabar'. *Working Papers* id:2921, *eSocialSciences*, 2010.

Menon, Priya. ' "*Pravasi* Really Means Absence": Gulf-*Pravasis* as Spectral Figures in Deepak Unnikrishnan's *Temporary People*'. *South Asia: Journal of South Asian Studies* 43, no. 2 (2020): 185–198, doi: 10.1080/00856401.2020.1719628.

Metz, Christian. *Psychoanalysis and Cinema: The Imaginary Signifier*. London: Macmillan Press, 1982.

Mezzadra, Sandro and Brett Nielson. *Border as Method, or, The Multiplication of Labor*. Durham, NC and London: Duke University Press, 2013.

Miller, Roland E. *Mappila Muslims of Kerala: A Study in Islamic Trends*. Bombay: Orient Longman, 1976.

Mini, Darshana Sreedhar. 'Public Interest Television and Social Responsibility: The Search for the Missing Person in Indian Television'. *International Journal of Digital Television* 7, no. 2 (2016): 173–191.

Mini, Darshana Sreedhar. 'The Spectral Duration of Malayalam Soft-porn: Disappearance, Desire, and Haunting'. *BioScope* 7, no. 2 (2016): 127–150.

Mini, Darshana Sreedhar. 'Transnational Ethical Screens: Empathetic Networks in Malayalam Short Films from the Gulf'. *Film History* 32, no. 3 (2020): 141–169.

Mishra, Vijay. *The Literature of the Indian Diaspora: Theorizing the Diasporic Imaginary*. New York: Routledge, 2007.

Moretti, Franco. *The Way of the World: The Bildungsroman in European Culture*. London and New York: Verso, 2000.

Morris, Maeghan. 'Transnational Imagination in Action Cinema: Hong Kong and the Making of a Global Popular Culture'. *Inter-Asia Cultural Studies* 5, no. 2 (2004): 181–199, doi: 10.4324/9780203960981-31.

Mottehedeh, Negar. *Displaced Allegories: Post-Revolutionary Iranian Cinema*. Durham, NC and London: Duke University Press, 2008.

Mulvey, Laura. 'Visual Pleasure and Narrative Cinema'. In *Film Theory and Criticism: Introductory Readings*, edited by Gerald Mast, Marshall Cohen, and Leo Braudy, 746–757. New Delhi: Oxford University Press, 1992.

Mumthas, Khadeeja. *Barsa* (3rd edn). Kottayam: DC Books, 2021.

Munif, Abdul Rahman. *Cities of Salt*. Translated by Peter Thoreaux. New York: Vintage International, 1989.

Naffis-Sahely, André. *The Promised Land: Poems from Itinerant Life*. London: Penguin Books, 2017.

Naficy, Hamid. *A Social History of Iranian Cinema, Volume IV: The Globalizing Era, 1984–2010*. Durham, NC and London: Duke University Press, 2012.

Nail, Thomas. *The Figure of the Migrant*. Stanford, CA: Stanford University Press, 2015.

Nail, Thomas. *Theory of the Border*. New York: Oxford University Press, 2016.

Nair, M. T. Vasudevan. *Naalukettu*. Kozhikode: Current Books, 1958.

Nair, M. T. Vasudeva, *Asuravithu*. Kottayam: DC Books, 1962.

Nair, P. R. Gopinathan. 'Asian Emigration to the Middle East: Emigration from India', Working Paper no. 180, Centre for Development Studies, Trivandrum, 1983.

Nair, Rajesh V. 'Remapping the Land: Displacement and Memory in Benyamin's *Aadujeevitham* and Khadeeja Mumtaz's *Barsa*'. In *Indian Literatures in Diaspora*, edited by Sireesha Telugu, 100–118. London: Routledge, 2022.

Nancy, Jean-Luc. *Being Singular Plural*. Translated by Robert D. Richardson and Anne E. O'Byrne. Stanford, CA: Stanford University Press, 2000.

Negt, Oskar and Alexander Kluge. *Public Sphere and Experience: Analysis of the Bourgeois and Proletarian Public Sphere*. London and New York: Verso, 2016.

Nora, Pierre. 'Between Memory and History: Les Lieux de Mémoire'. *Representations* 26 (1989): 7–24.

Ong, Aihwa. *Spirits of Resistance and Capitalist Discipline: Factory Women in Malaysia*. Albany, NY: State University of New York Press, 1987.

Ong, Aihwa. 'The Gender and Labor Politics of Postmodernity'. *Annual Review of Anthropology* 20 (1991): 279–309.

Ong, Aihwa. *Flexible Citizenship: The Cultural Logics of Transnationality*. Durham, NC and London: Duke University Press, 1999.

Osella, Caroline. 'Memories of Luxury, Aspirations towards Glamour, and Cultivations of Morality: How south Indian Muslim women craft their style'. In *Fashion India: Spectacular Capitalism*, edited by Tereza Kuldova, 119–135. Oslo: Akademia, 2013.

Osella, Filippo and Caroline Osella. 'Migration, Money and Masculinity in Kerala'. *The Journal of Royal Anthropological Institute* 6, no. 1 (2000): 117–133, doi: 10.1111/1467-9655.t01-1-00007.

Osella, Filippo and Caroline Osella. *Social Mobility in Kerala: Modernity and Identity in Conflict*. London: Pluto Press, 2001.

Osella, Filippo and Caroline Osella. 'Islamism and Social Reform in Kerala, South India'. *Modern Asian Studies* 42, nos 2/3 (2008): 317–346, doi: 10.1017/S0026749X07003198.

Osella, Filippo and Caroline Osella. 'Muslim entrepreneurs in public life between India and the Gulf: making good and DOIng good'. *Journal of the Royal Anthropological Institute* 15, s1 (2009): S202–S221.

Osella, Filippo and Caroline Osella. 'Migration, Neoliberal Capitalism, and Islamic Reform in Kozhikode (Calicut), South India'. *International Labour and Working-Class History* 79, Labour Migration to the Middle East (2011): 140–160.

Panikkar, K. N. *Against Lord and State: Religion and Peasant Uprisings in Malabar, 1836–1921*. New Delhi: Oxford University Press, 1989.

Parayil, Sujith. *Photography in 20th Century Kerala*, Unpublished PhD Diss., Manipal University, Manipal, 2007.

Parayil, Sujith. 'Family Photographs: Visual Mediation of the Social'. *Critical Quarterly* 58, no. 3 (2014): 1–20.

Parida, Jajati K., Merry Elizabeth John, and Justin Sunny. 'Construction Labour Migrants and Wage Inequality in Kerala'. *Journal of Social and Economic Development* 22 (2020): 414–442, doi: 10.1007_s40847-020-00104-2.

Phu, Thy and Elspeth Brown. 'The cultural politics of aspiration: Family photography's mixed feelings'. *Journal of Visual Culture* 17, no. 2 (2015): 152–165, doi: 10.1177/14704192918782352.

Pinney, Christopher. *Camera Indica: The Social Life of Indian Photographs*. Chicago, IL: The University of Chicago Press, 1997.

Pinney, Christopher. *'Photos of the gods': The Printed Image and Political Struggle in India*. London: Reaktion Books, 2004.

Pinney, Christopher. *The Coming of Photography in India*. London: British Library, 2008.

Pinney, Christopher. ' "What Time is the Visual?" Photography and the History of the Future', *Visual Anthropology Review* (2023): 3–34, doi: 10.1111/var.12288.

Poole, Deborah. *Vision, Race, and Modernity: A Visual Economy of the Andean Image World*. Princeton, NJ: Princeton University Press, 1997.

Prabhu, Gayathri. 'A gulf of secrets: Priya Kuriyan's graphic memoir "Ebony and Ivory" '. *Journal of Commonwealth Literature* 58, no. 1 (2023): 22–35, doi: 10.1177/002198942211452.

Prakash, B. A. 'Gulf Migration and Its Economic Impact: The Kerala Experience'. *Economic and Political Weekly* 30, no. 50 (1998): 3209–3213.

Prange, Sebastian R. *Monsoon Islam: Trade and Faith on the Medieval Malabar Coast*. New Delhi: Cambridge University Press, 2018.

Prasad, M. Madhava. *Ideology of the Hindi Film: A Historical Construction*. New Delhi: Oxford University Press, 1998.

Prasad, M. Madhava. 'From Cultural Backwardness to the Age of Imitation: An essay on film history'. In *Routledge Handbook of Indian Cinemas*, edited by K. Moti Gokulsing and Wimal Dissanayake, 7–18. Oxford and New York: Routledge, 2013.

Prasad, M. Madhava. *Cine-Politics: Film Stars and Political Existence in South India*. Hyderabad: Orient Blackswan, 2014.

Promodh, Irene Ann. 'FM radio and the Malayali diaspora in Qatar: at home overseas'. *Journal of Ethnic and Migration Studies* 47, no. 9 (2021): 1957–1975, doi: 10.1080/1369183X.2020.1838268.

Puravur, Vijayan. *Salalah Salalah*. Thrissur: Green Books, 2014.

Puri, Shamlal. *Dubai on Wheels: Speeding Headlong on a Dangerous, Slippery Road*. New Delhi: Diamond Books, 2010.

Puthan Purayil, Mufsin and Manish Thakur. 'The strength of strong ties: wasta and migration strategies among the Mappila Muslims of northern Kerala, India'. *Journal of Ethnic and Migration Studies* (2022): np, doi: 10.1080/1369183X.2022.2069090.

Puthan Purayil, Mufsin and Muhsin Puthan Purayil. 'Return migration amidst a Pandemic: Reflections on Kerala's Gulf Migration'. *Journal of Migration Affairs* 3, no. 1 (2020): 99–107, doi: 10.36931/jma.2020.3.1.99-107.

Radhakrishnan, Ratheesh. '"Looking" at Mohanlal: Spectatorial Ordering and the Emergence of the "Fan" in Malayalam Cinema'. *Deep Focus* (December 2002): 29–38.

Radhakrishnan, Ratheesh. 'The Gulf in the Imagination: Migration, Malayalam Cinema, and Regional Identity'. *Contributions to Indian Sociology* 23, no. 2 (2009): 217–245, doi: 10.1177/006996670904300202.

Radhakrishnan, Ratheesh. 'What is Left of Malayalam Cinema?'. In *Cinemas of South India: Culture, Resistance, Ideology*, edited by Sowmya Dechamma C. C. and Elavarthi Sathya Prakash, 25–48. New Delhi: Oxford University Press, 2010.

Radhakrishnan, Ratheesh. 'Soft Porn and the Anxieties of the Family'. In *Women in Malayalam Cinema: Naturalising Gender Hierarchies*, edited by Meena T. Pillai, 194–220. Hyderabad: Orient Blackswan, 2010.

Radhakrishnan, Ratheesh. 'Aesthetic dislocations: A re-take on Malayalam cinema of the 1970s'. *South Asian Popular Culture* 10, no. 1 (2012): 91–102, doi: 10.1080/14746689.2012.655111.

Radhakrishnan, Ratheesh. 'The "Worlds" of the Region'. *Positions: East Asia Cultures Critique* 24, no. 3 (2016): 693–719, doi: 10.1215/10679847-3618240.

Radhakrishnan, Ratheesh. 'Habits and Worlds: Malayalam cinema's travels with the Gulf'. In *Industrial Networks and Cinemas of India: Shooting Stars, Shifting Geographies, and Multiplying Media*, edited by Monika Mehta and Madhuja Mukherjee, 167–180. London and New York: Routledge, 2021.

Rafeek, Sonia. *Herbarium* (4th edn). Kottayam: DC Books, 2018.

Raj, Jayaseelan. 'Categorical Oppression: Performance of identity in South India'. *The Australian Journal of Anthropology* 31, no. 3 (2020): 288–302, doi: 10.1111/taja.12375.

Raja, Md Selim and Bhaswati Das. 'Labour Migrations Within India: Motivations and Networks'. *South Asia Research* 39, no. 2 (2019): 125–142, doi: 10.1177/0262728019842018.

Rajadhyaksha, Ashish. 'The Phalke era: Conflict of traditional form and modern technology', *Journal of Arts and Ideas*, nos14–15 (1987): 47–78.

Rajadhyaksha, Ashish and Paul Willemen. *Encyclopaedia of Indian Cinema*. New Delhi: British Film Institute and Oxford University Press, 1994.

Rajadhyaksha, Ashish. 'Who's Looking? Viewership and Democracy in the Cinema'. *Cultural Dynamics* 10, no. 2 (1998): 171–195.

Rancière, Jacques. *Dis-Agreement: Politics and Philosophy*. Translated by J. Rose. Minneapolis, MN: University of Minnesota Press, 1998.

Ravuthar, Nisamudheen. *Arabyayile Atima*. Thrissur: Green Books, 2013.

Reiss, H. S. (ed.). *Kant: Political Writings*. Cambridge: Cambridge University Press, 1991.

Rowena, Jenny. 'The "Laughter-Films" and the Reconfiguration of Masculinities'. In *Women in Malayalam Cinema: Naturalising Gender Hierarchies*, edited by Meena T. Pillai, 126–152. Hyderabad: Orient Blackswan, 2010.

Rushdie, Salman. 'Imaginary Homelands'. *London Review of Books* 4, no. 18 (1982).

Sagar, Pooja. 'Images of Deaths and Marriages: Syrian Christian Family Albums and Oral Histories in Kerala'. In *Photography in India: From Archives to Contemporary Practice*, edited by Aileen Blaney and Chinar Shah, 63–74. London: Bloomsbury, 2018.

Sageer. *Gulfumpadi PO*. Kozhikode: Olive Books, 2005.

Sageer. *Gulfumpadi PO*. Kottayam: Don Books, 2021.

Said, Edward W. *The World, the Text, and the Critic*. Cambridge, MA: Harvard University Press, 1983.

Saidalavi, P. C. 'Status claims among Muslims in Malabar, South India'. *Anthropological Notebooks* 23, no. 2 (2017): 103–105.

Sakai, Naoki. *Translation and Subjectivity: On 'Japan' and Cultural Nationalism*. Minneapolis, MN: University of Minnesota Press, 1997.

Salazar, Noel. 'The Power of Imagination in Transnational Mobilities'. *Identities: Global Studies in Culture and Power* 18 (2011): 576–598, doi: 10.1080/1070289X.2011.672859.

Santhosh R. 'Contextualising Islamic Contestations: Reformism, Traditionalism and Modernity among Muslims of Kerala'. *Indian Anthropologist* 43, no. 2 (2013): 25–42.

Sater, James. 'Citizenship and migration in Arab Gulf monarchies'. *Citizenship Studies* 18, nos 3–4 (2013): 92–102, doi: 10.1080/13621025.2013.820394.

Satrapi, Marjane. *Persepolis: The Story of a Childhood*. New York: Pantheon, 2003.

Schlote, Christiane. 'Writing Dubai: Indian labour migrants and taxi topographies'. *South Asian Diaspora* 6, no. 1 (2014): 33–46, doi: 10.1080/19438192.2013.828500.

Schmitt, Carl. *Political Theology: Four Chapters on the Concept of Sovereignty*. Chicago, IL and London: The University of Chicago Press, 1985.

Seccombe, Ian J. 'Labour migration to the Arabian Gulf: evolution and characteristics 1920–1950'. *British Society for Middle Eastern Studies. Bulletin* 10, no. 1 (1983): 3–20, doi: 10.1080/13530198308705359

Seyhan, Azade. *Writing Outside the Nation*. Princeton, NJ and Oxford: Princeton University Press, 2001.

Shafeeq K., Mohamed. 'Can the Migrant Exist? Reading Gulf Migrant Memoirs in Malayalam'. In *Reimagining Marginality: Exploitation, Experience, Expression*, edited by Mohan Dharavath and Achuth A, 144–153. New Delhi: Authorspress, 2022.

Singh, Asha. 'Of Women, by Men: Understanding the "First Person Feminine" in Bhojpuri Folk Songs'. *Soociological Bulletin* 64, no. 2 (2015): 171–196.

Spiegelman, Art. *Maus: A Survivor's Tale: 1. My Father Bleeds History*. New York: Pantheon, 1986.

Spiegelman, Art. *Maus: A Survivor's Tale: 2. And Here My Troubles Began*. New York: Pantheon, 1992.

Spivak, Gayatri Chakravorty. 'Can the Subaltern Speak'. In *Colonial Discourse and Postcolonial Theory: A Reader*, edited by Patrick Williams and Laura Chrisman, 66–111. New York: Columbia University Press, 1998.

Srinivas, S. V. *Politics as Performance: A Social History of the Telugu Cinema*. Ranikhet: Permanent Black in association with The New India Foundation, 2013.

Steyerl, Hito. *The Wretched of the Screen*. Berlin: Sternberg Press, 2012.

Strassler, Karen. *Refracted Visions: Popular Photography and National Modernity in Java*. Durham, NC: Duke University Press, 2010.Subrahmanyam, Sanjay. *The Career and Legend of Vasco Da Gama*. Cambridge: Cambridge University Press, 1998.

Sukenick, Ronald. *In Form: Digressions on the Act of Fiction*. Carbondale and Edwardsville, IL: South Illinois University Press, 1985.

Sumeetha M. 'Exploring the Capital-Labour Dynamics: Migrants in the Gold Jewellery-making Industry in Kerala'. In *India Migration Report 2017*, edited by S. Irudayarajan, 279–288. New Delhi: Routledge, 2018.

Taussig, Michael. *Defacement: Public Secrecy and the Labor of the Negative*. Stanford, CA: Stanford University Press, 1999.

Tilly, Charles. 'Transplanted Networks'. In *Collective Violence, Contentious Politics, and Social Change*, edited by Ernesto Castaneda and Cathy Lisa Schneider, 307–325. New York: Routledge, 2017.

Unnikrishnan, Deepak. *Temporary People*. Brooklyn, NY: Restless Books, 2017.

Unnikrishnan, Deepak. 'Abu Dhabi: The city where citizenship is not an option'. The *Guardian* (13 December 2017).

Vadakepat Menon, Devaki and Vanaja Menon Vadakepat. 'Migration and reverse migration: Gulf Malayalees' perceptions during the Covid-19 pandemic'. *South Asian Diaspora* 13, no. 2 (2021): 157–177, doi: 10.1080/19438192.2020.1820668.

Vallikkunnu, Balakrishnan and Dr Umar Tharamel. *Mappilappattu: Paadavum Padanavum*. Kottayam: DC Books, 2006.

Varghese, V. J. 'Migrant narratives: Reading literary representations of Christian migration in Kerala, 1920–70'. *The Indian Economic and Social History Review* 43, no. 2 (2006): 228–255.

Varughese, E. Dawson. *Visuality and Identity in Post-millennial Indian Graphic Narratives*. London: Palgrave Macmillan, 2018.

Varughese, E. Dawson and Mohamed Shafeeq Karinkurayil. 'Editorial'. *Journal of Commonwealth Literature* 58, no. 1 (2023): 3–8, doi: 10.1177/00219894221145.Vasudevan, Ravi. *The Melodramatic Public: Film Form and Spectatorship in Indian Cinema*. Ranikhet: Permanent Black, 2010.

Vinai, Maya and M. G. Prasuna. 'Re-mapping the Anxieties of the Gulf Diaspora: A Study of Benyamin's *Goat Days*'. *South Asian Review* 36, no. 2 (2015): 121–129, doi: 10.1080/02759527.2015.11933021.

Vollmann, William T. 'I am here only for working: Conversations with the petroleum brotherhood in the UAE'. *Harper's*, December 2017.

Vora, Neha. *Impossible Citizens: Dubai's Indian Diaspora*. Hyderabad: Orient Blackswan, 2013.

Warner, Michael. *Publics and Counterpublics*. New York: Zone Books, 2002.

Willoughby, John. 'Ambivalent Anxieties of the South Asian—Gulf Arab Labor Exchange'. *Revista de Economia Mundial* 14 (2006): 31–56.

Wright, Andrea. *Between Dreams and Ghosts: Indian Migration and Middle Eastern Oil*. Stanford, CA: Stanford University Press, 2021.

Zachariah, K. C. and Irudaya Rajan. *Kerala's Gulf Connection, 1998–2011: Economic and Social Impact of Migration*. Hyderabad: Orient Blackswan, 2012.

Zachariah, K. C. and S. Irudaya Rajan. *Emigration from Kerala: End of an Era*. Kochi: RedInk, 2018.

Žižek, Slavoj. *Tarrying with the Negative: Kant, Hegel, and the Critique of Ideology*. Durham, NC: Duke University Press, 1993.

Index

For the benefit of digital users, indexed terms that span two pages (e.g., 52–53) may, on occasion, appear on only one of those pages.